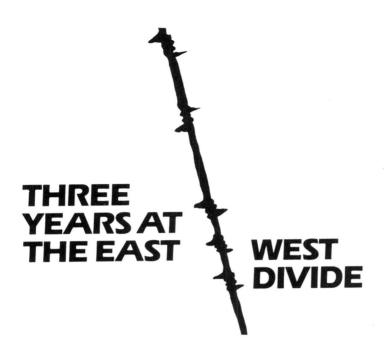

THREE
YEARS AT
THE EAST
WEST
DIVIDE

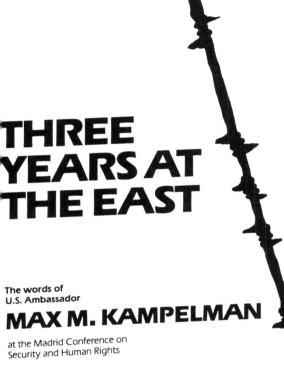

THREE YEARS AT THE EAST

WEST DIVIDE

The words of
U.S. Ambassador

MAX M. KAMPELMAN

at the Madrid Conference on
Security and Human Rights

with Introductions by

RONALD REAGAN

and

JIMMY CARTER

edited by Leonard R. Sussman

Perspectives on Freedom
A Freedom House Series
20 West 40 Street
New York, N.Y. 10018

Paperback edition: International Standard Book Number: 0-932088-05-8

Hardcover edition: International Standard Book Number: 0-932088-04-X

Library of Congress Catalog Card Number: 83-82249

Freedom House, 20 West 40th Street, New York, New York 10018

First published in September 1983, in both
paperback and hardcover editions.

Printed in the United States of America

Dedication

To all the courageous monitors
of the Helsinki Accords who are
now known to be in prisons, labor
camps, psychiatric institutions,
or internal exile in the Soviet Union.

Eduard Arutunyan
Vyacheslav Bakhmin
Oles Berdnyk
Vyacheslav Chornovil
Balys Gajauskas
Rostislav Galetsky
Irina Grivnina
Olha Heyko
Mykola Horbal
Mecislovas Jurevicius
Vitaly Kalynychenko
Ivan Kandyba
Merab Kostava
Anatoly Koryagin
Ivan Kovalev
Zinovy Krasivsky
Malva Landa
Yaroslav Lesiv
Levko Lukyanenko
Yuri Lytvyn
Anatoly Marchenko
Myroslav Marynovych
Mykola Matusevych
Osana Meshko
Robert Nazaryan
Viktor Nekipelov

Yuri Orlov
Tatiana Osipova
Vasyl Ovsienko
Valentina Pailodze
Viktoras Petkus
Aleksandr Podrabinek
Oksana Popovych
Bohdan Rebryk
Petro Rozumny
Mykola Rudenko
Feliks Serebrov
Anatoly Shcharansky
Yuri Shukhevych
Danylo Shumuk
Petro Sichko
Vasyl Sichko
Vytautas Skuodys
Ivan Sokulsky
Algirdas Statkevicius
Vasyl Striltsiv
Vasyl Stus
Alfonsas Svarinskas
Sigitas Tamkevicius
Leonard Ternovsky
Oleksy Tykhy
Vytautas Vaiciunas

Father Gleb Yakunin

Contents

Preface

The cold war between East and West began in 1917.

Marxism-Leninism declared ceaseless struggle, by whatever means necessary, to achieve the death of one social system—that which prevailed mainly in the democracies of Europe, the Americas and their associated states—and assure the supremacy of communism.

The cold war was enshrined at Yalta in 1945.

Roosevelt and Churchill observed the 1,500-mile "iron curtain" extending from the North Sea to northern Turkey. To the east of that curtain lay the Soviet-occupied part of Germany, a once-free Czechoslovakia, three Soviet-occupied Baltic states, and nations which had just lost Nazi yokes—Poland, Rumania and Hungary—but hoped to seek more democratic futures. At war's end, Soviet armies dominated all these lands.

A cornerstone of the Yalta agreement was fully ignored in practice: Stalin agreed to permit the peoples of Eastern Europe to choose their new forms of government, and their leaders. In country after country, however, Soviet troops, political puppets and assassinations of local leaders and nascent democracies insured Moscow's hegemony over Eastern Europe.

President Truman's Point Four Program halted Soviet efforts to extend its domination to Greece and Turkey. But the cold war continued. It was not essentially a war of words, but of deeds; for example, Soviet efforts to subvert free Greece and Italy after World War II; America's attempt to contain communism in Korea, Cuba and Vietnam; Soviet invasion of Hungary in 1956, overturning popular will in Czechoslovakia in 1968, dominating Ethiopia from 1977, invasion of Afghanistan in 1979, and, today, pressure on Poland and the use of Cuban-surrogate troops in several African and Central American countries.

Such deeds notwithstanding, the era of "détente" in the 1970s reflected the Western hope that the two major sociopolitical systems—the democratic and the communist—could somehow compete without military challenge, or the use of Soviet weapons to force a system of government on people who did not choose it.

The West's view of détente as peaceful competition proved an illusion.

During the era of détente in the 1970s when Republican and Democratic Presidents demonstrated restraint in weapons development and deployment, the Soviet Union dramatically increased its weaponry and deployed troops in lands well outside its Eastern European sphere of influence.

Yet détente—as Westerners interpreted it—seemed an attractive formula for peaceful competition. Western Europeans, the Vatican, Canada and the United States agreed in the early 1970s to stage the Conference on Security and Cooperation in Europe (CSCE). Preliminary debates lasted two years. The Final Act, known as the Helsinki Accords, was signed by 35 delegations at Helsinki on August 1, 1975.

The Final Act called for another meeting in Belgrade two years hence to review the implementation of the accords. The Belgrade review (1977-78) ended with a declaration that added little to the Final Act, but it had permitted the Western delegations to spotlight the violations of the accords by the Eastern bloc. Belgrade was followed by a review at Madrid beginning in October 1980 with final addresses in September 1983. The draft of a concluding declaration was stalled for much of 1982 because the NATO countries refused to conduct business as usual after Poland imposed martial law.

The reviews became known as the Helsinki process, and took on a life of their own. They afford a rare context for official spokesmen frankly, fully and publicly to debate East-West issues for the record. As America's representative at Madrid Max M. Kampelman played a key role. His addresses provide an extraordinary contribution to the Helsinki process. That process is perhaps the major accomplishment of the Final Act.

This volume includes about ninety percent of the speeches delivered by Ambassador Kampelman at the Madrid review. We have eliminated those which dealt mainly with procedural matters.

Other significant addresses were made at Madrid by Secretary of State Alexander M. Haig, Jr., Attorney-General Griffin B. Bell, and other members of the American delegation: Jerome J. Shestack, Dante B. Fascell, Warren Zimmerman, Philip Handler and Spencer Oliver, as well as the leaders of other delegations— allied, neutral or Soviet-bloc. But we feel the tone and content of Ambassador Kampelman's papers carry the thread of the debate, and suggest the tone and content introduced by the adversaries.

Ambassador Kampelman, who became Chairman of the Board of Freedom House in April 1983, was a member of the organization when the Madrid review opened in October 1980. He welcomed to Madrid a number of prominent human rights activists from Eastern Europe. Freedom House had brought them to a week-long citizens' conference paralleling the opening week of the official meeting. A pall was cast over that citizens' meeting as it began. Andrei Amalrik, one of the most sensitive and dedicated of the Soviet dissidents, was killed in an early-morning automobile accident as he dashed to the citizens' meeting. Some of Amalrik's colleagues regarded his death as an ominous portent for the CSCE.

Publication of this volume in the Perspective series of Freedom House is a natural continuation of our interest in the Helsinki process. Barely weeks after the Final Act was signed in 1975 Freedom House coined the phrase, "Helsinki Watch," and pledged to monitor the accords from then on (see editorial in the appendix, *Freedom at Issue* (Nov.-Dec. 1975).

This volume is not a history of the Madrid conference, but it conveys the realities not only in the Helsinki process, but in the world. Deeds count, Kampelman reminds us, but words are important too. They contain pledges to be tested against performance, and serious clues to goals sometimes hidden and at other times clearly revealed, yet ignored by the inattentive democrat.

We ignore both the words and deeds of adversaries to our detriment.

—L.R.S.

Introduction
Ronald Reagan

In 1975 the United States and Canada joined with the nations of Europe in proclaiming a new charter of freedom. They signed the Helsinki Final Act—a bill of rights for Europe—and they pledged their best efforts to its implementation.

Recently, the United States and the other 34 states participating in the process of increasing security and cooperation in Europe concluded the Madrid conference. The three-year effort in Madrid was aimed at measuring compliance with the Helsinki Final Act and at extension of its provisions. Under the masterful leadership of Max Kampelman, our Ambassador to the Madrid Conference, we and our Western allies conducted a thorough stock-taking of international respect for the Final Act. The results were anything but encouraging. Despite glimmers of hope here and there, the overall picture which emerged was one of frequent disregard by the Soviet Union and the East European states for many of the most elemental human rights.

We were confronted at Madrid with a difficult decision—whether in the face of these human rights violations to give in to frustration, and to dispense with the Helsinki process, or to bend our best efforts toward making that process more effective. The decision was difficult. In the end, however, we chose the path of hope, and not the one of despair. The United States and its Western colleagues were able, in the face of constant Soviet resistance, to negotiate a new document which gives additional meaning to the concepts of the Final Act.

In the months and years to come, we intend to follow the path which has been blazed in Madrid. We intend to preserve the Helsinki process and never to shrink from calling attention to actions and policies which violate the Helsinki and Madrid accords. Freedom House and organizations like it have an important continuing role to play in this effort.

Introduction

Jimmy Carter

The Helsinki Accords signed in 1975 were a significant achievement. This one document embodied the two most fundamental concerns of men and women everywhere: the yearning for a better life for the individual citizen, and for nations to live at peace with one another.

There had been many declarations on national security, and some on social and political rights. For the first time with such clarity and in such detail, the Helsinki Accords irrevocably linked human rights and national security.

My administration from the beginning reaffirmed America's commitment to human rights as a fundamental tenet of our foreign policy. We also sought to reduce the threat of military encounter by offering mutually verifiable reductions in armaments. We regarded these objectives as two halves of a whole. Neither America nor our sister democracies, large or small, are free because we are strong and prosperous. I believe we are strong and influential because we are free.

Our freedom, moreover, is not the vestige of a passing era. It is the true wave of the future. The Helsinki Accords, laboriously negotiated prior to 1975 and long debated at the Belgrade review conference in 1977–78, reflect the yearning of widely differing peoples of thirty-five nations. They are united in these accords despite diverse social, political and economic systems. The common bond are the rights which people hold simply by virtue of their humanity.

I asked Max M. Kampelman to serve as my Ambassador to the Madrid review conference of the Helsinki Accords that opened in September 1980. His instructions were simple: to reflect at Madrid the traditional support of the United States—its people and its government—for enhancing human rights, and creating confidence-building measures that reduce the likelihood of war.

We had no illusion that the Ambassador's assignment would be easy. The Universal Declaration of Human Rights certainly does not reflect the realities of the world today. Nor have the Helsinki Accords changed the behavior of those countries that have regularly ignored or violated commitments made at Helsinki and renewed at Belgrade.

On the contrary, even as the Helsinki review proceeded, the Soviet Union became more repressive at home, continued its invasion in Afghanistan, and threatened the movement toward social reform in Poland.

The three-year review conference at Madrid has, however, provided every country with a far clearer understanding of which countries abide by their commitments by earnestly extending human rights to their own and other citizens.

Ambassador Kampelman delivered a series of significant addresses at Madrid. I am glad Freedom House is making it possible to read these addresses as a single, flowing document. They are at once informative and inspiring. Ambassador Kampelman's papers reveal the nature of democracy's adversaries, even as they provide a reasonable and moving description of America's beliefs, strengths and yearnings.

Why Did We Go to Helsinki and Madrid?

Leonard R. Sussman

At the White House, on the morning of July 25, 1975, President Jerry Ford explained why he would fly to Helsinki the next day to sign the Final Act of the Conference on Security and Cooperation in Europe (CSCE). After two years of negotiating, 32 European nations, the Vatican, Canada and the U.S. approved by consensus the 68-page document. Few Americans seemed to understand the purpose of the President's trip, and some who did objected. It was, said George Ball, "a defeat for the West." Advised the Wall Street Journal, "Jerry, Don't Go."

President Ford acknowledged the fear of many Americans that "the Conference will put a seal of approval on the political division of Europe that has existed since the Soviet Union incorporated the Baltic nations, and set new boundaries...by military action in World War II." He also acknowledged, "There are critics who say the meeting is a meaningless exercise because the Helsinki declarations are merely statements of principles and good intentions which are neither legally binding nor enforceable and cannot be depended upon. They express concern, however, that the result will be to make the free governments of Western Europe and North America less wary and lead to a letting down of NATO's political guard and military defense."

Declared the president, "If I seriously shared these reservations I would not be going." He stated categorically, "The United States has never recognized the Soviet incorporation of Lithuania, Latvia and Estonia and is not doing so now."

Why had the Soviet Union pressed so hard for a security conference? Since the Berlin meeting of Foreign Ministers in February 1954—more than 20 years before the Helsinki Accords were signed—the Soviet Union had repeatedly proposed a European security conference. Obviously, the Soviets sought Western European and American recognition for the territorial status quo. They also sought through such a conference to bring the German Democratic Republic formally into the community of nations. For their part, Western European nations were eager to advance détente. They were increasingly interested in discussing with the Soviets military confidence-building measures and humanitarian issues. The United States was skeptical, and awaited some proof of relaxed tensions over Berlin and reduction of Soviet forces facing West.

The signing of the Four Power Agreement on Berlin in September 1971 was regarded by the three Western signatories as proof that concrete progress had been made in the most sensitive European area of East-West confrontation —Berlin. Improvement in the relations between the people on both sides of the Wall, and between Bonn and East Berlin, raised Western European hopes of better relations with East Germany, the Soviet Union and other Eastern European countries. Consequently, on a visit to Moscow in May 1972 President Nixon approved not only the CSCE but also Mutual and Balanced Force Reduction talks (MBFR).

Before the CSCE concluded in 1975, many of the USSR's earlier objectives had already been achieved. The Oder-Neisse line between the GDR and Poland was settled in 1970. The GDR was admitted to the United Nations in 1973, and recognized by the United States in 1974. Numerous bilateral exchanges with the Soviets in many fields had begun. The euphoria of détente prior to CSCE helped facilitate those East-West arrangements, and they, in turn, produced a climate in which CSCE could be held.

If one had regarded East-West relations in 1975 as confrontational, there would have been little justification for accommodating the Soviets at Helsinki. President Ford did not view the trip in that manner. The president read the editorial advising, "Jerry, Don't Go," and responded, "I would rather read that than headlines all over Europe saying, 'United States Boycotts Peace Hopes.'"

The United States had long avoided participating in a European security conference, and went along after Western European countries persisted in meeting the Soviets at the CSCE. Indeed, the Americans during two years of negotiations insisted that the Final Act would not be legally binding. UN Secretary-General Kurt Waldheim underscored in his Helsinki speech that "the Final Act is not a document which is legally binding on governments (and) provides for no enforcement mechanism."

The Soviets, it would seem, were eager to produce a document that could be said to reflect Western acceptance of the post-war geography, whether or not accompanied by formal legal status. Moreover, the USSR seemed ready to discuss a broad spectrum of humanitarian issues as the price for some document on sovereignty and the inviolability of present borders.

For their part, the Western Europeans seemed eager to soften the disputes over borders and particularly press for a document on humanitarian questions.

What was done at Helsinki?

Representatives of Eastern, Western and neutral Europeans, the Vatican, Canada and the United States approved the Final Act composed of three main sections (nicknamed "Baskets"). The first related to security in Europe. This included a document on confidence-building measures, security and disarmament. Basket II deals with cooperation in the fields of economics, science and technology. Basket III, by far the most controversial, applies to cooperation in humanitarian and information fields.

Perhaps the most revealing part of the Final Act is the preamble in Basket I called the Declaration on Principles Guiding Relations Between Participating States. It must be remembered that the entire document was intended to be morally compelling if not legally binding. One cannot escape the conclusion, however, that after two years of laborious negotiations there emerged a document that sounds like a legally binding instrument, and may in time be regarded as a source of customary international law. Though the principles are said to serve as "guiding" relations between states, the declaration is widely regarded as consistent with international law.

What, then, does the Declaration on Principles tell us?

The first principle discusses sovereign equality and respect for the rights inherent in sovereignty. While a statement on the inviolability of frontiers presumably was the primary objective of the Soviet Union for twenty years, the first principle does not support the absolute retention of present European boundaries. "Frontiers can be changed," says the declaration, "in accordance with international law, by peaceful means and by agreement."

The main issue of inviolability of frontiers is dealt with in principle 3 under that title. That two-sentence section says solely that states "will refrain now and in the future from assaulting" one another's frontiers. When read with principle 1, the document opposes changes in borders by force but upholds changes resulting from peaceful agreements. In the view of Harold S. Russell, the principal American negotiator for the principles, he and "all the Western negotiators" believe that the "USSR failed in large part to achieve the kind of language it originally sought." He added, "the document does not depart materially from previous international agreements on frontiers and does nothing to recognize existing frontiers in Europe."Said Russell, "Negotiation of the two sentences comprising the inviolability principle occupied four months," and eliminated "virtually all" of the essential elements in the Soviets' initial draft.

What the Soviets failed to achieve in the CSCE negotiations, said Russell, they "almost totally recouped at Helsinki through the North American press." He quotes West German Foreign Minister Hans-Dietrich Genscher warning the Bundestag, "The Conference has not finalized the status quo in Europe. And what the Conference did not do by texts we should not do by words."

The words, indeed, were harsh. For example, the New York Times' columnist, C. L. Sulzberger,said the Helsinki Summit "signalizes a personal triumph for Leonid Brezhnev" who "brought to a legal conclusion the process of gaining recognition for all Russia's World War II territorial conquests— as well as the ideological ascendance Moscow has since reaffirmed in that area." Looking forward to four years from then, Sulzberger predicted, "In 1984 the Russians are not going to be less tough about what they consider their private business than they were in Hungary (1956) or Czechoslovakia (1968). Nor is the deal...ratified (in Helsinki) going to alter Soviet determination." That determination was set forth in the 1968 Brezhnev Doctrine. It sought to justify Soviet military actions to prevent another communist society from opting out of the communist camp.

The doctrine declares, "nobody interferes in the concrete measures taken to improve the socialist system" and if a "danger arises to socialism itself in a particular country...its defense is the common cause of all communists..." Cross-border military action, says the doctrine, is necessary to defend "social-ism." The doctrine argues, in effect, that present international law is operable only if it advances "socialist" objectives.

Yet such actions would violate the CSCE. The first principle conveys the promise of the signatories to "respect each other's right freely to choose and develop its political, social, economic and cultural systems'— hardly a support for the primacy or permanence of communism or any particular political or social system. Moreover, the declaration pledges—"irrespective of their political, eco-nomic or social systems'—to put all the principles into practice "with all other participating states." No exceptions for certain social systems or for a threat to a particular social system. Principle 2 clearly rejects "any manifestation of force for the purpose of inducing another participatory state to renounce the full exercise of its sovereign rights." Principle 8 is most specific when read against the Brezhnev Doctrine. Principle eight, paragraph two, states:

> By virtue of the principle of equal rights and self-determination of peoples, all people always have the right, in full freedom, to determine, when and as they wish, their internal and external political status, without external interference, and to pursue as they wish their political, economic, social and cultural development.

But if that sounds like an iron-clad rejection of the Brezhnev Doctrine—and it does—how can one explain Mr. Brezhnev's own words to the CSCE the day before the Helsinki Accords were signed? He used the occasion to counterattack, to utter words that have become the classic Soviet response to the West's call for implementation in the East of human rights pledges. The same words, if spoken in a different context, might have been taken to mean a repudiation of the Brezhnev Doctrine. Said Brezhnev, "No one should try to dictate to other people, on the basis of foreign policy considerations of one kind or another, the manner in which they ought to manage their internal affairs. It is only the people of each given state and no one else, who have the sovereign right to resolve their internal affairs and establish their internal laws." Brezhnev likened the principles of the CSCE to Lenin's "principles of peaceful coexistence."

Far from being a repudiation of the Brezhnev Doctrine—the Afghanistan invasion is but the latest reaffirmation of it—that speech at Helsinki was Brezhnev's first warning to the West that the Soviet Union would regard insistence on compliance with the humanitarian commitments of the accords as an intrusion in the internal affairs of the Eastern bloc. It was as specious for him to use the CSCE text to reject human rights démarches as it was for him to sign the CSCE document without withdrawing the Brezhnev Doctrine. For while principle 6 of the CSCE declaration refers to "nonintervention in internal affairs," that very text provides specific definitions of intervention. Not one includes exhortatory expressions of concern by one nation at human rights violations in another country. Intervention is there defined as "armed intervention or threat of such intervention" or "coercion designed to subordinate" one nation to another, or "direct or indirect assistance to terrorist activities, or to subversive" acts "directed towards the violent overthrow of the regime." Thus, to invoke principle 6 Brezhnev would have to prove, for example, that Western pleas on behalf of Andrei Sakharov are intended to generate terrorism or other armed force in order to overthrow the Soviet system.

Since the Soviet Union had insisted on a separate principle on intervention in internal affairs, the Western nations firmly tied human rights to the mainstream of the entire Final Act. In principle 7 the states "recognize the universal significance of human rights, and fundamental freedoms, respect for which is an essential factor for the peace..." Thus, "fundamental freedoms"—a reference to full political rights and civil liberties—are included along with other human rights as essential to international peace and security. As though to underscore this, the declaration's first of several concluding paragraphs states that "all the principles"—certainly including the respect for human rights—"will be equally and unreservedly applied, each of them being interpreted taking into account the others."

Thus, the fate of human rights sections should determine the future of the entire CSCE process. By the terms of that process, every section and every clause in every paragraph of every section has equal weight. Every word in the long document was approved by consensus—unanimously. By the very presence in the document of the human rights and information issues, the Soviet Union acknowledged that these rights are a legitimate international concern. One nation's expressing that concern about another nation can no longer be considered interference in domestic affairs.

Why did we go to Madrid?

The CSCE review has been called a process. Like most processes, the CSCE has objectives: not only the inviolability of frontiers, but greater respect for human rights and fundamental freedoms (principle 7), for equal rights and selfdetermination of peoples (principle 8) and an extensive list of additional human rights commitments. These pledge the signers to discernible movement toward reunification of families separated by political and military actions, removal of restrictions on cross-border marriage and travel, freer and wider dissemination of information, improvement in the working conditions of journalists, and more cultural and educational exchanges.

This is a brief summary of the extensive objectives established in CSCE. If taken seriously, these undertakings could, over time, produce significant alteration in closed societies and minor correctives even in generally free countries. Why then did the Soviet Union accept the human rights commitments? Was it only because it wanted the security section and believed human rights could be sloughed off as only rhetoric? Yet Basket I was itself not a legally binding instrument either. It required no action by the Western allies. But it did provide an opportunity for the Soviets to claim that the geographic status quo was permanent. And the Western press did immediately accommodate—despite the quiet objection of the Western negotiators—by interpreting the CSCE as formal acceptance of postwar boundaries.

We are left with human rights commitments—or nothing!

The review conferences are not solely to place on the record the compliance, noncompliance or violation by the several states of the standards set by the Final Act. The review conferences should also draw the ultimate conclusions from that record. The 1978 review conference at Belgrade devoted most of its time to the presentation of cases deemed to be violations of the Helsinki Accords by the Soviet Union and other Eastern-bloc countries. This was, at that time, an essential exercise. When examined on a limited case-by-case basis, however, such clear violations of the Accords nevertheless appeared to be aberrations of established policies of the respective countries. There was insufficient time or resources to list many examples of the harsh maltreatment of dissenters within the Soviet Union; or cite many cases of foreign journalists harassed or denied travel permission within the Soviet Union, or across its borders and back again; or dwell on many family reunions prevented; or indicate the breadth of denials of ethnic and religious rights. Yet the presentation of only a few cases at Belgrade—just a sampling of violations of the CSCE—inevitably implied that these were not the result of formal policy and administrative decisions at the highest levels in the Soviet Union and the other Eastern-bloc countries.

The review at Madrid went much farther in revealing whether the signatories are making good-faith efforts to move discernibly toward ever higher levels of compliance with the Final Act. Retrogressive acts or lack of perceivable movement could now be regarded as tantamount to formal policy commitments by the particular country against compliance and in direct violation of the Final Act.

The Madrid conference was, therefore, expected to place the numerous examples of violations of the CSCE process in the proper context. The retrogressive acts, and the failure to implement CSCE objectives or move noticeably toward them, should be regarded as blatant undermining of confidence in the CSCE process. That process is as important to sustain and strengthen as it was in 1975 or again at Belgrade in 1978. The process is not worth retaining if it is seriously compromised and made a sham.

Although abrogation of the process and an ending of the CSCE was not ruled out by some American observers, there are advantages to renewing the process and assisting it to function as stipulated in the Final Act. The Kampelman addresses illuminate that value. The future conferences scheduled under the aegis of the CSCE could provide continuing opportunities to hold the signatories to their words. There must be perceived movement toward the higher objectives of human rights, wider dissemination of diverse information, improved cultural and trade exchanges, and verifiable steps toward a reduction in military threats.

Most important, the Brezhnev Doctrine must be repudiated if the Helsinki Accords are to have meaning.

The Words of
U.S. Ambassador
Max M. Kampelman

The unique ingredient of the Helsinki Final Act is that it reflects the integrated totality of our East-West relationships. It assumes that the commitment to the human dimension is as necessary to peace as is our commitment to respect one another's borders and to refrain from the use of force against any state. The emphases of the Act on cultural and scientific exchange, human contacts, trade, emigration and the reunification of families, represent essential components in the weaving of the fabric of peace in Europe. The competition between the systems in the East and the West must be one without violence if our objectives of peace and security are to be achieved. This was what all the peoples of Europe, East and West, hailed when they welcomed the Act and looked at the word "détente." Here was to be the formula for peace.

The Soviet Union signed the Act. But its disdain and defiance of the Act since its signing by Mr. Brezhnev must alert us to the threat to peace represented by that disdain and defiance. There is every reason to believe that the Soviet authorities meant something different from what we had in mind when they joined us in signing the agreement.

Within the context of the Act, we must examine the Yalta Agreement and the obvious Soviet interpretation of that agreement to justify and legitimize "spheres of influence." To them, the "Socialist World" (in itself a distortion of the word) has an identity of its own which must not be interfered with in any way by the West because that would be internal intervention by outsiders.

The partition of Europe along predetermined lines cannot and should not become a permanent part of our geopolitics. The myth of Yalta and the "Brezhnev Doctrine" are dangers to peace. They stand in the way of necessary peaceful change and, if allowed to remain, can only produce later upheavals which will threaten stability, in the East as well as in the West.

The provisions of the Helsinki Final Act were accepted by all thirty-five states, signed individually by each. There was no separate set of undertakings based on whether a nation was East or West. There were no two standards. The sovereignty recognized by the Act was the sovereignty of thirty-five nations whose independence was not modified by "spheres of influence."

Our message from Madrid to Moscow has been that those of us who have faith in our societies and have a commitment to peace must find ways to harmonize with one another as we strive to accommodate our systems to the movements of civilization. Change is inevitable. It will come. It will come to the East as it comes to all of us because life requires change. The challenge is whether that change can come peacefully.

The awesome question is whether anything we say gets heard, absorbed and understood in Moscow. And here we come to what I consider to be the ultimate test of our diplomacy.

The West cannot and must not avoid the reality that those who are influenced or adhere to the teachings of Lenin look upon the systems of the East and the West as irreconcilable.

Leninism asserts that world peace can be assured only after "just wars." It believes that the ultimate defeat of capitalism and our Western culture, which will require violence, is a prerequisite to the achievement of a "just peace."

Our society must make it clear to the Soviet authorities that we cannot accept declarations of peace as genuine if those who make those declarations accept the doctrine that war is a law of history and that there is a duty to prepare for, encourage and fight that war to inevitable victory over those of us who proclaim the values of free societies, free elections, free enterprise.

We have an obligation to reveal the hollow hypocrisy of Soviet peace propaganda in the face of its ideology and its aggression. If there is constancy, consistency, and continued Western unity in that message from Madrid to Moscow and from Madrid to the peoples of Europe, then the message will be taken seriously and will have the prospect of contributing to effective diplomacy.

Max M. Kampelman
*Adapted from an address honoring former Secretary of State Dean Rusk
at the University of Georgia, May 8, 1982*

Acronyms Used in the Text

CBMs	Confidence-Building Measures
CMDD	Conference on Military Détente and Disarmament
CW	Chemical Warfare
CSCE	Conference on Security and Cooperation in Europe
FRG	Federal Republic of Germany
GDR	German Democratic Republic
ICBM	Intercontinental Ballistic Missile
ILO	International Labor Organization
KOR	Komitet Obrony Robotnikow (Committee for the Defense of Workers)
MBFR	Mutual and Balanced Force Reduction
MIG	Soviet aircraft
MIRV	Multiple Independently Targetable Reentry Vehicle
NATO	North Atlantic Treaty Organization
PAP	Polish Press Agency
PLO	Palestine Liberation Organization
RM	Registered Madrid
SALT	Strategic Arms Limitation Talks
SMOT	Free Interprofessional Association of Workers
TASS	Telegraphnaya Agentstva Sovetskovo Soyvza (Official Soviet News Agency)
TKK	Temporary Coordinating Commission
VONS	Committee for Defense of the Unjustly Persecuted

Preparations

The Madrid review faced an impasse soon after it began on September 6, 1980. The preparatory sessions scheduled to run until November 11 could not agree on an agenda. The Western delegates (from all fifteen NATO states, and Spain and Ireland) and most of the neutral and non-aligned (Austria, Cyprus, Finland, Liechtenstein, Malta, Monaco, San Marino, Vatican, Sweden, Switzerland, and Yugoslavia) approved using the rules that governed the Belgrade review three years earlier. They sought an agenda for the main sessions that would assure ample time to examine how well the countries had implemented the 1975 Act. The Soviet Union and its associates (Bulgaria, East Germany, Hungary, Poland, Romania,and Czechoslovakia) strongly objected. As days of acrimonious debate passed, there was some question whether the review meetings might be held. The Soviets particularly sought to limit time devoted to discussions of human rights issues. To avoid passing the November deadline for opening the review, the clocks in the negotiating hall were stopped.

At 3:00 a.m. on the morning of November 11, Ambassador Kampelman emerged to announce an agreement: The formal sessions would begin that day and run until December 19. Those weeks would be spent reporting and discussing implementation of the 1975 act.

Ambassador Kampelman made fourteen interventions during the nine-week preparatory meetings. Two of these appear here. They reflect the divisions that grip not only the conference but the world, and the relation of the United States to these.

September 11, 1980 Guidelines for Negotiation

I rise in my capacity this afternoon as a representative of the government of the United States. We are now in the third day of our deliberations. I find myself with a greater degree of conviction that the CSCE process is alive and healthy.

I came here on behalf of my government determined to assert our view that we are committed to the process and to its continuation as an integral and indispensable part of our international commitments. It is clear to me that this conviction of my government is shared by the other nations who are signatories to the Helsinki Final Act of 1975. This gives me great personal satisfaction and gives my government an even more profound appreciation that we are, all of us, jointly committed to a noble process in behalf of peace.

We are prepared for our meetings in Madrid this month with that in mind and with sensitivity because we all desire that the main meetings which begin in November be successful. We may, each of us, have varying interpretations of how we would measure success, but I believe that the element common to that definition is one of commitment to peace, to security, and to the eternal principles of human dignity which are an integral part of the Helsinki Final Act.

It is with immense gratitude as a citizen of the United States and as a representative of my country, that I tip my hat to those of you present today who helped build the CSCE fabric which weaves its way through the international community. It assists us in our striving for peace. Those of you who had the privilege of participating in the Geneva, the Helsinki, and the Belgrade deliberations, have earned the gratitude and appreciation of all of us.

What began as something of an experiment in international relations has become a living institution, one that is evolving and growing as our problems intensify and also as our opportunities present themselves. Our presence here today in Madrid is testimony to that fact.

Our institution is a unique one. It has no staff. It has no continuing formal structure. Yet, for the first time in history, a process has evolved under which the thirty-five nations who are represented around this table, come together on a regular basis to discuss the full range of their relations.

Our forum is unique, not just because it affords an opportunity to meet, to review our behavior, and to renew our commitments. It is also unique because we are united in appreciating that all our citizens share the aspiration for human dignity and for fundamental human freedoms.

We have differences. We will continue to have differences. Those differences will manifest themselves, hopefully, with clarity and dignity, at our main meetings in November. It would be misleading—indeed, disastrous—were we to deny the existence of those differences and the need for us to help lead them toward a mechanism and a procedure under which our differences can be resolved with peace and with the values we share protected.

Our task is to find a means of recognizing the existence of our differences and, even to some extent, the profound depth of those differences, and, at the same time, renew our commitment to the process of peace symbolized by the Helsinki Accords.

It is, therefore, without hesitation that I assert our own determination and conviction that the end result of our process must be a decision to meet again under the terms of the Final Act. This may not be the diplomatic time and place for such a statement as I am aware, but this is the one indispensable way to demonstrate our commitment to the process and our determination that it shall continue to live and to meet our needs. To do anything less would be a disservice to our citizens, to our values, and to future generations. But it is timely to move to the specifics.

We have all listened with pleasure and satisfaction to the statements of our colleagues made around this table: pleasure because of their eloquence, satisfaction because of the far-reaching apparent agreement which has been expressed here on the way we should proceed and the goals we should seek. Mr. Chairman, allow me to summarize the points of that consensus, as they appear to me.

First of all, there seems to be wide agreement among us on the advantages of the Yellow Book, which governed our meeting at Belgrade. Some of my colleagues have indicated areas in which those procedures might be improved; others have urged us to adhere closely to the Belgrade procedures. But there seems to be agreement that they are the proper starting point of our deliberations.

Let me say that my government is in complete agreement with this approach. The Belgrade procedures—as several of my fellow representatives have pointed out—were not perfect. Indeed, we have been strongly tempted to propose changes to meet our needs and our appraisals. But those procedures worked well. I needn't remind you again of the differences which had to be overcome to create this body of procedural rules; but surely our awareness of those difficulties should make us all extremely reluctant to seek changes in those procedures, other than those changes indicated by the obvious, such as changes in time and locale.

My delegation is confident that the rule of reason will prevail in our proceedings. There are beneficial changes to meet our needs and our appraisals which can and should be accommodated within the *mutatis mutandi* formula. We would hope that those changes need not be the subject of controversy between us. But if others believe they are controversial, we will, of course, not insist and be guided by that reality.

I offer for your thoughtful consideration this suggestion: it is far better, from our point of view, to adopt the procedures that we had previously agreed upon as represented in the Yellow Book without change than to open this meeting to recommendations which would undo past work and plunge us into a lengthy—and perhaps fruitless—debate. For our part, we will do nothing to put in jeopardy the agreement on procedures which prevailed at Belgrade and which provide, in our opinion, the only reasonable foundation for Madrid.

There seems, as well, to be a growing feeling among us that we should conduct our deliberations in a spirit of reason and pragmatism, and that we should discharge our duties quickly and return home to our preparations for the substantive discussions which will begin in November. Let me assert calmly as a matter of fact: Madrid is beautiful. We are willing to spend as much time here as is necessary to our task—if not quite the forty-nine weeks which our British colleague indicated as the limit of his endurance. But I doubt whether that would be constructive for our process.

I must note as well, Mr. Chairman, what I perceive as a general agreement which seems to be emerging from many of the statements we have heard and the informal conversations we have had. This agreement concerns the need to bear in mind that this is a preparatory meeting, devoted—according to both mandate and precedent—to establishing the date, duration, agenda, and other modalities for the main meeting which will follow. We are not here to discuss substantive issues. Indeed—and here again, I believe there is widespread agreement among us—it is essential to the success of our efforts that we respect the distinction between the task for which we have assembled here in September, and the wider tasks which our governments will address beginning on November 11.

To say that the task of this preparatory meeting must be a limited task is not to say that it will not be an important task. Indeed, the very fact that we do our work well in this meeting will underlie our collective commitment to the CSCE process. It is a commitment which will be reinforced at Madrid, and at the follow-on meeting which will come after Madrid.

Mr. Chairman, I trust that in these short remarks, I have not misinterpreted what I believe the prevailing mood here to be. If I have, I have no doubt that my colleagues will correct me.

Mr. Chairman, challenged by the examples of several delegations, I have searched for a classical quotation to serve as a conclusion to my remarks. It would have been good were I able to cite an appropriate Spanish source. Given a more personal familiarity, I am confident something suitable and Spanish could have been found. Let me offer as a substitute a quotation from another rich culture represented in our CSCE framework. Hippocrates laid down for the medical profession a maxim which should govern our minimum aspirations in this preparatory meeting: above all, do not harm.

November 5, 1980 U.S. Elections

I ask for the floor to comment briefly on the elections that took place in the United States yesterday and their possible effect on these Madrid meetings and the CSCE process itself.

Yesterday, the citizens of the United States made a choice which has traditionally been one of the strengths of our democratic system. For the nineteenth time in the history of our country, they have voted to change their president and their party.

We are a young country compared to most of those around this table. But in one thing we are old. We have the oldest written Constitution in the world. That document has now endured nearly two hundred years.

Under our Constitution, we have elected forty presidents. And in nineteen of those elections, the people of the United States have voted for a change. The principle of democratic alternation—the right to change our leaders peacefully and by democratic vote—is one of the fundamental elements of our political system and of the Constitution which spawned it. Yesterday, we saw that principle confirmed once again. I returned to my country and yesterday exercised my right to vote.

Last night, minutes after learning that his defeat was inevitable, President Carter conceded the victory of President-elect Reagan and pledged to work as hard as he could to ensure a smooth transition. With those words has begun for us a transition which will be marked by both continuity and change.

Mr. Chairman, it is legitimate to ask what all this means for the Helsinki process and for the Madrid conference.

The government of the United States is committed to the CSCE process which was formalized with the Helsinki Final Act in 1975 and is in full support of the positions taken by this delegation at these preparatory meetings. My government's policy today is the same as it was yesterday and as it has been from the very first day of these meetings. This commitment will remain the position of the United States under President Jimmy Carter until January 20. And this commitment will remain the position of the United States under President Ronald Reagan after January 20.

I make this statement with conviction and on the basis of both instruction and firm advice.

Mr. Chairman, I conclude this statement by reminding this distinguished body of its immense responsibility to the Helsinki process. We are now in the midst of our ninth week. We have only six days remaining before the main meeting begins. My delegation continues to believe and to assert that the delays we have experienced are unnecessary and have been harmful to the process. The goals of the Helsinki Final Act would have been better served, in our opinion, had we agreed expeditiously to the rules arrived at by compromise on the part of all of us in Belgrade.

To those who have sought substantive changes in that previously agreed upon compromise, I must again respectfully state that my delegation has insisted and will continue to insist on adequate time for a thorough review of implementation and we will not agree to weaken the Helsinki process by accepting proposals designed to alter that essential element of the Helsinki Final Act. On that, Mr. Chairman, and the issue of human rights which it represents, the American people—Democrats and Republicans, supporters of President Carter or President-elect Reagan—are united.

Implementation

In his opening address, Attorney-General Griffin B. Bell called the CSCE a "dynamic and positive process" that is "slowly but surely breaking down the barriers which grew up at the height of the cold war; a process which is bringing people together across the East-West divide."He added, the delegates "will hear often over the next several weeks that the words of the Final Act on human rights and human contacts must be interpreted in different ways when applied in different social systems. This argument is untrue—and profoundly harmful to the spirit of our enterprise." He stated, men and women "do not possess human rights because they are members of this or that social system. They possess human rights because they are human beings."

Congressman Dante B. Fascell, vice-chairman of the U.S. delegation, told an opening session that "the Soviet invasion of Afghanistan cannot be reconciled with the principles of the Helsinki Final Act." He listed six principles that were "openly flouted."

Ambassador Kampelman fashioned his opening address on détente. Interestingly, it was to be the first subject mentioned in the final declaration of the Madrid conference.

November 17, 1980 **Détente**

We meet here today in the eleventh consecutive week, the second week of our main meeting. We have, all of us, been emphasizing our differences at the same time as we have been reaffirming our joint desire to revitalize the spirit of Helsinki which is today badly tarnished. The word *détente* appears in the Helsinki Final Act to describe a relationship of growing cooperation among the thirty-five nations who are a part of this process. I should like to address myself to the concept and word *détente*.

It is a feature of our times that the developed world is divided between two great political systems and that those two systems happen to be represented by the two most powerful nations on earth: the United States and the Soviet Union. Ever since World War II our systems and our two nations have been locked in a military competition and an ideological struggle. Indeed, to a large degree, the history of the postwar period is a chronicle of that competition and that struggle.

Ironically, the United States and the Soviet Union have much in common. We are both continental countries, sprawling across a vast land mass and washed by distant seas. We are explorers by nature—settlers, adventurers, cossacks, and cowboys. We have never fought a war with each other, and were indeed allies in the largest foreign war in which either of us has ever been engaged. And we are, finally, revolutionary nations wtih a political tradition which draws sustenance from our respective revolutions.

Nevertheless, our political systems are incompatible and, to a large degree, antithetical. The American system, which derives from French philosophy and English experience, is rooted in the importance of the individual. As Jefferson said, "the care of human life and happiness, and not their destruction, is the first and only legitimate object of good government." The Soviet system, if I may be so bold as to characterize it, is typified by collective values: the proletariat, the party, the state. In practice, those collective values have produced achievements in education, in health care, and significant accomplishments in the technology of space travel. But those collective values bring with them the suppression of the individual who is thus deprived of the freedom which is his by natural right, even by Soviet law, and indeed, by the Helsinki Final Act. Hence, the incompatibility to which I referred.

Despite our incompatibility, we are compelled to coexist and to cooperate. War, not peace, has historically been the typical human condition. But the prospect of war in a nuclear age must give pause. And here again, I turn to the Helsinki Final Act. Our hope was that, out of the cooperation and understanding called for by that agreement, there would develop confidence between us which would strengthen our sense of security and trust with one another.

My government, Mr. Chairman, took that agreement seriously. We signed it in 1975 because it had within it the essential ingredients necessary for détente. In the Principles and in Basket III it reaffirmed and codified the historic yearning of men and women, from the beginning of time, to strive for greater freedom and to be a part of that evolutionary process which stretches mankind from its early animal beginnings into what many would call that which is God-like in all of us, a higher form of civilized behavior. The fact that the Helsinki Final Act implicitly recognized that definition of man's role in the universe, was basic to the decision that led my government to sign that agreement.

Détente to us was indivisible and we were pleased that the Helsinki Final Act, approved by all thirty-five nations, was itself an indivisible whole. The second Basket of our basic document was part of that whole. It aimed to forge growing cooperation among all of us in the day-to-day intercourse that is an integral part of our lives, all of our lives, whatever system or form of government we may be organized under. And we all understand that, with the modern weapons of horror created by the technology which has absorbed the talents and energies of our societies, it was indispensable that we pledge ourselves to peace and that we renounce in a steady and ever constant course the use of war to resolve our differences.

We take these responsibilities seriously, but the American people, Mr. Chairman, have increasingly begun to question whether all of the nations who signed the Helsinki Final Act in 1975 took that commitment seriously. It is with deep regret that we have increasingly become skeptical. Détente is not only indivisible, it is only meaningful if it is universally understood, accepted, and acted upon. If détente as a concept is to be interpreted one way by us and another way by the Soviet Union, then it is a meaningless word which cannot govern our relationships. It becomes a propaganda weapon rather than a set of principles to guide international behavior. That, I fear, is what has indeed become the reality of our relationship and what is at the root of the serious differences between us that have become so evident at these meetings.

Representatives of a few states stood before this body last week, and again today, indignantly objecting to the fact that practically every other participating state at these meetings made adverse reference to the Soviet invasion of Afghanistan. The references were made by us earnestly and with deep feeling arising out of a conviction that we share, that a basic and indispensable ingredient of détente is to forego unilateral military action against any other state. The invasion of Afghanistan, no matter how it may be denied by verbal obfuscation, is a threat to peace and a direct violation of the principles of the Helsinki Final Act. For clarity, let me read from that Act: "The participating States declare their intention to conduct their relations with all other States in the spirit of the principles contained in the present Declaration."

We have reason to question the depth of the commitment made, when we learn that in a speech delivered in Prague early in 1973, a leader of the Soviet Union described détente as a device to bring about a decisive shift in the international balance of power. This is a far cry from the definition of détente which led my government to reduce its armed forces and moderate its military power in an effort to demonstrate our commitment to peace. I quote from that talk in Prague: "We have been able to achieve more in a short time with détente than was done for years pursuing a confrontation policy with NATO... trust us, Comrades, for by 1985, as a consequence of what we are now achieving with détente... we will be able to extend our will wherever we need to."

When the Helsinki Final Act was signed by the United States in 1975, we were aware of that statement and fully aware of Lenin's 1921 statement that the cultural strata of Western Europe and America, along with the capitalists of the entire world, are "deaf mutes" who "will close their eyes to the realities" and thus become blind as well as deaf as they "open credit... and provide us with essential materials and technology thus restoring our military industry, especially for our future victorious attacks on our suppliers." The West, he said, would thus work to prepare its own suicide.

We were aware of this 1921 teaching of Lenin, a useful revolutionary tool, but our desire for peace and understanding and cooperation and mutual security was so great that we were prepared to accept the written commitments of the followers of Lenin in the hope that experience had and would moderate those teachings. My government agreed to increase economic and technological exchanges in order to advance the process of peace. Instead, we have seen those benefits distorted to stimulate more military aggression in support of national and ideological goals.

There will be criticism of my government's recent actions restraining our commitments under Basket II of the agreement, but I suggest, Mr. Chairman, that this action is required and indeed demanded if we are to maintain the indivisibility of détente and preserve the fabric of the Helsinki Final Act. Aggression and continued violations of commitments made must be condemned by effective responses if the integrity of the agreement is to be preserved.

It has also been greatly disturbing to us that, during the periods when we enthusiastically participated in growing cultural and economic exchanges with the Soviet Union, the so-called high period of détente, the commitments under Principle VII and Basket III were undermined as internal repression in the Soviet Union increased with a tightening of censorship and an intensified use of prison, psychiatric institutions and exile to deal with dissension.

Indeed, Mr. Chairman, during the course of this very meeting on Thursday of last week, in brazen disregard of its commitments, Dr. Viktor Brailovsky, a scientist and editor, a leading figure in the Jewish emigration movement was arrested in Moscow, two days after announcing that a three-day fast would take place by scores of Jews refused permission to emigrate, a demonstration linked to the opening of this Madrid Conference. For the past eight years, Dr. Brailovsky has been denied an exit visa. Since that visa application, Brailovsky's son, Leonid, who is now nineteen years old, has been forced to leave school and has been banned from any university. Viktor Brailovsky himself has not been allowed to pursue his teaching career. His arrest makes him the twelfth Jew currently in prison in the Soviet Union for attempting to emigrate. All twelve of those cases are in direct violation of the Final Act.

And during the past decade, Mr. Chairman, the Soviet Union has strengthened its war machine by spending about 150 billion dollars more than the United States on military equipment; and its armed forces are a threat to the peace of Europe and the world. The Soviet Union today devotes an astonishing 14-15 percent of its gross national product to its military machine, while the United States spends 5 percent of its gross national product on defense. Today, the Soviet Union has a new catalogue of major weapons systems, including four intercontinental ballistic missiles, three submarine-launched missiles, four new classes of submarines, and four new fighter bombers.

I raise these facts today, Mr. Chairman, again, not to be confrontational. I state them because they are facts, facts that must be faced if we are to turn from the growing spirit of mistrust and dissension which characterizes international relations today. Only through understanding can we face reality, and only through facing reality can we hope to achieve the harmony which we all seek. We are moving precipitously toward confrontation and it is to all of our interests that this movement cease and be redirected toward the spirit of détente which, regrettably, no longer is today the reality we all hoped for in 1975.

There should be no misunderstanding. The United States of America has embarked and will intensify its efforts in the days ahead toward strengthening our military capacity. The Soviet Union must understand that the United States and its allies will match its military effort. There can be no question but that we will not concede military superiority. We are proceeding, and will continue to proceed with great reluctance, but the will to do so is there—and it is a will which unites the American people. In our society, Mr. Chairman, our leaders reflect public opinion and do not have the instruments of propaganda and coercion to create it.

We are embarked on our program of renewed military strength because we have been forced to do so in the light of massive military build-up, unparalleled in world history, and regrettably one prepared for use. The Afghanistan invasion was a symbol of that preparation, and its seriousness to us, therefore, must not be underestimated.

We will pursue our program of military preparedness with determination and we will mobilize the resources of the American people, American wealth, American ingenuity and technology, so that it is effective and can serve as the deterrent so necessary to avoid war. We had hoped that this spirit of Helsinki would serve as a sufficient deterrent and that the attraction of security, cooperation, and peace would persuade the Soviet Union to join us and all thirty-five nations here in a determined common effort to achieve international stability and security. Regrettably, that has not proven to be the case, and we are reluctantly forced to the conclusion that we must, once again, depend upon our military strength to serve as the necessary deterrent.

I use this occasion to reiterate, however, that my government under President-elect Reagan and under President Carter stands ready to negotiate significant, verifiable and balanced arms control agreements once a mutual determination to do so becomes evident. We are prepared to enter into negotiations at any time to explore the existence of that mutuality. This forum is one of those available to us, and there are other forums.

The reality of military competition does not make arms control impossible, it makes arms control imperative. The first major arms control agreement of the postwar period—the limited nuclear test-ban treaty—was signed in 1963, at the height of the cold war. Today, the United States is currently engaged in two major disarmanent negotiations, on Mutual and Balanced Force Reductions, and on Theater Nuclear Forces, and President-elect Reagan has expressed his readiness to enter into renewed SALT negotiations.

We stand ready to reduce the level of our armamemts and move toward the disarmament that our people all yearn for, but we will only do so if this is universally accepted and acted upon. There will be no unilateral action by the United States in this area. It will be joint and it will be meaningful and verifiable, or it will not take place.

Our ideological differences are sharp. It would be folly for us to consider it realistic that we can persuade one another of the virtues of our respective beliefs. We, in America, do not shrink from the competition of ideas. Americans are as free to read the works of Marx and Lenin as to read the works of Franklin and Jefferson; all are available in our book stores and libraries. We are as free to vote Communist as to vote Republican; and the 11,738 votes the Commumist candidate received in our presidential election two weeks ago accurately reflect, it seems to me, his true support in our country. We are as free to listen to Radio Moscow as to our own networks. Does a Soviet citizen have the same freedom? To ask the question is to answer it.

We believe that, in the long run, the aspirations of mankind toward greater individual freedom will inevitably be attalned and cannot be defeated no matter how severe the repression. Helsinki monitors may be arrested in Moscow but in doing so, they create a situation in which those of us all over the world who cherish human freedom join our voices with theirs and become with them Helsinki monitors.

We are convinced that the historic inevitability for the human being is the inevitability of human rights, of individual freedom, and not of some ideologically defined doctrinal concept of revolution.

Others differ with us and have developed a modern faith of their own. We urge those who differ with us that these differences, fundamental as they are, be pursued in the competition of ideas and in the competition of performance. Let us devote our energies toward demonstrating within each of our societies the superiority of our models to meet the needs of our peoples. That kind of competition can help us all. The competition of armaments and the use of force for aggression has the potential of destroying us all.

I close this presentation with a plea on behalf of my government that we return to the foundation of the Helsinki Final Act as a basis for our relationship, all of that agreement, in its totality, indivisible. Only by demonstrating a commitment to its provisions, all of its provisions, by performance, can we hope to establish the trust that will lead us forward to new commitments. We deeply and genuinely hope that the beginning of that rebirth can begin here in Madrid.

December 19, 1980 Review of Implementation Phase
* * *

... At this transition point, ... it is natural and proper to pause and reflect upon the meaning of what has transpired to this halfway point and to indicate the course of the next phase.

By one measure, it is easy to see whence we have come and whither we go. We have worked here for more than three months. They have been difficult months, but also productive ones. And we now prepare to return to our homes for renewal and for consultations, after which our delegations will come back to Madrid for the next phase of our deliberations.

By that same measure, it is clear that we established the ground rules for our main meeting in an unnecessarily difficult and prolonged preparatory gathering, which ultimately proved to be successful. We reviewed the implementation of the Final Act thoroughly, forthrightly, and constructively. We thus made the important review of implementation phase of our work an integral and permanent part of the CSCE follow-up process. And we have brought forward new proposals designed to strengthen our commitments and hopefully to advance the process. We next are faced with the task of considering these proposals, examining whether we believe they advance the process, and exploring possible areas of agreement. Finally, we expect to draft and adopt a concluding document, and to establish the date, the place, and the terms of the next follow-up meeting.

But a deeper look is called for. Our meeting is indeed in a transition week. The significance of that transition and of these meetings requires an awareness that the European order, of which the CSCE process is so important a part, is also in profound transition. And my country, the United States of America, is in its own interrelated transition.

President Carter, under whose authority and instructions this delegation has acted, will leave office on January 20. When our delegation returns on January 27, it will be under the authority of President Ronald Reagan. In one vital sense, I have already assured this body that my government and its people will remain true to the commitments we undertook in Helsinki five years ago. No one should doubt American constancy to the powerful ideals of the CSCE process, to the preservation and enhancement of human freedom, to respect for the sovereignty and independence of all states, and to the effort to establish greater military security and cooperation among us. Those will be President Reagan's objectives, as they have been President Carter's. They are my country's objectives.

But, Mr. Chairman, neither the CSCE process nor this Madrid meeting exists in a vacuum. As important as it is and committed as we are to it, the Helsinki process constitutes but a part of a larger movement of politics and history. It affects, and is affected by, the relations between the states of this most developed portion of the world. We must understand that it has all the fragility of a process which is taking place in a geographic area which has twice spawned global wars, which has endured a thirty-five-year period of tension following the second of those wars, and which is now beset by a new crisis of confidence.

That crisis of confidence must be faced if we are to achieve understanding. It has three aspects and these have dominated our thoughts and our discussions during these last fifteen weeks of our meeting.

The first manifestation of this crisis of confidence reflected itself in the reality, a surprise to some, that human rights has been a fundamental theme of our Madrid meeting's work to date. This issue is an ever-present and permanent part of the East-West agenda. Never before have so many governments examined the practical aspects of this question with such comprehensiveness. We have laid to rest forever the notion that the way a country treats its own people is its own affair alone and that such treatment is not a proper subject for international discussion. The notion is wrong that human rights has no effect on interstate relations or on international security.

The message that my delegation has sought to convey—and which we have heard spoken by the vast majority of states represented here—is our profound displeasure with the failure by some countries, and particularly the USSR, to implement Principle VII and Basket III, the human rights provisions of the Final Act. We, and others, have presented sober and incontrovertible evidence of this failure to perform.

My delegation has reviewed, inter alia, the repression which the Helsinki monitors have suffered; the restrictions on religious freedom; the pressures on the rights of national minorities; manifestations of anti-Semitism and indications of officially sanctioned so-called "anti-Zionism"; the jamming of radio stations that seek to make available more information in the spirit of the Final Act; the restrictions on international mail which isolate people from friends, colleagues, and family; and the human suffering represented by continuing obstacles to family reunification.

With free men and women all over the world, we are thankful for the Scharanskys, for the Orlovs, for the Mendelvichs, for the Slepaks, and for the Sakharovs. In suffering untold indignities for their principles, they unselfishly give something precious to us. They give us a warning about the incredible cruelty that man is capable of inflicting on man. They also give us reassurance that the human spirit cannot be crushed by force; it can be imprisoned, but it cannot be annihilated.

We have said a great deal. We could have said more. We could have discussed in greater detail the abuse of psychiatry for the purpose of controlling nonconforming citizens, a particularly cruel and inhuman form of punishment which requires overwhelming moral condemnation. We could have discussed the imprisonment of Soviet workers for their efforts to form independent labor unions, a movement which cannot long be denied. But we felt that the case was clear enough; and the realization is clear that the U.S. and other nations of the West are profoundly disappointed in the conclusions we have been forced to draw.

Mr. Chairman, the subject of human rights should draw us together, not drive us apart. Whatever disagreements the participating states may have about philosophical and ideological issues of how society should be organized, we should be able to identify in human rights a unifying factor. We were able, after all, to agree in Principle VII and Basket III on clear language setting forth our obligations in this area. It is doubly disappointing, therefore, that during the months since we first convened in Madrid, even as we discussed review of implementation, there were more than twenty instances of arrest, conviction, or other serious harassment of individuals in the Soviet Union that have been brought to our attention—individuals who have sought only to exercise rights confirmed to them in the Final Act.

Let me recall the words of Alexander Herzen, the nineteenth-century Russian patriot who struggled for the rights of the Russian people. He said in 1851: "Russia's future will be a great danger for Europe and a great misfortune for Russia if there is no emancipation of the individual."

Mr. Chairman, progress in the human rights area would encourage progress in bilateral relations and progress in the security area. If we could observe a willingness to achieve practical improvements in the humanitarian sphere, to the direct benefit of individuals, then my government and the American people would be quick to respond positively. I have every confidence that other peoples and governments would be similarly inclined. The prospects for cooperation in other spheres would be significantly increased. On the other hand, ignoring this yearning for greater human freedom would inevitably perpetuate the crisis of confidence.

There is a second component of the crisis of confidence that grips us. It is the armed intervention in Afghanistan by the Soviet Union, which has been seriously discussed at length by a large number of delegations. Many of us have submitted irrefutable textual evidence from the Final Act itself that the principles basic to the Helsinki process must be observed in relations with all states, whether they are signatories or not. Standards for proper international behavior cannot be selectively applied, and the Act makes that clear. The verdict of the vast majority of governments represented here is clear. The Soviet military aggression in Afghanistan does come within the competence of CSCE. It does threaten European security and cooperation. It does adversely affect the relations which the Soviet Union seeks with all of us. To attempt to justify that aggression by a supposed special code of conduct within the so-called "Socialist Community" of states, as if military aggression is justified when it protects or advances their ideology, is not merely unacceptable. It imperils the very existence of the CSCE process and world peace.

Mr. Chairman, the third aspect of the crisis of confidence concerns the essential area of security. Security—whether military security or security in a broader sense—has been addressed by many delegations here. Arms control and disarmament are objectives which must be mastered. But the wish, even the intention, is not always father to the deed. We have a common expression of goals. But we also have a marked difference in the assessment of how to achieve those goals and in the analysis of why we are far from realizing them.

Our delegation has described in detail our deep concern arising out of the unprecedented Soviet expenditure on armaments—the largest military build-up the world has ever seen. The response of the United States and our friends has been twofold. We have undertaken and will continue to undertake the necessary steps to maintain an adequate level of our own military strength. And we have offered and continue to stand ready to negotiate seriously to enhance mutual security at substantially lower levels of armament.

We must not fail to note, however, that the degree of our confidence in the intentions of the Soviet Union is vital to our perceptions of what is necessary for defense and what is feasible for diplomacy. That confidence, as we have often stated, has been shaken. In recent weeks, that confidence has further eroded.

The preamble to the Document on Confidence-Building Measures and Certain Aspects of Security and Disarmament of the Final Act recognizes "the need to contribute to reducing the dangers of armed conflict and of misunderstanding or miscalculation of military activities which could give rise to apprehension particularly in a situation where the participating States lack clear and timely information about the nature of such activities." The same preamble—as well as the language of Principle II—commits the signatories to refrain from "the threat or use of force against the territorial integrity or political independence of any state."

Mr Chairman, in recent weeks the movements and preparations of sizeable Warsaw Pact forces in Central and Eastern Europe have caused us all deep concern.* This action is totally inconsistent with the commitments of the Final Act that I have just quoted. It has aroused widespread apprehension. As our disting-

*These movements were regarded as threats to invade Poland to prevent further gains by the Solidarity labor movement in that country.-Ed.

uished colleagues from France and other countries have said, the CSCE process would make a significant contribution if it were to adopt significant, verifiable confidence-building measures, covering all of Europe, measures that could effectively cope with such a threatening development.

CSCE can be relevant to East-West relations only if, in the words of the Final Act, its principles are put into practice by all the participating States "irrespective of their political, economic or social systems as well as of their size, geographical location or level of economic development."

The obligations to refrain from the use of force are not new and are not theoretical obligations. They were violated in Europe in 1956 and again in 1968. If they should again be violated—and we pray they will not—East-West relations as we know them could not continue. And the contribution which CSCE could make to the security and cooperation in Europe would be, I am afraid, a certain casualty of that disaster.

Mr. Chairman, I have described three areas which contribute to a crisis of confidence that puts at issue the course of events in East-West relations. Our delegations return to their capitals at a turning point. As with all turning points the direction that is to be taken is not inevitable. Our governments are not the captives of fate alone. We have the capacity to determine the course of events.

We, the CSCE signatories, some with a heavier responsibility than others, have it within our power to pursue courses of action that will convert each of these crises of confidence into renewed efforts at cooperation that can contribute to mutual security.

It is against this realistic and disturbing background that we will be returning to Madrid next month to consider and discuss new proposals that can help resolve the lack of confidence which has led to the crises. All of the proposals introduced, co-sponsored, or supported by the United States are directed to this objective. The most important of these proposals would: recommit us all to respect for human rights and fundamental freedoms and to the opening of a true dialogue, both bilateral and multilateral, on this important subject; lead to practical improvements in the areas of human contacts, including family reunification, and to a freer flow of information; encourage decisions for dealing with the problem of terrorism, a threat to all our societies, and indeed to civilized behavior on our planet; and put us on a path to expanding and strengthening significant, verifiable, and geographically broadening confidence-building measures which would, among other things, make more difficult the use of military force for political intimidation.

When our main meetings began on November 11, my country was in transition. We were under the leadership of a president who was in office; and we were about to welcome a president-elect who was preparing to assume office. I stated then that our government was deeply concerned over the fact that the provisions of the Helsinki Final Act were being blatantly violated and that those violations cast a shadow over our meetings. The American people, along with peoples elsewhere, had come to question the validity of seeking new commitments from a state which had not lived up to commitments it had previously made.

This meeting is only a piece of a larger picture. What we may do here can affect that larger picture. Our successes or failures in talking to each other here and in putting words on paper will have an effect on the course of East-West relations. But obviously determining will be actions taken by our governments outside this conference hall.

The United States looks at the world realistically. We do not seek to change the social system of any other state represented here. We understand that the Soviet Union, for example, is proud of what it considers the accomplishments of its society and its way of life. We believe the actions we have proposed would not threaten its security. On the contrary, with confidence in the appeal of its ideology, greater freedom within its society may well enhance its security. We wish to work with the Soviet Union as a partner in helping to achieve security and cooperation in Europe and throughout the world. We are deeply conscious of the shared responsibility that our respective military capacities impose upon our two nations.

We wish to ask of the Soviet Union only the possible and the necessary. On human rights, there are steps which we and others have indicated which, if taken, would change the climate of our relations in a fashion that can scarcely be overstated. If prison doors open, if families are reunited, if defenders of human rights are recognized as such—and at least released from imprisonment, psychiatric detention, or exile—if emigration restrictions are more tinged with humanity, then the American people will respond enthusiastically with a willingness to improve, in renewed faith, the entire range of our relations.

If the Soviet Union will ponder and act upon the implications of its actions in Afghanistan, then a great impediment to true peace can be set aside.

In every problem there is an opportunity. With human rights, with Afghanistan, with the current situation in Central Europe, there are solutions readily available. They are not mysterious. They are fully spelled out in the Helsinki Final Act. The Act spells out our ideals and the realistic pragmatism to achieve those goals and all of our interests.

If this meeting has helped all of us to face the reality of our position—and to realize the strength of our process—and to act upon that realization, then the CSCE will have made a great contribution. We can then share the confidence that it will make even greater contributions in the future.

Proposals

The review-of-implementation sessions recessed December 19, 1980. When the conference reconvened January 19, 1981, the United States had a new president, and Ambassador Kampelman was retained at his post in Madrid. At the reopened meeting in January he discussed the continuity of U.S. policy, and in subsequent sessions addressed new proposals. He particularly rejected the moral and legal standing of the Brezhnev Doctrine. The second phase of the main conference ended on April 10, 1981.

January 27, 1981 Continuing U.S. Objectives

One week ago today Ronald Reagan was inaugurated as the fortieth president of the United States. I speak at this first plenary session of our renewed meetings here in Madrid to assert once again that the position of the government of the United States, expressed at these meetings during our preparatory sessions and during the first phase of our main meeting, remains a constant one.

When our delegation first addressed this body during the first day of our preparatory meeting in September, I stated that our government was fully committed to the provisions of the Helsinki Final Act; to the continuation of the processes which that Act initiated; to the success of this Madrid meeting; and to further follow-up meetings after Madrid. I asserted then, Mr. Chairman, and reassert today, that these are objectives of the American government, reflecting the deep desires of the American people to achieve peace, security, and stability in Europe and in the world.

There is a heritage that all of us represented at this conference share. Our civilization is characterized by optimism, by a faith in the process of history, by a conviction that the forces for the emancipation of the human being from the shackles of slavery—whether it be an imprisonment of the body, the mind, or the spirit—will in the end prevail. This aspiration for freedom is an integral part of the yearnings of all peoples.

The Helsinki Final Act earned its place as a significant document for history because it recognized the indivisibility of peace and security and human dignity. It wove a seamless fabric for cooperation among us by establishing standards for moral and civilized behavior among us as nations and within our own societies for those who reside in our societies.

If this document is to be preserved as a vehicle for realizing our goals of peace and security, it must be guarded with care. For that reason, Mr. Chairman, we agree that the first six weeks of our main meeting would require a full and thorough and detailed and frank review of its implementation.

During the course of these meetings, Mr. Chairman, we, and all but a few of all the other participating states, asserted that the invasion of Afghanistan was a gross violation of all the principles of the Helsinki Final Act of 1975 and was a serious burden across the full spectrum of East-West relations. We expressed our serious concern about the unprecedented Soviet expenditures on armaments, the largest military build-up the world has ever seen. The movements and preparations of sizeable Warsaw Pact forces in Central and Eastern Europe, in direct violation of Principle II of the Helsinki Final Act, drew our sober attention and deep concern. Delegation after delegation took the floor at these meetings, furthermore, to note with deep regret the evidence of growing repression in the Soviet Union in direct defiance of the first and third chapters of the Helsinki Final Act.

I made those statements then and I reassert them now, Mr. Chairman, with my government under the direction of a new president. The government of the United States and the American people continue to deplore these violations of the Helsinki Final Act. They are barriers to international harmony and peace.

The review of implementation phase of this meeting ended on December 19. It was therefore our hope, Mr. Chairman, that it would not be necessary at this reconvened meeting to refer in specific terms to violations and challenges to the integrity of the Helsinki Final Act. The violations, however, continue and intensify, and we have no choice but to respond in this forum.

Just prior to our recess, our delegation noted sadly the large number, more than twenty, of arrests, trials and related persecutions in violation of the Helsinki Final Act that had occurred in the Soviet Union since these CSCE preparatory meetings began in early September. I regret to say that there have been nine additional trials and at least two arrests since our meetings ended on December 19. Indeed, the Moscow Helsinki Watch Committee, whose activities should never have been interfered with and whose personnel should have been respected rather than persecuted, has now been reduced in number to two individuals willing to identify themselves openly with that organization.

We have learned that on January 6, Feliks Serebrov, geologist, a member of the Moscow Helsinki Watch Group and a founding member of the Working Commission to Investigate the Use of Psychiatry for Political Purposes, was arrested. In December Oksana Meshko, a member of the Ukrainian Helsinki Watch Group, was transferred from a psychiatric hospital to a prison and an imminent trial—and I note for us all that this courageous lady is seventy-five years of age. In December an Odessa regional court ordered the two young children, ages four and twelve, of baptist Maria Drumova to be removed from her custody on the ground that she was giving her children a religious upbringing. This is the first recorded court order of its kind since the signing of the Helsinki Final Act in 1975. And in recent days the distinguished writers Vasily Aksyonov and Lev Kopelev were stripped of their Soviet citizenship.

These acts of repression will not work. The voices from the prisons are heard. The human spirit is strong and cannot long be denied. Others come forward to replace those who are taken away. And they know they have friends wherever men and women think of freedom. And yet the repression continues.

It would appear, Mr. Chairman, that a conscious decision has been taken to violate the Helsinki Final Act and to defy those of us who urge compliance with it as the only realistic basis for international stability and peace. East-West relations, Mr. Chairman, are already severely troubled. Systematic continued violation of the Helsinki Final Act adds to that tension and makes our task here more difficult. Describing this reality is not confrontational. It is the violations that lend themselves to confrontation. Recognizing and describing reality is a necessary prerequisite for later cooperation.

No one should doubt American constancy to the powerful ideals of the CSCE process, to the preservation and enhancement of human freedom, to respect for the sovereignty and independence of all states, and to the goal of military security and cooperation among us. Those are my government's objectives. They are the objectives of the American people.

At the closing day of our first session, I made a plea in behalf of my government. It was that the subject of human rights draw us together and not drive us apart. Whatever philosophical and ideological disagreements we may have about how society should be organized, we should be unified on the principle of human dignity. For that is, after all, not only the guiding premise upon which democratic theory is based, but it was also the motivating ingredient which led Karl Marx to challenge the economic truths of his day and seek a society of greater justice. I repeat that plea today.

Practical steps taken to improve human dignity and freedom and to confirm the integrity of sovereign states would produce a significant improvement in the international atmosphere and would lead the American people to respond positively. Reference was made here this morning to "détente." The word appears in the Final Act. If the word has any significance, we must realize that it does not today exist as an accurate description of East-West relations. It remains, however, an objective to be sought, yet to be achieved.

Mr. Chairman, our agenda calls for us to proceed, beginning today and for the next six weeks, to discuss and negotiate new proposals and hopefully to fashion a significant concluding document arising out of those new proposals. Our delegation will pursue that task diligently and responsibly. We all realize, however, that words alone will not accomplish our purpose if they are not accompanied by proper constructive action by all signatories of the Final Act. Positive action is called for if we are to rebuild the confidence necessary for agreement.

Our objective is clear. We seek a balanced set of new undertakings, which respect the interrelated pattern of our commitments in the areas of military security, human rights, economic cooperation, information, educational and cultural exchange.

Our task is not to seek a collection of illusory and meaningless words around unimportant and insignificant proposals designed to hide the realities of our problems. Our task rather is together to work here and elsewhere to improve the international atmosphere and build a web of interrelationships based on the Helsinki Final Act and thus designed to assure us the peace and security we seek.

On behalf of my government, Mr. Chairman, I pledge that we will make a serious effort to find a common ground, within the guidelines of our principles, upon which all thirty-five participating states can stand. The distinguished chairman of the Soviet delegation spoke of "realistic diplomatic negotiations." We fervently hope we will be joined in this effort by all assembled here today.

There is much to be done, here and elsewhere. Our peoples are looking to all of us for the leadership to help achieve the peace and liberty we all seek. Our delegation is ready to begin.

February 6, 1981 Review of Proposals

At the conclusion of our delegation's statement to this body on the opening day of these renewed sessions, I stated that we would proceed in a responsible fashion diligently to pursue the task of discussing and negotiating the new proposals that had been submitted to us for consideration by the participating states assembled here. In reasserting the constancy of the American commitment to the CSCE process, I pledged in behalf of my government that we will make a serious effort to find a common ground, within the principles of the Helsinki Final Act, upon which all thirty-five of us can stand.

This was said in the context of a broader message: that my government cannot easily separate its consideration of new proposals from the realization that proposals previously agreed upon have not been lived up to. I noted seriously—and repeat—our grave concern that the continuation of those violations casts doubts upon the good will and the commitment of those who have not lived up to their responsibilities.

This meeting cannot proceed in a vacuum, free from the atmosphere of tensions, repression, and military threats that surround us. It would, therefore, be misleading to our publics and to ourselves to seek superficial agreement on secondary, noncontentious proposals. This would create an appearance of progress not consistent with the reality we must face if we are to attain the peace, security, and cooperation envisaged for us by the Final Act five and a half years ago.

With this in mind, the United States is proceeding to work soberly and seriously to achieve constructive results in Madrid in the hope that we may see tangible indications that the Helsinki Final Act will be followed in letter and spirit. Such indications would help break down the distrust and concern that have paralyzed East-West relations and that today reflect a world more dangerous and less secure than the one which greeted the birth of the Helsinki process in 1975.

We, of course, all proceed from a premise of national self-interest as we see it. None of us will accept a proposal or a concept that we believe to be contrary to our national interest or to that of our peoples—and we respect that criterion for all of us. It is, furthermore, accepted in our CSCE process that results, if they occur in the form of new proposals and a concluding document, must be balanced so as to give equitable weight to all major components of the Act. It is constructive that we all seem to appreciate the wisdom of that simple and noncontentious point.

Two alternative courses lie open to us. The concepts of balance and of national self-interest can be used to bargain down to a lowest common denominator. Alternatively, they can provide the motive force behind an effort to construct a higher and more meaningful level of agreement. The United States delegation believes that the stakes before us are so high as to call for us to stretch our horizons, and reach for the higher and more meaningful level of agreement. We are prepared to make our best effort to explore that route.

Clearly one aspect of such a balanced result, as virtually every delegation has stressed, is a substantive military security element. The issues involved are complex and we expect to address them separately in the near future. The United States shares the conviction, however, that the challenge we face requires that we avoid cosmetics and propaganda and concentrate on militarily significant and verifiable confidence-building measures, applicable to the entire continent of Europe. That is the kind of boldness and scope that is required to provide us with the confidence we need to help us achieve the security we all seek.

Further, the confidence which the governments and the peoples of the CSCE states have in each other's credibility and intentions is crucial to security. The political will, or the statement by a delegation that it has the will, to conclude meaningful agreements is inadequate—and any agreements reached would hold the seeds of their own failure—if they are not founded on mutual confidence. We are now burdened by a lack of confidence, indeed, as I noted on December 19, by a crisis of confidence. This is the corrosive influence at work in East-West relations. And it has been fostered by the obvious failures to implement our CSCE undertakings.

Confidence, it is clear, is the basis for agreement. With that in mind, the United States delegation sponsors and has joined with other delegations in supporting a broad program of proposals designed to make concrete progress in areas where we know that implementation has been deficient. Many of these proposals deal with issues of human rights, humanitarian cooperation, and the freer flow of information, because these are areas where the credibility of participating states and of the CSCE process itself is very much at stake. Acceptance by all of significant new proposals in these areas would go far to communicating a desire to restore the confidence we need.

What are these proposals? There are three in the realm of Principle VII, which asserts our respect for human rights and fundamental freedoms.

One (RM.19) would identify two areas where immediate progress is possible and urgent: first, the treatment of private citizens who seek to encourage their governments to implement the Final Act more completely. The other area covered by the proposal is religious freedom. The purpose of RM.19 is to instill a sense of perceptible progress while recognizing that, realistically, no society is perfect and that the full implementation of this part of the Final Act is a complex and lengthy process. I commend the delegation of the United Kingdom for its leadership in advancing this proposal.

A second proposal (RM.16) is intended to intensify the dialogue among us which has only just begun at this meeting and at the Belgrade meeting before it. It would bring together both governmental and private experts seriously to discuss how we can work to fulfill our commitments to implement Principle VII. We would then report, either as a group or separately, on our findings to the next follow-up meeting. Our object here is to bring us together and help us to communicate over our differences.

A third proposal (RM.26) is based on experience. It would encourage bilateral discussions of human rights between participating states, with frank and open discussion on a direct country-by-country level. We hope that understanding can be increased and that diplomatic means can be explored to achieve practical progress. Human rights is a sensitive area, but we are convinced it would advance, when attained, mutually beneficial results for our societies and our peoples. The bilateral discussions called for by our proposal have been shown to be effective. They have already been tried successfully by the United States and Romania.

None of these proposals we support would threaten any state. Each would make its own contribution, not to the creation of Utopia, but to beginning the difficult task of converting human rights from an issue that divides us into one that brings us closer together.

Closely related to these proposals are several that are based on specific humanitarian provisions of the Final Act's third basket.

One (RM.11) would build upon the significant progress that has been achieved, despite regrettable setbacks, in human contacts. It would call for improved efforts to process applications within each society for emergency visits out of the country; and to help expedite family reunification and binational marriages. It would protect the rights of applicants, ensuring that they would not be disadvantaged because of what they sought to do and would allow them promptly to reapply if their initial request, for some exceptional reason, could not be granted. It would provide a target goal to carry out the existing Final Act commitment progressively to lower travel document fees, so that they are less than the equivalent of a week's wage. For family visits, it would waive what can be onerous hindrances to human contacts, such as the requirements that exist in some states for advance hotel reservations or currency exchange. It would encourage greater openness and understanding by requiring that relevant laws and regulations be published and readily available to all who need to make use of them.

Our delegation also urges (in RM/H.1) the holding of a post-Madrid experts meeting that would consider specific measures to further improve the operation of the Final Act's commitments on family reunification. To ensure a businesslike and productive meeting, each participating state would prepare a written submission outlining its own internal pertinent laws and regulations. This would provide a factual basis for the task that our experts would face, to prepare practical recommendations for consideration by our governments.

In a third major area, the United States, in conjunction with many other delegations, has advanced proposals concerning the acquisition and dissemination of information. Our delegation believes that the Madrid meeting should build upon the undertakings in the Final Act and benefit from the lessons gained during our review of implementation. It proposes, therefore (in RM.12), improved access to all forms of printed matter. It further proposes that the participating states adopt a positive attitude toward the acceptance of agreements in the private sector facilitating the distribution of printed matter. Our objective is to see greater protection of journalistic activity and to facilitate that activity by assuring the freer movement of journalists and their right to contact sources without prior governmental approval.

Finally, we believe that the participating states should agree that jamming of radio broadcasts is not consistent with the Helsinki goal of encouraging the freer flow of information and that, therefore, jamming should cease in those states where it is still practiced. The strength and breadth of the opposition to jamming which has been expressed in the Basket III working group illustrates the depth of concern on this issue.

All of these proposals are specific and carefully designed efforts to bring greater reality to the lofty objectives of our CSCE process. They are meant to be constructive. They would not undermine the political, economic, or social order of any participating state. They are practical and realistic. They should be adopted. We are convinced, Mr. Chairman, that, if adopted, they would help turn around the atmosphere of distrust and tension that is today paralyzing East-West relations.

This now leads us to another area. It is clear that all of us share an interest in identifying areas where cooperation is equally vital to each of the participating states. No such area is more obvious than the effort to banish terrorism from international life. No state here can profit if terrorism is tolerated, let alone nurtured and encouraged. Terrorism is a threat not only to the stability of international intercourse, but to the very basis of individual and institutional security in civilized societies. It is a challenge to stability, to the stability of all societies, no matter what social system they espouse. Hardly a state represented here has not been affected by the scourge of terrorism.

The United States delegation, therefore, considers the proposal on this subject which Spain has developed (RM.14) highly important, both for its own sake and for the positive example its adoption could set across the spectrum of relations between the states in the CSCE process. We will address this subject again, because its importance to all of us is intense.

Another area encompassed by the Final Act is economic cooperation, a field fundamental to our well-being as states. The United States is co-sponsoring proposals designed to improve the conditions under which trade between us takes place.

We have suggested, for example, ways (RM/E.4) in which the participating states can develop more direct and meaningful access between sellers and buyers in the East and West. We would encourage broader participation in technical symposia. We call for after-sales training of personnel of end-user firms at the seller's training centers. We note the need for agreement on improved working conditions and facilities for representatives of foreign firms. There is a need to ease accreditation procedures, to provide telecommunication links, and to improve the treatment of temporarily resident staff.

We express our belief in another of the proposals we support (RM/E.2) that the Madrid meeting should urge the United Nations Economic Commission for Europe to examine ways to overcome certain specific problems with regard to the practice of compensation trade, which has come to be employed frequently in East-West transactions.

We are seeking (RM/E.3) a measure of comparability in the scope and nature of statistical data published by the participating states. If the CSCE states are serious in pursuing the expansion of trade, then we must ensure that our business communities have the fundamental tools, including adequate commercial information, to conduct business.

The proposals which I have outlined during the course of these comments do not constitute an exclusive list of what we need to strengthen the CSCE process. The United States delegation sponsors and will support other proposals which are before the Madrid meeting, both in these fields and in others such as cultural and educational cooperation. My comments this morning, rather, are meant to indicate that we approach this second phase of our meeting with a desire to seek substantial and meaningful action on the full range of subjects with which the Final Act deals.

In so doing, the United States delegation is guided by a desire to recapture the spirit of our process by dealing with the serious inadequacies and problems indicated so clearly as necessary by the review of implementation which was conducted during the fall. We are ready seriously to try. But our effort and that of other delegations will serve no practical purpose if it were to be made without all of us as participants understanding the difficult conditions under which this negotiation begins. Realism and a sense of measure and balance must guide the meeting's work. The meeting cannot, as was suggested here by one delegation last week, consign our first phase of implementation review to history. What is attempted now must be grounded upon what has been discussed all these many weeks.

This same sense of realism causes us to state that the United States delegation is aware that no negotiation is possible unless all participants make a sincere effort to accommodate the important interests of others. Accordingly, we will seek in good faith and imaginatively to take appropriate account of proposals introduced by all other delegations. We proceed from the assumption that such proposals are as seriously meant as our own and that their proponents will likewise seek in good faith and imaginatively to take account of the very serious interests that we have. It does not serve this objective to characterize proposals as "confrontational" or having a "war psychosis," as has unfortunately already been done at this meeting.

If all of us work in a constructive manner and if we are assisted by positive developments outside of this forum, there is a chance that another beginning can indeed be made here in Madrid. We must proceed not on wishes alone, nor on unproven assumptions, but on the realities of the world around us. One of those primary realities is the unsatisfactory history of implementation that has hitherto been established.

There is, and my government regrets this dearly, a crisis of confidence in the relationship between East and West. Our task as participating states is pragmatically to create a sense of confidence by attitude and action, here and elsewhere. The well-being of all our peoples, the health of our relations as sovereign states, the stability of the international community—all these are affected by our capacity and willingness to help meet and solve this crisis of confidence. For that task, we must first understand its dimensions and its roots. To help communicate that message has been the objective of the American delegation since we first assembled together in September. Without understanding there can be no cooperation. And it is cooperation, and security, and peace, that my delegation seeks.

February 9, 1981 Terrorism

On Friday I stated our delegation's support for RM.14, the proposal on terrorism submitted by the Spanish delegation; and I stated our intent to discuss the subject in greater detail as an indication of my government's serious concern about the problem it addresses.

Terrorism as a political instrument is a blight on our standards of civilized political behavior. Its immorality cannot be justified. It has become a serious phenomenon and is a threat to the very basis of individual and institutional security in modern life. It has become a tool for irresponsible fanatical groups whose object is to use cruelty and violence to impose their will upon individuals, institutions, and societies whom they could not otherwise influence or persuade.

There was a time, Mr. Chairman, when terrorism was limited to individual acts by desperate and usually depraved minds. The terrorist was sometimes looked upon as a person in the grip of passion. It was all too common to think of him as a romantic individualist, acting alone. And there was a time when we could properly seek to contain terrorism within national borders. It has become increasingly clear, however, that most terrorists today belong to disciplined groups, cynically employing terrorism as an instrument of policy. Today, it is well-organized and well-financed. And the terrorist is not confined by national boundaries; indeed, all too often he is able to flee across borders for refuge. Terrorism has become international in scope. As such, it is real and terrifying and dangerous to us all; and there is every reason to believe that its most extreme manifestations are yet to be experienced.

We must all realize that the danger of international terrorism is among the most serious of all the problems on the international agenda facing us here at Madrid. None of us is safe from it. No social, economic, or political system and no nationality group is immune from its destructive impact. Few of us have not been affected by its violence and cruelty. It undermines national and international stability; and stability is the basis for peace and understanding among us.

Terrorism does not favor a particular ideology. It is not a friend of one side or another. It knows no boundaries and it respects no values. No nation is sacrosanct. It can be practiced, and rationalized, by all races, creeds and faiths. It is self-perpetuating, with incident breeding incident and violence breeding violence. Indeed, terrorists often seek to provoke a response in the hope that the response itself will undermine the stability they seek to destroy.

Terrorism is a tactic of those who have neither the humanity, nor the tolerance, nor the understanding to seek solutions through the established institutions which form the basis for stable civilized relations among nations and peoples.

Terrorism must be opposed by nations and by peoples if they have any commitment to decency, and certainly if they have any concern for the stability of their own societies. The task of defeating international terrorism requires an international effort. RM.14 is an important step in that direction. It calls for our support.

Today's advocate of terrorism, I respectfully warn, can easily become tomorrow's victim. It is gruesomely impartial in effect, striking its victims indiscriminately. It most often strikes at the innocent: the bus filled with tourists, the passerby in the park, the shopper in the market. It seeks to intimidate and brutalize; and all of us, literally and figuratively, are its potential victims.

The terrorist feeds on silence, ignorance, psychological indulgence, expediency, and the cynicism of those who would foolishly and for shortsighted purposes look the other way. No apologies or excuses for terrorism can make less abhorrent the facts which they ultimately encourage. No justification can be accepted for policies which, for whatever reason—"'national liberation" or any other political rationalization—provide encouragement, weapons, instruction or refuge to those who spread terror through random violence for political ends. Terrorist groups may profess different ideologies and attack different human targets, but it is what they have in common that is a danger to us all. Terrorist bands must be treated as such. We must not tolerate the death, mayhem, and instability which is the trademark of the terrorist.

It is tragic and reprehensible when governments, within their own borders and elsewhere, support such groups by providing financial assistance, explosives sophistication, sabotage instruction, other training, arms, and even targets. It is unconscionable when they use their media to support groups which employ terrorism as an instrument of policy. Surely it must be clear that such activity can only fan the flames of terrorism in the world and thus endanger the lives of still more innocent people as well as the stability of all governments, including those whose support or equivocal attitude fosters the atmosphere on which it thrives.

Mr. Chairman, you are aware that my government has within the past few days in Washington expressed its concern over terrorism. Those statements speak for themselves. Secretary Haig placed the problem well within the scope of our agenda when he described terrorism as the ultimate abuse of human rights as well as a threat to our security as it tears at the very fabric of our society and stability.

There is understandably a widened consciousness in my country today because of the recent holding of fifty-two American diplomats as hostages in Iran. We have also had five of our ambassadors killed by international terrorists since 1968. Other diplomats and citizens have been victims of these attacks. But we all know that other governments have had similar experiences. The Spanish and Turkish statements to this effect here have been eloquent.

A number of international measures have already been taken to deal with the problem of terrorism. More measures are needed. Here in this meeting we can play a vital role in mobilizing public and governmental consciousness against this outrage. We have a fundamental and common interest in cooperating to face this challenge. RM.l4, introduced by Spain and supported by the Federal Republic of Germany, Italy, Portugal, Turkey, Canada, the United Kingdom, and the United

States, merits the unanimous endorsement of this body. I congratulate Ambassador Ruperez and his colleagues on their constructive effort in putting together this valuable and important proposal. It notes the need for improving international cooperation in order to meet the threat of terrorism. It calls on us to commit ourselves openly and resolutely to this present task. My government welcomes this call.

I can see no reason for standing apart from such an urgent task. Agreement here will serve as an important symbol to our peoples and to the world. It will send a message that the nations represented in Madrid have confirmed their resolute opposition to the tactics of barbarism and terror, as well as their determination to cooperate in overcoming the terrorist challenge to peace, security and cooperation among all of our peoples. RM.14 provides us an opportunity to reaffirm that terrorism cannot and will not be condoned.

February 11, 1981 Military Security

. . . The Final Act refers to the role of military confidence-building measures (CBMs) in strengthening confidence, stability, and security in Europe. We have now had five years of experience with them. It is clear that the CBMs now in force are insufficient to fulfill their purposes and our hopes for them. Five years after their adoption, the Soviet Union has yet to notify of a single smaller-scale maneuver. It has yet to implement adequately the measure for the invitation of observers to major maneuvers. It has yet to provide anything more than the sparest information in its notifications of major maneuvers. Even as this meeting was getting under way, Mr. Chairman, the Soviet Union undertook significant military preparations, including the mobilization of reservists, in Eastern Europe; and none of this activity was accompanied by notification under the Final Act.

A change in the character and stringency of CBMs is needed if they truly are to improve confidence, dispel doubts, and prevent misunderstandings about the intent of military activities in Europe. For such measures to make real contributions to security, they must in fact inhibit actions that threaten the confidence of other states in their own security.

Given the importance of this issue, in our consideration of the various proposals before us, we have looked closely at RM.6, supported by the Soviet Union, for some indication that its proponents recognize the type of CBMs which would further the goal of a more stable and secure Europe and reduce the risk of surprise attack. We find no such indication. Indeed, RM.6 itself gives no idea at all that its authors view CBMs as a serious vehicle for security.

Recent declarations of the Warsaw Pact countries give some picture of what CBMs they have in mind. It is not encouraging. One proposal would lower the threshold for maneuver notifications by 5,000 men, a number that would leave untouched the significant military activities that occur when military formations, such as divisions, are in the field. The possibility of other types of measures is mentioned, but the context in which these proposals are given, and the paucity of detail on their parameters, indicate that the sponsors of RM.6 contemplate nothing more than minor adjustments of the current CBMs, with perhaps some additional measures that would have little or no effect on the Warsaw Pact's ability to undertake military activities for political intimidation or to threaten the security of other states.

There is also a remarkable absence from RM.6 (and from previous declarations of its authors) of any mention of the need for verification measures. Indeed, two days ago, we heard the representative of the Soviet Union question the need for CBMs to be verifiable. Verification is an essential element of a security agreement. If an agreement on CBMs is to increase security and confidence, the CBMs must be verifiable. And they must obviously be accompanied by provisions which provide means to assure they are being observed.

It is abundantly clear to us, Mr. Chairman, that the purpose of the CMDD under RM.6 is not to negotiate concrete steps to improve security. Evidently it is rather to provide a platform for eventual adoption of so-called "political and legal" steps, designed, they say, to reduce the danger of the outbreak of war in Europe. Noble words. But RM.6 does not specify what these "political and legal steps" might be. We, therefore, look for guidance to the plenary statement of the Soviet Union of two days ago.

It would appear that in some cases, these words would merely reiterate commitments already undertaken in the Final Act and the U.N. Charter, such as the non-use of force or the threat of force. In other cases, such as the proposal for non-expansion of alliances, they would infringe on the recognized rights of states under the Helsinki Final Act to arrange for their collective defense. In still others, they would offer a vague and unverifiable commitment to freeze military forces at their present levels. We understand, of course, Mr. Chairman, that this commitment has an exception to it: the freeze is not to apply to forces in all but a small part of the European USSR.

It is absurd to believe that confidence in Europe can be built by such declaratory measures. Such assurances are especially hollow in the face of the Soviet Union's brutal invasion of Afghanistan, its determined and continuing military expansion, its dismal implementation record of commitments it previously undertook under the Final Act, and its obvious reluctance to accept the concepts of "military significance," "verification," "binding," and "to the Urals."

The conference proposed in RM.6 apparently would have us progress from a set of inadequate confidence-building measures, to empty "political and legal" steps, to a third condition—and I quote— "measures aimed at lowering the level and intensity of military confrontation in Europe, including the limitation of military activity and disarmament." Let us look carefully at this third element, that dealing with disarmament. Here the utter poverty of RM.6 becomes most apparent.

The Final Act indicates the necessity to take effective, and I stress *effective*, measures in the CBM's field which by their *scope* and by their nature constitute steps toward disarmament. Instead, RM.6 seeks to lure us with words, the word *disarmament*, as a goal which the substance of RM.6 itself and the history of the Warsaw Pact military preparations deny. It seeks to induce us to abandon what is surely a more believable and useful form for our efforts, the development of more effective and significant CBMs. It seeks also to impose an erroneous and wholly unacceptable conception of the geographic scope of European security.

In one of his plenary interventions during this phase of our discussions, the distinguished chairman of the Soviet Union delegation indicated that the arms race had gone beyond acceptable limits on what he referred to as "our continent." One might assume that the proposal would include the area of all of Europe, "our continent." But, unfortunately, we have learned that the Soviet Union maintains that for the purposes of such a conference, Europe ends 250 kilometers inside the European borders of the USSR. One is tempted to ask, is not Moscow a European capital?

We owe it to our own peoples to consider the implications of a proposal which would define European-wide arms control as reaching only 250 kilometers inside the Soviet Union. All other European states would be called upon to reduce their forces on all their European territory. Non-European states, the United States and Canada would be required to reduce their forces in Europe. But the largest and most militarily powerful European state of all, the Soviet Union, would only participate in the arms control process in the 250 kilometers adjacent to its European borders—a tiny fraction of the European area which contains the human and material resources for its vast military establishment.

We respectfully suggest that such a restrictive interpretation of the geographical dimensions of military security directly contradicts Principle I of our Act, which indicates that all participating states have equal rights and *equal duties*. Such an arrangement would not at all improve the military security of other participants in CSCE. It would rather intensify the danger.

Let us look further at this proposal to see what it could mean for the future of our CSCE process. RM.6 makes no mention whatsoever of a continuing link between its proposed conference and future CSCE follow-up meetings of the type we are now conducting. We cannot help but wonder if this deficiency is intentional; and whether the authors of this proposal seek to give the proposed conference a life of its own so that issues on the military aspects of security are separated from the CSCE process. This would seriously undermine the integrity of the Final Act and the CSCE process.

The conference proposed in RM.6 offers no real program to further security and cooperation in Europe. Indeed, by its deliberate vagueness, it would permit evasion of the concrete and specific measures that could improve military security in Europe. We believe, therefore, that such a conference ultimately would set back the effort to improve security and cooperation in Europe.

I don't wish to end this intervention, Mr. Chairman, on a negative note, although I believe the clarity of our message should help bring us together toward the later understanding and agreement that we all seek. The American delegation puts a high value on achieving progress in the military aspects of security. We believe that militarily significant, verifiable confidence-building measures covering all of Europe and possessing a high degree of political obligation provide us a means of achieving the security we seek. We commend all those delegations who have submitted serious security proposals for our consideration. The discussion of those proposals, frank as it may be, helps achieve understanding. We note with satisfaction the fact that the French delegation shares our views on the substantive criteria for future confidence-building measures and that its proposal, RM.7, which suggests a post-Madrid conference, reflects those criteria.

Our task in the days ahead will be to discuss the appropriate forum and means by which we can advance our security interests and our desire for cooperation. That is a subject that deserves and is receiving our delegation's most serious study and attention.

It is the hope of the American delegation that we may end our meeting here with significant progress in all of the areas of our concern—on questions of military security as well as on the other subjects of our agenda. We pledge our best efforts toward this end. That can only be achieved, however, by maintaining realistic standards for progress and by emphasizing for all to understand that our study and our deliberations are within the framework of the hard facts, the realities which we have attempted to share with this body this afternoon.

February 16, 1981 RM. 7—French Proposal for a Military Conference

On February 11, the United States in this plenary discussed aspects of European military security as that issue has been reflected in our discussions here and in the security proposals before us. As I noted then, it has been a constant desire of my government to expand and strengthen military confidence-building measures (CBMs) as a way of attaining that security we seek. But efforts to build confidence have floundered, and for good reason. Efforts to build confidence are greatly hindered if there is a weak underlying foundation of confidence to build upon. And, as has been noted here often, by us and by others, this underlying confidence has been severely damaged by actions of the Soviet Union in recent months and years.

A few here have argued that under these circumstances, our common interests are best served by beginning with CBMs of little significance—with voluntary measures or measures which cannot or will not be verified. The argument is made that such CBMs would be at least again a start; and that we can move on later to more significant measures.

My government disagrees. We join with many other participating states here who are convinced that unless this meeting mandates a negotiation with specific and firm criteria, those who dislike effective CBMs will keep us talking about words, about vague declarations, and about pious but meaningless pronouncements for generations to come; and all without coming to grips with the basic requirements for real security. For our part, we cannot depend upon security by pronouncement, by declaration, or by promise—unless those pronouncements involve specific obligations, unless we can be assured that those declarations will be honored, and unless there are means to verify that what has been promised will be done.

We have the opportunity starting here in Madrid and within our CSCE process to explore the new and promising field of confidence-building measures. Because this field is new, we must be sure to structure our discussions carefully. Because we are interested in genuine arms control, we view laxness and imprecision as contrary to our purposes amd counterproductive to confidence-building. And we will absolutely not lend our support in this meeting to a cosmetic and meaningless negotiation.

It was this clear requirement that any negotiations be carefully structured to make a real contribution to security that led the administration of President Reagan to give intensive and detailed study to RM.7, the proposal of France for a Conference on the Military Aspects of Security in Europe.

I would like now to describe to this plenary meeting the critical elements in our consideration.

• First of all, the French proposal prescribes a mandate for a post-Madrid meeting which will focus discussion on confidence-building measures that are of true military significance. It is clear that measures which are not "militarily significant"—which would not deal effectively with military activities that could threaten the security of other states—are the kinds of cosmetic proposals that would contribute nothing to security and might well detract from it.

• Second, the mandate in RM.7 calls for "provisions ensuring appropriate verification of commitments." Effective verification has been at the heart of the American approach to every arms control negotiation we have undertaken since World War II. We, therefore, agree with the emphasis which this proposal gives to verification. All forces in Europe must be covered, including, of course, our own. And I want to note here, in connection with some misleading comments and implications made by some delegations, that, outside the complete European area proposed to be covered by the French proposal, many more Soviet than American forces would be *exempted* from coverage.

• Third, RM.7 places a strong political obligation on all the participants reliably to implement the confidence-building measures. We all know from our own experience regarding the implementation of discretionary measures that any new measures must be founded on a commitment to this full and consistent implementation, or they simply will not be lived up to.

• Fourth, the French proposal lists specific categories of confidence-building measures to be examined or negotiated. We believe it concentrates attention on the three areas where productive results are most likely: on measures of information on the strength and positioning of the military forces of the parties; on measures to increase stability, such as by more stringent and precise prenotification of military activities of immediate security concern to the rest of Europe; and on measures of observation and verification. Moreover, a separate post-Madrid conference, as France proposes, would seem to provide the best forum for effective consideration of these measures.

• Fifth, the French proposal will make confidence-building measures applicable to all of Europe, from the Atlantic to the Urals. The Final Act describes confidence-building measures as measures to ". . . strengthen confidence . . . and thus contribute to increasing stability and security in Europe." This statement means all of Europe, including the European areas of the Soviet Union. It makes no sense to us that CBMs should exempt some portions of Europe. CBMs will not build confidence if they ignore large portions of the European Soviet Union, where there are considerable military forces which have a direct and immediate potential threat to security in Europe.

• Sixth, RM.7 clearly establishes a link between a post-Madrid conference and the CSCE process. It states that measures agreed at the conference would be referred to the next CSCE follow-up meeting. This procedure is indispensable for the continued vitality of the CSCE process, which must not be bypassed.

• Finally, the French proposal specifies that further steps in the arms control area will be considered only after we have had the opportunity to evaluate the results of the CBM negotiation and to review other developments in the arms control field. We consider this course to be in the best interest of genuine security. The need is to concentrate on achieving a successful CBM outcome; we must not be distracted from the important immediate task of building confidence by diversionary attempts to lay out plans for a vague second phase sometime in the future in an atmosphere and under conditions we cannot now foresee.

Mr. Chairman, careful consideration of all the factors I have just cited has led my government to one conclusion: President Reagan has resolved to commit the full support of the United States government to the French proposal, RM.7. We support it because it offers the prospect of serious and productive negotiations to achieve security in Europe.

We are pleased to join our French and other colleagues in supporting RM.7. As we do so, we most emphatically also join them in insisting that the essential criteria the French have established for CBMs are the minimum conditions for our approval of any post-Madrid security meeting of CSCE states.

We stand with France and the many others here who have joined in opposing a post-Madrid security meeting unless it is determined in advance that there will be serious negotiations. For us this means negotiations of militarily significant, verifiable confidence-building measures applicable to all of Europe with a high degree of political obligation. To accept less than these criteria would be to fail to serve the interests of true security.

There is one additional criterion which cannot be included in a formal mandate, but it is important nonetheless. This is the criterion of balance. CSCE cannot survive in the future solely as a security negotiation. The genius of the Final Act is its recognition that true security depends upon a balance of progress on security, on human rights, and on economic cooperation. The post-Madrid conference of CBMs, as outlined in RM.7, is, as our French colleagues have pointed out inherently linked to CSCE. This means that the progress we contemplate in the security area must be matched by significant steps forward in the other areas of CSCE if balance is to be maintained.

Mr. Chairman, recent occurrences have made progress on security a much more difficult task than it seemed only a few years ago. We all know the reason for this; and we know where the responsibility lies. In this situation, we strongly believe that the burden of performance must be on those who have disturbed the peace and damaged the atmosphere of international trust. The French proposal offers an opportunity to discharge this burden, because it is designed to make more difficult the use of military power for intimidation or aggression. And it is designed to increase warning of surprise attack in Europe.

We are convinced that European security will be served if all the states participating in CSCE accept the criteria for CBMs set forth in the French mandate criteria which will apply equally to all nations here. If they do, they will open the way for a serious negotiation aimed at increasing confidence and enhancing security on the entire European continent. That is our objective.

March 13, 1981 Criteria for CBMs

... By recognizing that a significant portion of its area is in Europe, the Soviet Union is recognizing a fact. In accepting that the principle of sovereign equality calls for the application of CBMs to all of Europe, the Soviet position becomes consistent with the basic assumptions and spirit of the Final Act. We would welcome that position. But it does not justify any "payments" to be made to the Soviet Union in the form of unreasonable demands which fly in the face of common sense. No conditions attached to the Soviet recognition that CBMs should apply to all of Europe are either legitimate or acceptable.

The United States of America, Mr. Chairman, wants a careful and conscientious negotiation on the military aspects of security within the sponsorship and direction of CSCE. We believe the criteria in RM.7 offer the best hope that a conference built around them can make a genuine contribution to security.

Mr. Chairman, had we had any doubts about the need for stringent parameters for future CBMs, such doubts would have been erased by the events of recent days.* In that period has come word of military exercises planned in an area of Europe where tensions have been increasing. We have not been informed of the scope or purpose of these exercises, but we do know that under the present CBM regime the lack of obligation and verification forces us to cope with uncertainty precisely when better information could help decrease tensions. These developments reinforce our concern that CBMs of the sort we now have—even with minor improvements—are not effective in building confidence and stability.

We hear much talk of "political will" in this body. If everyone really shares that "political will," then let us all sit down and write a mandate for a conference based on the reasonable criteria that I have discussed. The simple act of drafting—rather than ambiguous speeches or vague hints—will be the proof of political will, of sincerity, and of a desire for real security.

Even as we continue our efforts to produce such a draft, we must also strive to make comparable progress on human rights, human contacts, and other issues of concern here, since a balanced outcome must remain an essential objective of our work. In that connection, we listened with interest—and some concern—to the absence of any reference to human rights in the major intervention of a few days ago by the delegate from the Soviet Union.

I referred at the outset of this statement to the deteriorated international

---

* Renewed movement of Soviet-bloc troops around Poland.-Ed.

atmosphere in which we find ourselves. It is necessary to recognize this reality if we are to establish a basis for meaningful agreement between us. Soviet troops remain in Afghanistan and violations of human rights continue within the Soviet Union on what appears to be an intensified scale. We had hoped for some positive response to our frequently expressed concerns about these violations of the Helsinki Final Act. We have found none. The barrier, therefore, remains, and we are no closer to an atmosphere conducive to confidence and understanding than we were when our meeting began.

We cannot pretend, in these circumstances, that normal business can be transacted in this building. Nevertheless, my government is prepared to continue to work for meaningful agreements, here and elsewhere, agreements which can reduce tension and rebuild the confidence which is so sorely lacking. We will respond affirmatively to any positive acts which would signal a realistic effort to work with us to eliminate the causes of the crisis of confidence that today pervades East-West relations.

The principles of the Helsinki process provide a solid basis for peace and confidence. Let us abide by them. Let us strengthen them. Let us reaffirm our commitment to them. Those are the objectives of the American delegation at this meeting.

March 24, 1981 Objections

I regret asking for the floor again this morning, but I must do so to express my keen disappointment at the many unhelpful comments made a few moments ago by the delegate from the Soviet Union. The delegate expresses his opposition to "confrontation," but he engages in it. He expresses support for the Helsinki process, and then subtly injects the threat of abandoning the process if the result does not satisfy him and his government.

We hear reference by him to "peace-loving action" by the Soviet Union at the 26th Congress, but I suggest that all we heard was words and not "action." Action would mean withdrawal of Soviet troops from Afghanistan. That would be peace-loving action. It would mean a decided improvement in the implementation of human rights commitments undertaken by all of us in 1975.

We heard an attack against the earlier phase of our meeting, that dealing with implementation review. For my delegation and for the American people we represent, we test the worthwhileness of whether to take new promises seriously by judging what promises previously made have been lived up to. To call this essential activity of the Helsinki process "polemics" is to once again persuade us that this word, too, has been redefined by those who use it to mean any statement with which they disagree.

Once again, the American delegation reaffirms its commitment to the Helsinki process—and looks forward to the introduction of the paper discussed by a number of delegations this morning, in the expectation that the product of their work will indeed be a strengthening of the Helsinki process to which the United States is committed.

March 27, 1981 Brezhnev Doctrine

Our delegation has joined many others at this meeting in stating that understanding among us can only be achieved if we keep in mind that our meeting is taking place in a wider international context and that this context is marked by a crisis of confidence in East-West relations. In my intervention of last Tuesday, I said that what was needed to overcome that crisis of confidence was action for peace, and not words. In the few days following these remarks, it has become increasingly evident how imperative this is.

The Final Act sets out clearly certain principles of behavior to which all the states represented here have pledged themselves. When those principles are not applied, it is not just the Final Act that is violated, it is the overall standard of human behavior without which no state can pretend to be a member of a civilized international community.

It is thus a matter of the utmost seriousness that states recall and act in accordance with the principles of the Final Act—refrain from the use of force, respect for sovereignty, the inviolability of frontiers, non-intervention in internal affairs, and all the other principles which we have been noting and reviewing here. It is a matter of utmost seriousness when states ignore or forget that all of us committed ourselves at Helsinki to respect those principles in "relations with all participating states, irrespective of their political, economic, or social systems as well as their size [or] geographical location."

Neither creed nor religion, nor ideology nor doctrine, nor any other factor exempts any of us from the obligation to observe these solemn commitments. There were occasions in the years preceding the Final Act when tragic developments in Europe resulted from the failure to apply these principles. Indeed, we witnessed the creation of a "doctrine" which sought to codify and legitimize interference in the internal affairs of other countries.

Given the Helsinki Final Act, nobody can argue with even a shred of justification that such a "doctrine" can have any moral or legal standing. So it was with extreme regret that a few weeks ago we read a statement with an ominous and familiar ring: that the defense of the Socialist community "is a matter not only for every single state but for the entire Socialist community as well."

Mr. Chairman, let me draw your attention to a profound irony. Those who allege that history is on their side betray their lack of confidence in such a historical inevitability, and in their faith itself, when they resort to threat and intimidation to try to offset the failure of their system to function for the benefit of the working men and women of their society.

No state represented here has special "rights." But all states represented here—including the biggest and strongest of us—do have certain responsibilities: responsibilities to set an example of restraint in respecting the sovereignty of others, responsibilities to promote equal rights for all, responsibilities to respect the contributions that all people and nations—big and small—can make, responsibilities, in short, to honor the specific commitments in the Final Act. Only if these commitments are honored outside this meeting hall can we expect cooperation and understanding and agreement inside it.

Negotiations

First attempts to frame a concluding document for the Madrid review began April 10, 1981 and would not be completed until September 1983.

Ambassador Kampelman reviewed, April 3, the work of the previous phase of the conference which he called not "adequately productive."He welcomed the efforts being made by eight neutral and nonaligned states to achieve a comprehensive agreement. He warned that this may be the "last hope" for continuing the CSCE process.

He said the firmness of the U.S. position is not a "transitory firmness," but is based on "principle and the realities of the regrettable crisis in East-West relations which flow from the invasion of Afghanistan and the violations of the Helsinki Final Act...particularly in the area of human rights."

He spoke April 10 as the new phase of negotiations opened. The meeting recessed for Easter and resumed in early May. Clearly, no steps were taken to relax tensions in the world outside the conference room. Instead, there was growing repression and intensified military activity in the Soviet bloc. The U.S. delegation, therefore, sharpened its expression of outrage at the increasing violations of human rights and military excesses. Ambassador Kampelman particularly emphasized Soviet military threats in his address of June 12.

This phase of the negotiations ended without agreement on July 28, 1981.

April 10, 1981 Human Rights

* * *

Let me reiterate that our delegation favors and we would agree to participate in a conference to advance the military element of security.

* * *

There is another element of real security—the element of human rights. As we take inventory of where we are, we must again remind ourselves that the issue of human rights and humanitarian concerns is an indispensable part of our security and of our search for peace. In a conference of thirty-five nations, it is natural that political systems should be different one from another; and our perceptions may be different as well. But we all did agree in 1975 to commit ourselves to the clear and unequivocal language of Principle VII on human rights and fundamental freedoms. The delegate of the Holy See, at our last meeting, brought us face to face with the fundamentals of the issue as he referred to the universality of human rights, encompassing the complete harmony of the human person in a framework of freedom and social justice. He reminded us that this is basic to the nature of man and to his dignity, no matter where he or she may live. He emphasized that this understanding is indispensable if the term "human rights" is to have any meaning at all.

There can be no doubt that any progress achieved in military security, or any other area, must be balanced by progress in human rights, a balance which may be composed of ingredients from outside this hall as well as concepts agreed upon inside it. Our delegation will not settle for language in this vital area that is token or trivial; and, unfortunately, the language that has been provisionally negotiated so far is of that sort. It must be supplemented by language that is significant in pointing the way to effective improvements. The proposals calling for experts' meetings on subjects of human rights and family reunification, a proposal for the removal of obstacles to the right of citizens to monitor the implementation of the Final Act and to practice their religion—these are the kinds of proposals that would carry out our objective.

When we reconvene in May, our work will be greatly aided and stimulated by the draft final document presented by a number of neutral and non-aligned states. We will continue constructively to improve that document in the areas where that is called for, but that effort does not obscure the fact that the document provides the opportunity to bring this meeting to a successful conclusion in a reasonable timeframe. If, after such a reasonable timeframe, it becomes apparent that our differences are too great, we should then turn our thoughts to a creative effort to bring the meeting to an end in a way that strengthens the CSCE process rather that subjecting it to futile, counterproductive and interminable debate.

Mr. Chairman, no delegation in this room is more devoted to a positive outcome of this meeting than the delegation of the United States of America. But we must not deceive ourselves with the repetition of pious platitudes. Events in the world outside have made and continue to make our task more difficult. Soviet troops continue to be reinforced in Afghanistan, thus compounding the violation of that country's sovereignty. And we have witnessed the threat of military force as a form of political intimidation against the sovereignty of a participating state by a more powerful neighbor. Furthermore, solemn commitments undertaken in the human rights area are, even as we meet, being flouted.

These events bring to mind our agreement of last November that our Madrid meeting would be a balance between a review of implementation phase and a negotiating and drafting phase. Our delegation is willing to continue negotiating and drafting as long as there is a reasonable prospect of agreement, because agreement is our objective here. But tragic developments since we returned to Madrid in January, as well as the need to restore a semblance of substantive balance to our proceedings, compel us to speak candidly.

Two weeks ago today, the learned chief of the Soviet delegation acknowledged the importance of human rights and humanitarian concerns to our process. He also thereby provided a good basis for understanding the extent of our differing perceptions of the issue. During that intervention, he vigorously asserted that his country looked upon human rights and freedom as one of "the main operative aspects" of the "right to life." He stated that the Soviet Union, contrary to its critics, has a keen interest in "humanitarian issues."

On many occasions, including today, this delegation has stressed that words are by no means as significant as action in helping us come to grips with the problems that divide us and thus achieve the cooperation we seek. In this area of humanitarian concerns particularly, and with all respect and deference to a most able spokesman for his government, we believe it is only fitting to put the words of the Soviet delegation to the test of whether they are accompanied by consistent action.

Several weeks ago Oksana Yakovlevna Meshko, a 75-year-old woman, one of the founders of the Ukrainian Helsinki Group, was sentenced to six months in a strict regimen camp and five years of internal exile. This old woman, sick with heart disease and with severe inflammation of the lungs, and now sentenced to a lonely existence in the harsh conditions of distant exile, has been subjected to systematic persecution for her human rights activities. She has been held illegally in psychiatric hospitals. Why? Because she has worked to collect and distribute accurate information about human rights violations in her country, thus exercising rights and freedoms proclaimed in the Soviet Constitution and encouraged by the Helsinki Final Act. Where, in this tragic event, is there a sensitivity to "humanitarian issues"?

A few weeks ago, on March 17, Anatoly Marchenko, whose 1966 book *My Testimony* was the first expose of labor prison camps in the post-Stalin era, was arrested in Aleksandrov and is apparently now in prison in the city of Vladimir. This man has already spent fifteen years in labor camps and in exile. He suffers from the effects of meningitis, is partially deaf and has undergone surgery on several occasions. We ask how long this man will be punished for his convictions, as we again fail to see in this action a concern for "humanitarian issues."

Two weeks ago, we learned of the death in a Soviet labor camp of Yuri Kukk, forty-one years old, whose only crime was to focus attention on human rights violations in his native Estonia. Where in this unfortunate death was there a sensitivity to humanitarian concerns? Several days ago, a number of delegations received an appeal to save the life of Dr. Yuri Orlov, who founded the Helsinki Watch Group in 1975, and who is today imprisoned in the Soviet Union. In that appeal, which is signed by Nobel Laureate Dr. Andrei Sakharov and by Moscow Helsinki Watch Group member Dr. Naum Meiman, Dr. Orlov's prison is described as "a form of extended torture." A letter from Dr. Orlov's wife, Irina, dated January 17 and addressed to our conference, reads:

"I appeal once again to the Conference to save my husband from the undeserved and barbaric treatment which threatens his health and even his life.... The senseless, cruel and petty harassment by the camp administrators has deteriorated to the point where my husband is prohibited from resting by lying down, even though the medical commission previously granted him permission to rest two hours daily. He can now only rest sitting down, but he is not even allowed to place his head in his hands...."

Where in the treatment of this noble and humane man is there sensitivity to "humanitarian issues"?

Andrei Sakharov himself remains in exile, isolated from friends and associates. For the first time since his exile, telegraphic communications with relatives have been cut off. His three diaries containing his current scientific work on theoretical physics have been taken away from him. His autobiographical writings have been confiscated. Telegrams have not been delivered to him or to his wife, including a telegram informing his wife of her aunt's death in Moscow. Not only is Dr. Sakharov treated thus, but his son's fiancée (and in effect his wife), Yelizaveta Alekseyeva, is persecuted and threatened, in an obvious effort to put pressure on Dr. Sakharov. Mr. Chairman, I ask, is this the way a society which supports "humanitarian issues" treats one of its most distinguished citizens and his family?

* * *

Finally, I read an excerpt from a letter addressed to our delegations by a citizen of the Soviet Union, Ida Milgrom, the mother of Anatoly Shcharansky, now in a Soviet prison:

My son, like many other freedom-loving and courageous people... believed in the reality of the agreement concluded in Helsinki. He believed in you, conference participants, who ratified the Final Act with your signatures, and proclaimed the unbreakable link between détente and observance of the fundamental human rights. My son believed in, and took upon himself the obligation of monitoring and bringing to the notice of governments all violations in implementation of the agreement.

You, the conference participants, implanted in them (my son and other honest people) hope, and they have ended up... in bondage....

In the years since the Helsinki Agreement was adopted, the most courageous people have found themselves behind bars, are now languishing in prisons, forced labor camps, and exile. ... You gathered together in Belgrade, argued, delivered speeches, and then went your separate ways. And since that time, new honest people have stood in the dock and received "terms." Now you are in Madrid, and again there are speeches, academic arguments. . . .

Since the letter by his mother was written, Anatoly Scharansky has been moved to a "strict regime barrack" in his prison camp, where he receives reduced rations and can write home only once every two months. His mother, who had looked forward to a visit with her son this month, has been told that her visit has been canceled and that her son is in solitary confinement for six months. What kind of concern for "humanitarian issues" is it that can treat this young man, who believes in the Final Act, this way?

Mr. Chairman, I have by no means today raised all the issues involving human rights which have arisen in the weeks since our December recess. The British delegate, for example, has already brought to our attention the decline in the rate of emigration of Jewish persons from the Soviet Union, particularly following the 26th Party Congress. All of these issues are highly disturbing in their severity and in their implications. I respectfully suggest, furthermore, that they are hardly consistent with the aspirations of a "worker's state." They impose a heavy burden on our meeting. We raise the issue in the hope that it can be squarely faced and then constructively dealt with. Doing so would make an immense contribution to a productive outcome for this Madrid meeting. Meanwhile, we will not ignore our obligation, in the words of the delegate from the Holy See, to acknowledge the silence of those who cannot speak.

Mr. Chairman, we hold in trust the future of our CSCE process. To preserve and strengthen that process, our commitments under the Helsinki Final Act must be respected. Governments and peoples asked to consider new proposals and new promises must have their confidence restored by having old promises kept. We earnestly make that observation in the hope that this realization can help Madrid become a constructive turning point in improving relations among all of us, thus moving closer to our goal of disarmament and peace. Two additional steps are expected of us when we return in May. First, a commitment to the CSCE process requires us to make every effort to achieve a final agreement which reflects positive results. My government pledges itself to that effort.

Second, a commitment to the CSCE process also requires us—whatever the result of our effort here in Madrid—to make adequate and timely provision for the next follow-up meeting. My government pledges itself to that objective as well. It is indispensable if we want to demonstrate our commitment to the process as a whole. If we do not demonstrate that commitment, we will have failed the millions of our citizens for whom the process offers hopes of a better future. There is still time for our Madrid meeting to produce constructive results if we choose to use that time efficiently, more expeditiously, and more productively than we have up until now. We will have one more opportunity to do so when we reconvene in May. Let us work together to accomplish that objective.

May 12, 1981 Helsinki Monitors

On May 12, 1976, five years ago today, in Moscow, nine citizens of the Soviet Union met to organize the Moscow Group to Promote Observance of the Helsinki Accords. Their intent was to express their strong support for the decisions made by their government and thirty-four other governments the previous year in Helsinki. They committed themselves to strengthen the Helsinki process by monitoring its observance.

Other men and women of courage soon joined this group. They and countless others in their country, in my country, and in all the countries of Europe looked upon the Helsinki Final Act as a new impulse in man's evolution toward a higher form of civilized international behavior. The CSCE offered a means to encourage peaceful, gradual evolution away from the roots of East-West confrontation.

These men and women in Moscow were not the only ones who saw it as their duty, as well as their right, to form Helsinki monitoring groups in their own country. Similar groups were formed in other parts of the Soviet Union, in the United States, and in many other countries. Americans were particularly pleased because of the early indications that the Soviet Union would at least tolerate the formation of those groups within its borders. This seemed to us to be a sign of maturity, a concrete indication that the "détente" which the Final Act set as a goal could, in fact, be achieved. We looked with favor upon the formation of these groups in the United States. I remind the delegates to this body that members of the Helsinki monitoring groups in the United States served as public members of the American delegation during the first phase of our Madrid meeting.

But this was not to be. This delegation and others have already expressed their deep and profound regret that the Helsinki monitors in the Soviet Union were not at all tolerated. Instead, they faced repression, exile, arrest, imprisonment and ostracism in their pursuit of that which they had a right to pursue under the Final Act. The power of the Soviet state has, in these past five years, been used to oppress these men and women of compassion rather than to protect their rights.

The Moscow group was not the only Helsinki monitoring group to be formed and then forcibly harassed and persecuted in the Soviet Union. A Ukrainian group, a Lithuanian group, a Georgian group, an Armenian group, the Christian Committee for the Defense of Believers, the Working Commission on Psychiatric Abuse, the Group for the Legal Struggle of the Faithful and Free Seventh Day Adventists, the Catholic Committee for the Defense of Believers—were all formed. And those who joined them found themselves punished for their conviction that the commitments of the Helsinki Final Act were to be taken seriously. They have been told that their activities, in behalf of the observance by their government of the Helsinki Final Act, are considered by the authorities to be "anti-Soviet." There are now forty-seven Soviet Helsinki monitors from this group either in prison or in internal exile, a number of them tried and sentenced during our Madrid meeting.

Moscow monitor group members imprisoned today are Vladimir Slepak, Yuri Orlov, Anatoly Shcharansky, Viktor Nekipelov, Tatyana Osipova, Leonard Ternovsky, Malva Landa, and Feliks Serebrov; and they are serving a total of fifty-seven years of labor camp and exile sentences. Many other names have here been mentioned by us and by other delegations. And they are representative of endless numbers of other nameless men and women whose rights are being violated and whom our delegation today remembers as we mark the anniversary of the founding of the Helsinki monitoring group.

In Czechoslovakia, too, a group of individuals formed what became known as the Charter 77 Human Rights Movement to engage their government in peaceful dialogue about the fulfillment of its pledges to its people and to all of us under the Helsinki Final Act. During the convening of the Belgrade CSCE meeting in the fall of 1977, the world learned to its dismay that mass arrests of this Charter 77 group had taken place. We know that these arrests in no small measure adversely affected the atmosphere of that Belgrade meeting.

Now again we note with deep regret the arrest of former Foreign Minister Jiri Hajek and about thirty other Czechoslovakian supporters of the Charter 77 human rights movement in that country, persons of distinction and courage, now charged, we understand, with "subversion." We condemn with the utmost seriousness the arrests of these Helsinki monitors by Czechoslovakian authorities.

I do not know what message the Czechoslovak authorities are seeking to convey to all of us here with these arrests. It comes at a time when many delegations believe there is a sense of heightened commitment to end our meetings constructively. The news from Prague makes us wonder how real this is. It reminds us that there is a world outside our conference hall that must be taken into account during our deliberations.

The arrests are a tangible blow to the CSCE process. We call upon the Czechoslovak authorities to consider again carefully whether, with the mass arrests they have made, they are not denying their commitment to the CSCE process and their interest in the success of this meeting.

The government of the United States, Mr. Chairman, recognizes its obligation to those monitors who took the Helsinki Final Act seriously and have been imprisoned and otherwise seriously punished for doing so. We signed the Helsinki Final Act and earnestly undertook our commitments in the belief that the other signatory nations would do the same. We cannot permit the violations of that Act to escape unnoticed by us and to be free of our most serious condemnation.

We hope that those who act against Helsinki monitors come to recognize that they are acting against the Final Act, against security and cooperation in Europe. They construct new barriers of distrust between East and West. They make agreement here in Madrid more difficult. They convince us that ambiguous verbal formulae at Madrid will not be sufficient and require us to seek clear, meaningful words as well as action, if we are to end with the substantive, balanced results which we require.

Mr. Chairman, we use this occasion of the fifth anniversary of the forming of the Moscow Helsinki Watch Group to reaffirm our commitment to the Act; our friendship and deep respect for those citizens of the Soviet Union, Czechoslovakia and elsewhere who are being punished for believing in it; and our pledge that we will not cease to express our identification with them until such time as they are once again free to pursue their rights as human beings, rights recognized by the Helsinki Final Act.

May 19, 1981 Andrei Sakharov

Tonight in my nation's capital city, Washington, D.C., where I live, there will be a birthday celebration for a man whose name has come to be identified all over the world with the greatness of the human spirit. On Thursday, May 21, Dr. Andrei Sakharov will be sixty years of age. In New York a few days ago, under the sponsorship of the New York Academy of Sciences, a large number of the world's most distinguished scientists gathered at a three-day symposium to pay tribute to this giant of a man, the winner of the 1975 Nobel Peace Prize, who has been confined by the authorities of his government to "internal exile" since January 1980.

My country and its people could find no better way to express their profound admiration for Dr. Sakharov and his persistent and eloquent voice for justice, which rises above the babble of totalitarian sounds that surrounds him, than through the words of the president of the United States. In a message to the symposium, President Ronald Reagan called Dr. Sakharov "one of the true spiritual heroes of our time," who "was willing to risk all to speak out on behalf of human rights and freedom." The president wrote:

Dr. Sakharov is a Russian patriot in the best sense of the word because he perceived his people's greatness to lie not in militarism and conquests abroad but in building a free and lawful society at home. His principled declarations on behalf of freedom and peace reinforce our belief in these ideals. We hope and pray that his exile will be ended and that he will enjoy a long and creative life on behalf of science and humanity.

It would be inappropriate, Mr. Chairman, were our delegation today to note Dr. Sakharov's sixtieth birthday by limiting ourselves to the abhorrence we feel at his continued exile and at the harassment and petty punishments that accompany his exile. All of the communications from him that I have seen refer rather to the needs of others: the most recent refers to the plight of Alexander Bolonkin, an imprisoned mathematician and cyberneticist, who cruelly faces a third term in a labor camp, having been rearrested on April 10, ten days before he was due to be released.

The best way for us to note Dr. Sakharov's birthday is to reassert our commitment to the Helsinki Final Act, to which he attaches major significance in his tireless pursuit of peace, human rights, and justice.

But the provisions of the Helsinki Final Act, so enthusiastically welcomed by our peoples in 1975, have not been lived up to by all of the participating states. Delegation after delegation here has so testified. The symbols of those violations are the invasion and continuing military occupation of Afghanistan and the growing repression of human rights in the Soviet Union.

My delegation has documented our concern in significant detail. We did so on the closing day of our session prior to the Easter holiday, on April 10. It was with sadness that I read in the press the following day that at a press conference by the head of one delegation, the human beings whose rights, integrity, and freedom have been interfered with, and whose names I mentioned, were considered to be "castoffs, the throwaways of Soviet society." If the newspaper report is accurate, I remind this meeting that among those so-called "throwaways" was Dr. Andrei Sakharov, about whom I began these comments—who was the youngest person ever elected to membership in the Soviet Academy of Sciences, who was three times awarded by his government the honorific title, "Hero of Socialist Labor," and who is today one of the towering and, assisted by the excesses of his government, most influential men of our time.

We have heard a statement a few minutes ago about the commitment of the Soviet Union to disarmament—a strange claim by the government that has been and continues to be engaged in the largest military buildup in world history. I remind us all in that connection that it is the exiled and discarded Dr. Sakharov, the recipient of the Nobel Peace Prize, who has advocated, with all his energies, world disarmament—a genuine disarmament and not a propaganda instrumentality behind which to arm and to invade another sovereign nation.

In the treatment of Andrei Sakharov by the Soviet authorities and in our differing perceptions of what that means, we have a dramatic illustration of the serious problem we face at this meeting and in our process.

Many of us here continue to look for some concrete response to the violations we have identified, some indication that there will be a more serious effort to abide by the provisions of the Act that we all hoped would bring us together. But we see none. Rather, to look at recent events—the small and the large, and both are important—we see what may be considered to be deliberate defiance rather than a desire to seek accommodation and understanding. There have been at least forty-six arrests of human rights activists in the Soviet Union since the Madrid conference opened. In 1980, according to reliable sources, there were more such arrests (242) than in any one of the last fifteen years.

We have listened with care to the defense which is made here of such actions. We have heard an appeal to a broader good. We have heard that the welfare of the masses of people is superior to the rights of individuals. We are told that those who challenge their society by claiming their own individual human rights and supporting the rights of others are thus lawless and criminal, deserving to be punished by their authorities.

We must respond that no broader good can justify the systematic oppression of human beings; that the welfare of the masses cannot be distinguished from the rights of individuals (indeed, I suggest that those societies that espouse this distinction neither meet the needs of the individuals nor the needs of the masses); and we respond that those who exert their human rights—even to question and to challenge authority—deserve protection, not oppression.

As my wise countryman, Thomas Jefferson—like Andrei Sakharov, a scientist and a humanist—said: "The care of human life and happiness, and not their destruction, is the first and only legitimate object of good government."

Mr. Chairman, where the monopoly of economic and political power in a state or in a party is not tempered with a commitment to human rights as set forth in the Helsinki Final Act, where its legitimacy is then based primarily on police and military force, this tends to produce a dialectic of its own, an inner contradiction which undermines that monopoly. Such a system produces a denial of democracy to its peoples, except for a privileged ruling elite; it produces ideological self-righteousness and intolerance; and it stifles creative effort just as it stifles industrial and agricultural productivity.

The provisions of the Helsinki Final Act and their implementation are essential to the stability of all our societies as well as to the stability of the international order, yet we see these provisions violated. It is no wonder that many ask what good it does to meet for endless weeks in an effort to find language to strengthen and improve the Final Act when provisions already agreed to are not lived up to.

Nevertheless we meet; and we will continue to meet. We do so because those of us, like Dr. Sakharov, who take the Helsinki Final Act seriously, know that its guiding principles are the best remaining standards by which to ensure liberty and to reach peace among us.

We have the faith that our persistence, our talking with one another, our frank and sometimes unpleasantly candid exchanges, our halting but continuing efforts to reach new agreements—that all of these will help produce the adjustments

This exhaustive and extensive work is remarkable for a number of reasons. First, it was compiled under very difficult conditions of official repression. Its authors assumed grave personal risks to collect information from across Poland. But the report is most remarkable for its scope and content. The report's 600 pages analyze legalized and extra-legal means of repression employed in Poland before and after December 1981; it documents wide-scale rights abuses which violate Poland's domestic law as well as international law obligations; it traces the enactment of legislation designed to institutionalize the massive repression undertaken; it cites the cases of thousands of Polish citizens who have suffered severe punitive measures for attempting to know and act upon their rights.

This chronicle serves to expose to the stark light of world public opinion countless oppressive actions of the Polish regime against its own people. But the determination of Solidarity to endure and continue in their peaceful pursuit of basic democratic freedoms also shines through the pages of the report.

In the cover letter introducing the report, the authors write: "We send this report with the conviction that it will serve the cause of peace and security in Europe, for there is no peace without social justice." The American delega... United States government. He charged that my country had initiated an enormous arms race. He asserted that we were attempting to establish military supremacy. He claimed that we were embarked on a drive for global military control under the direction of the Pentagon. And he assailed the United States government and the American military establishment for spreading "myths" about the Soviet military threat and "slanderous rumors" about Soviet policy.

Monsignor Chairman, I do not intend to respond to this attack in the propagandistic and polemical way in which it was launched, no matter how justified such a response by us might be. I would prefer, rather, to challenge our Soviet colleague with facts; the absence of any facts in his statement was noteworthy.

Let us today consider—soberly and analytically—the serious charges that were launched on Wednesday against my country. Let us examine the military situation in his country and in mine, and the military policies each of our countries is pursuing. In this examination I will not cite a single conclusion not based on fact, nor a single piece of data that is not fully substantiated or readily available in reliable publications. The data will speak for themselves. And I will leave it to the distinguished delegates in this room to decide, on the basis of the facts, which government has unleashed an arms race, which government is attempting to establish military supremacy, and which government represents a military threat to the peace and security of our peoples.

I begin with general statistics, which should set the context for our examination. First of all, defense budgets:

Between 1968 and 1981—a period presumably corresponding to the charge that we have unleashed an arms race—the United States defense budget *declined* by 25 percent in constant dollars. It is unfortunately impossible to measure exactly the Soviet defense budget in the same period because, unlike Western defense budgets, the components of that budget are not made available for independent scrutiny. But the following estimates are reliable and generally accepted. In contrast to the U.S. decline of 25 percent during this period, since the 1960s the Soviet Union: has *increased* its defense budget at an average annual rate of 5 to 8 percent; has *outspent* the United States on conventional armaments at a rate that is double ours; has spent *three times* as much as the United States on strategic nuclear weapons; has devoted an average of *11 to 12 percent* of its gross national product to military expenditures; the comparable U.S. figure is under 6 percent.

A further general fact: the total armed forces of the Soviet Union number more than 4,300,000 men in the five branches of its forces and its KGB border guards, and this figure excludes some 500,000 internal security troops and railroad and construction troops. The total armed forces of the United States, in contrast, number 2,050,000. Translated into percentages, the figures show that, with a population 20 percent greater than ours, the Soviet Union has armed forces which are more than 100 percent greater than ours.

It is noteworthy also that the Soviet Union has built the world's largest officer training system. There are today 125 military colleges with five-year programs teaching the art of war to young people; sixteen military academies that offer doctoral degrees in military science; and seven special military institutes. Here are indeed the signs of a military society.

Let us look more closely, taking first conventional forces:

In conventional land warfare, it is generally agreed that the tank is the primary offensive instrument. When we think of invasion, most of us think of tanks streaming across borders. The United States has 10,500 tanks. The Soviet Union has 50,000—a ratio of almost five to one. Since a large number of Soviet tanks are being used to support the Soviet occupation of Afghanistan, or are deployed facing China, a breakdown for the European Theater alone is relevant. Here the ratio of Warsaw Pact tanks against all of NATO tanks is 2.8 to 1.

Moreover, the last new U.S. tank now operative, the M-60, entered service in 1959. While the M-60 is still produced in a modified version, we have had no new tank for twenty years. In contrast, two new Soviet tanks, the T-64 and the T-72, entered service with the Warsaw Pact in the late 1970s. Still another new Soviet tank, the T-80—heavier, faster, with increased fire power and a longer range—will enter service in the near future, and is expected to be produced at the rate of 2,000 tanks per year—twice the number of new tanks in U.S. projected production. In contrast to the Soviet Union, the U.S. has concentrated its investment in this area on antitank weapons, which are by definition defensive in purpose.

The Soviet preponderance in men and tanks, which I have just described, has, of course, reflected itself in the imbalance that now exists between NATO and Warsaw Pact forces in Central Europe. It was with the purpose of reducing that destabilizing and dangerous imbalance that the United States and several of its Allies entered the Vienna talks on Mutual and Balanced Force Reductions. Yet the Soviet Union has consistently refused to provide us even the most elementary data on the organization and strength of the Warsaw Pact ground forces. The fact that those talks have entered their ninth year should tell us something about the willingness of the Soviet Union to find a solution to the urgent need for force reductions in Europe.

The Soviet delegate referred several times during this meeting to a unilateral step, taken by the Soviet Union in 1980, when it withdrew approximately 20,000 troops, including a tank division from the GDR. He has told us that this was a major positive step. Unfortunately, he did not tell us that this tank division was not dismantled but was, according to published data by the International Institute of Strategic Studies, simply redeployed to a Western military district of the Soviet Union, where it still presents a considerable threat to the people of Europe. And he did not tell us that, in the GDR itself, the fire power and combat utility of the remaining units have been increased. The number of infantrymen assigned to tank divisions has been increased; reconnaissance sub-units have been strengthened with additional tanks; artillery sub-units have been assigned to infantry divisions; and obsolescent tanks have been replaced with newer models. The net effect of what the Soviet delegate would have us believe is a positive step—the net effect has been an increase in the Soviet ability to pursue a high-speed offensive in Western Europe. None of this has the Soviet delegation told us.

If we look at the respective air forces, we see similar trends. The Soviet Union is currently producing tactical aircraft at a rate of about 1,150 units per year—compared to about 500 such aircraft for the U.S. Air Force and Navy combined. Moreover, in the early 1970s, the Soviet Air Force in Central Europe began a process of rearmament that changed its orientation from a previously defensive role to a role in which it is capable of independent air operations to strike targets anywhere in Europe. Third generation attack aircraft such as the SU-17 FITTER, the MIG-27 FLOGGER, and the Sukhoy-designed FENCER-A (all of which are nuclear capable) were introduced during the last decade along with large numbers of late-model MIG-21 FISHBED and MIG-23 FLOGGER, plus many reconnaissance aircraft, including the MIG-25 FOXBAT. In many cases, these aircraft represent a threefold increase in range and offensive weapons payload over the aircraft they replaced.

In addition, several thousand helicopters have been added to this strike force, greatly expanding its mobility and further emphasizing its offensive role. These include the MI-8 HIP and the MI-24 HIND. These attack helicopters, the most heavily armed helicopters in the world, already have gained significant combat experience in an offensive role, since they are now being used extensively in the Soviet invasion of Afghanistan.

Let me make clear that we Americans are confident of our own capabilities in the air. We believe that our aircraft are more advanced technologically and our pilots extremely well trained. What disturbs us are the apparent Soviet efforts to achieve superiority in support of what is clearly an offensive air doctrine.

Let me now turn to the naval situation. In the decade of the 1970s the Soviet Union began an enormous effort which transformed it from a coastal defense force into a blue-water navy, present in all the seas of the world. A few facts will underline the results and the concern.

In the last ten years, in response to relaxation in tensions, the U.S. Navy deliberately reduced in size from 1,000 to 540 ships—nearly a 50 percent reduction. Our total tonnage dropped 20 percent. During the same decade, while we dropped, the Soviet Navy increased to the point where it now outnumbers the U.S. Navy in numbers of vessels by more than three to one. It has more principal surface combatants, more attack submarines (in this vital category the ratio is three to one), it has more auxiliaries and more ships and craft for mine warfare. Let us look at last year's figures. During 1980, the United States delivered one submarine to its operating forces; the Soviet Union delivered twelve—one a month. In the same year, we delivered eighteen major ships to our Navy; the Soviets delivered forty.

In asking ourselves the purposes of this massive naval buildup, we can do no better than to quote the man who has been commander of the Soviet Navy for some twenty-five years and was the architect of the buildup. In 1979, four years after our thirty-five states subscribed to Principle 11 of the Final Act on refraining from the threat of force, Admiral Sergei Gorshkov stated: "In many cases naval demonstrations have made it possible to achieve political goals, without resorting to an armed struggle merely by exerting pressure through one's own potential power and by threatening to initiate military hostilities." It was as if there were no Helsinki Final Act.

Turning now to the nuclear area, we see the same patterns of Soviet increase that we observed in the conventional area. In the three major categories of strategic weaponry, the U.S. has made no increases in deployment since the decade of the 1960s. While we have replaced some of our aging land-based missiles with the MIRV'ed Minuteman III, we have deployed no new nuclear ballistic missile-carrying submarines since 1966; and no new strategic bombers since 1962. Indeed our bomber B-52 fleet has been reduced from 935 to 400 since 1966, even though we were not required by SALT I to make such reductions.

By contrast, during the same time frame, the Soviet Union has developed and deployed three completely new ICBMs: the SS-17, SS-18, and SS-19, each of them with multiple warheads. The SS-18 is now deployed in approximately 300 launchers, each capable of carrying at least ten warheads, each of which has over a thousand times the destructive capacity of the Hiroshima bomb! This giant SS-18 missile, the biggest in the world, was clearly designed to eliminate the retaliatory capacity of U.S. missiles in deep underground shelters. Furthermore, just last year the Soviet Union launched the largest strategic missile submarine in the world—the TYPHOON, which will carry the largest sea-launched missile currently under development.

As observers ponder these strategic realities, it is reasonable for all of us to ask whether the Soviet strategic objective is mutual deterrence or whether its objective isn't rather a war-winning capability based on an effort to achieve nuclear and conventional superiority. My own views on this question are clear, but I would prefer to leave the answer to the experts.

Let us first look at the question of military superiority in general as a Soviet objective. One expert source here is Erich Honecker, the GDR's leader, who, in describing détente six weeks after the signing of the Helsinki Final Act, said, "In this struggle, the military *superiority* of Socialism is and will remain a major factor for preserving peace." Superiority, Monsignor Chairman.

Now let us turn to the issue of strategic nuclear superiority. I quote from *Military Thought*, the official journal of the Soviet General Staff. The author, Colonel A. Aleksandrov, writing in 1967, describes the procurement of large quantities of technologically advanced weaponry for the purpose of "maintaining superiority over imperialism in the field of the principal and decisive type of weapons, and first of all nuclear-rocket weapons."

Lest this view be deemed out of date, let me add that the objective of quantitative and qualitative superiority is also enunciated in Volume 2 of the current Soviet Military Encyclopedia, which is edited by Marshal of the Soviet Union N. V. Ogarkov, who is now chief of the Soviet General Staff and was formerly a member of the Soviet Union's SALT I negotiating team.

Finally, Mr. Chairman, there is one other significant category, and we have heard quite a bit about it from the Soviet delegation during these meetings. The category is that of theater nuclear forces. For two decades, the Soviet Union has had the capability to launch nuclear missile attacks with its SS-4's and SS-5's against Western European cities. Never in this period has the United States had, nor does it now have, the capability to launch similar land-based missile attacks from Western Europe against the Soviet Union.

Nevertheless, the Soviet Union is now replacing the SS-4 and SS-5 missiles with SS-20's. My government maintains that the SS-20 represents a significantly destabilizing and dangerous influence in Europe. Why? The answer is apparent when one considers the [greatly superior] capabilities of the SS-20 in comparison to the missiles it is replacing. . . .

* * *

Some mention of Soviet policy is in order. . . . For example, the Soviet invasion of Afghanistan, and the military occupation which has continued for the [past] year and a half, tell us something about Soviet policy toward their neighbors. The extraordinary political and military intimidation of another neighbor, even while we have been at this conference, provides an ominous commentary on the real policy of the Soviet Union toward what our Soviet colleague ominously referred to as the "Socialist Commonwealth."

It is clear from this review that during the past decade there has been an accelerated and massive accumulation of Soviet armaments in virtually every major military category. And we note that this accumulation coincided exactly with a period which the Soviet Union has characterized as a period of "détente." One is forced to ask whether, for the Soviet government, "détente" has been an objective or a camouflage.

Monsignor Chairman, the increased expenditures for our defense needs which President Reagan and the American people are now making have evoked censure from the Soviet Union. I have today set forth a few observable facts—they are not "myths"—which have made those expenditures necessary. We ask each delegate in this room to consider: If his government faced the same indisputable facts, could he seriously recommend to that government a different course from the one we and our Allies are taking?

Monsignor Chairman, the United States obviously has the ability to defend its interests and those of the free world. We have confidence in our strengths in such important categories as strategic warheads, in our technology, in our industrial and agricultural strength, in our human material, and in the determination of our government and people to maintain a strong defense in behalf of our own national interests and our values.

Our own position is clear. The course we are following is one we will continue to follow. We have no other course. But it is an essential part of our policy as well, and we reiterate the continuing commitment of my government to long-term arms control as a component of our national security policy. How far we can go in arms control, how far genuine détente is possible, will depend primarily on the Soviet Union—on its military programs and on its international behavior.

In closing, let me invite the attention of the delegates assembled here to a passage from a great work by Fyodor Dostoyevsky, who wrote a century ago:

Our fatal troika dashes on in her headlong flight, perhaps to destruction, and in all Russia for long past men have stretched out imploring hands and have called for a halt to its furious, reckless course. And if other nations stand aside from the troika, it might not be from respect, but simply from horror; from horror, perhaps from disgust. And well it is that they stand aside, but they will cease one day to do so and will form a firm wall confronting the hurrying aberration and will check the frenzied rush of our lawlessness for sake of their own safety, enlightenment, and civilization.

. . . Let us pray those words are no more than the creative product of a brilliant Russian imagination, rather than a prophetic description of things to come.

July 28, 1981 Negotiating Human Rights

* * *

Mr. Chairman, as I have suggested, a major reason why we have not reached agreement here in Madrid is the international atmosphere outside our conference hall. The invasion of Afghanistan and the continued occupation of that tragic country by Soviet troops have had a corrosive effect on our meetings. Recently, as the delegate of the United Kingdom noted on Friday, the European Community presented an imaginative plan for a political settlement of the crisis in Afghanistan. The Soviet Union has not responded to it positively. That, too, has its negative effect here.

Moreover, the Soviet Union is continuing its military buildup, which intensified while my country, in the spirit of "détente," took significant disarmament steps. That buildup, as I noted in this hall several weeks ago, is the most massive that the world has ever known. On behalf of my government I state with deep conviction that it must end. Continued military escalation and activity by the Soviet Union will not attain the security or respect they seek. It may instill fear in some; but it instills determination in many more. Military power, no matter how great, does not confer moral legitimacy.

There has been much debate at our meeting over the word I just used, détente. The word is meant to describe a condition of relaxation of tension between states. I submit again that the Soviet Union's actions and attitudes toward its neighbors and its massive military buildup demonstrate to us that such a condition does not exist today. If a general pattern of aggression and intimidation can be referred to as "détente," then surely the continued use of the word is bereft of any significance. That is why our delegation has been reluctant to use it in our final document. We will not permit its use as an attempt to camouflage a policy of force.

Within the Soviet Union, the repression of human rights continues with cruel relentlessness. Even if we look only at what has happened since April 10, when the last recess of our meeting began, we see that specific Soviet transgressions of the Final Act have increased in numbers and intensity.

Here in Madrid, we have had some movement in strengthening written commitments to reduce barriers to the reunification of families. But that movement on paper has not been reflected in the practice of Soviet authorities. Emigration figures for Armenians and for ethnic Germans who want to rejoin their families have dropped substantially. The number of Jews allowed to emigrate is dropping at an even greater rate. In the first six months of 1979, 24,794 Jews left the Soviet Union; in the first six months of this year only 6,668 left—a decline of 73 percent in only two years.

For those Jews remaining, conditions have continued to deteriorate. We and other delegations have already noted with deep regret and condemnation the sentencing on June 18 of Viktor Brailovsky. New arrests have taken place. My files are filled with names and letters reflecting individual human tragedy inflicted by an insensitive bureaucracy.

Here in Madrid, we have had difficulty in negotiating a text on religious freedom, in large part because of an insistance on a variety of loopholes which would enable real commitments to be evaded. One of the loopholes is that our commitments are to be qualified by the "national traditions" of participating states. Let us look at what that phrase "national traditions" might mean.

June 27, exactly a month ago, marked the third anniversary of the day two devout Pentecostal families from far Siberia sought refuge in the American Embassy in Moscow. This desperate action by the Vashchenko and Chmykhailov families culminated twenty years of frustrated attempts to emigrate to a country where they could practice their faith freely. There are at least 20,000 Pentecostals who want to emigrate and are denied the right to do so.

Devout Christian believers of all denominations have faced years of persecution, imprisonment, and systematic discrimination in education and employment. Indeed, during previous efforts to emigrate, four of the Vashchenko children were placed by the authorities in a state orphanage and their father was forcibly confined in a psychiatric hospital. During the last three years, at least 250 Christians, to our knowledge, have been imprisoned in the USSR for pursuing the dictates of their faith and conscience. These include Baptists, Adventists, Pentecostals, Russian Orthodox, True Orthodox, Greek Catholics, Roman Catholics, and Jehovah's Witnesses.

We have every reason to wonder whether this pattern of arrests may not be the "national tradition" we are asked to condone. This kind of "national tradition" has no place in any document brought forth by our meeting.

A major objective of many delegations at Madrid, including our own, has been to seek language in our final document that calls for the removal of obstacles preventing the individual from expressing his views and otherwise knowing and acting upon his rights and duties in the human rights area, including those concerning the implementation of the Final Act. The basis for this is in Principle VII of the Final Act. It is, therefore, relevant to examine what has happened to the human rights activists and groups in the Soviet Union, whose purpose is exactly to concern themselves with the implementation of the Helsinki Final Act.

Since early June, three members of the Psychiatric Watch Group, which was set up to monitor the abuse of psychiatric medicine to inflict political punishment, have been sentenced to prison terms. One of them, Anatoly Koryagin, a psychiatrist, was sentenced on June 5 to seven years in labor camp plus five years of internal exile for "anti-Soviet agitation and propaganda." Koryagin's crime was to attest to the sanity of Aleksei Nikitin, a mining engineer, who was forcibly committed to the Dnepropetrovsk special psychiatric hospital for protesting against unsafe working conditions of miners in the Donetsk region.

In a Plenary statement on May 12, I noted the fifth anniversary of the Moscow Helsinki Monitoring Group. Since then, that group, and the Lithuanian and Ukrainian monitoring groups as well, have been further decimated by arrests and trials. This is the occasion to remember that the health of the Moscow group's founder, Yuri Orlov, and of founding member Anatoly Shcharansky, continues to worsen in prison, as does the health of Estonian rights advocate, Mart Niklus, who is serving a fifteen-year sentence.

Raisa Rudenko, the wife of the founder of the Ukrainian Helsinki Monitoring Group, Mykola Rudenko, who is himself serving a twelve-year sentence, was arrested on May 12 in Kiev. We have only recently learned of the re-arrest on March 24 of Ivan Kandyba, founding member of the Ukrainian group, who now faces the possibility of yet another fifteen-year sentence, which would bring the total years he will have spent in confinement to thirty.

We learned, too, that two new members of the Lithuanian Monitoring Group, Vytautas Vaiciunas and Mecislovas Jurivicius, were arrested and charged with "anti-Soviet fabrications" and participating in religious processions.

And in Latvia on June 9, Juris Bumeisters, a sixty-three-year-old electrical engineer, was sentenced to fifteen years of strict regimen camp for treason, reportedly in connection with his involvement in the Latvian Social Democratic Party, which belongs to the Socialist International.

And Andrei Sakharov remains banished to Gorky, weaker in physical strength, isolated by the Soviet authorities—but not forgotten by the world.

I am aware, Mr. Chairman, that we have mentioned many names today. I only wish that the list of arrests and persecutions since April 10 were much smaller—indeed, nonexistent. Let me only state that the names mentioned were but a few, illustrative of many more men and women who have become victims of state oppression.

What we have witnessed during the entire life of this Madrid meeting—while the Soviet delegation has been professing its fidelity to the Final Act—is a systematic effort by the regime to destroy the entire human rights movement in the Soviet Union. No human rights group has been left untouched. But these men and women know they have friends. They are not forgotten. We remember them here. Their friends will continue to remember. Books published all over the world will recall their deeds for new generations to remember.

We have on another occasion noted that in Czechoslovakia, human rights champions are facing similar dangers. On July 9, Jiri Gruntorad, a young fighter for human rights and a signer of Charter 77, was sentenced to four years in prison for subversion. Following mass arrests on April 28, trials have begun for members of Charter 77 and VONS (the Committee for the Defense of the Unjustly Persecuted). Yesterday, the trial of spokesman Rudolph Battek took place. There are reports that other trials are imminent. We deeply hope that the Czechoslovak regime will reconsider before it does new damage to its standing at this Conference and its relations with the states represented here.

The head of the Soviet delegation has reminded us many times of the small number of human rights activists that exist in his country. Then why is his government so afraid of them? Has it so little confidence in itself that it cannot tolerate the activities of a handful of people? Why is a state that calls for peaceful coexistence unable to coexist with its own internal differing views? Why must it punish people for asking their government to observe the commitments it assumed of its own free will?

I will make a prediction—not a warning, a prediction. The regime can, by force, weaken and even come close to obliterating the formal human rights movement in the Soviet Union. We know from recent history that any totalitarian regime can, if it is ruthless enough, succeed with repression—in the short run. But the struggle for that review, and it was a thorough one. The Soviet invasion of Afghanistan and the record of human rights violations in the Soviet Union and Eastern Europe were explored and recorded in meticulous detail.

Continuing Soviet and other Eastern violations of the Helsinki Final Act made it necessary to extend this review of implementation throughout most of the Madrid deliberations.

The final document acknowledges that this review took place ("They . . . reaffirmed . . . the importance of the implementation of all the provisions . . . of the Final Act . . . as being . . . essential. . . . It was confirmed that the thorough exchange of views constitutes in itself a valuable contribution towards the achievement of the aims set by CSCE. In this context, it was agreed that those aims can only be attained by continuous implementation, unilaterally, bilaterally and multilaterally, of all the provisions and by respect for all the principles of the Final Act"), that the review is essential to the health of the process, and that there must be an improvement in compliance ("Serious violations of a number of these principles were deplored during the assessments. Therefore, the participating states . . . considered it necessary to state . . . that strict application and respect peoples, great peoples with profound cultures and proud histories. We pray that the government will gain the self-confidence and the moral courage to advance human rights rather than suppress them, because that is the key to the genius and greatness of any people. certain states, particularly the U.S.S.R. continue to

Mr. Chairman, the transgressions of the Final Act here cited, all of them applying to the short period since our last recess, are raised to underscore a point essential to the success of the Madrid meeting. Events outside our conference cloud the possibility of significant achievements here. Their improvement will be reflected in an improved spirit here.

The United States delegation will return in October with determination to fulfill its responsibilities under the Helsinki Final Act. We join nearly all of the delegations here in our determination to bring this meeting to a close with positive, substantial, and balanced results. What we need to accomplish this objective is a reciprocal commitment. We need a demonstration that the Soviet Union intends to abide by the provisions of the Final Act. Our peoples have every right to ask what good it does to talk about new promises when the old ones are not kept.

The delegation of the United States will persevere in our efforts here for peace, security, and understanding, and for the building of the CSCE process. What we have already done in a long ten months in Madrid is inadequate, but it can provide a good basis on which we can build.

It is our view that the best way to build is:

▶ By finding language which makes unmistakable reference to the important role that Helsinki monitors can play.

▶ By agreeing to discuss our problems in the human rights and human contacts areas in a serious, thoughtful, and constructive spirit at post-Madrid experts' meetings.

▶ By putting specific content into the Final Act language on freedom of religion.

▶ By reaching consensus on a strong information text. It is the unique gift of thought which distinguishes man from the animal world. The right to hear facts and ideas through, among other things, the unimpeded dissemination of broadcast information, is an integral part of that thought process; as is clear protection for professional journalists, a vital channel through which facts and ideas are communicated.

group of neutral and nonaligned states (RM-39). The amendments were designed to reflect the view that "business as usual" remained impossible. The essence of many of these proposals was incorporated in a revised neutral and nonaligned document, submitted on March 15, 1983, after martial law was ostensibly and technically suspended (RM-39 revised). That revised document, with improvements to it produced by the Prime Minister of Spain on June 17, 1983, has become the official concluding document of Madrid.

A number of provisions of that document reflect our Polish concerns. They deal with trade unions, religious freedom, and renewed obligation to refrain from the threat or use of force. Summary language in the preamble further reflects Western attention to developments in Poland. The United States and its Western allies never forgot during the course of the Madrid meeting that among the first of Solidarity's demands in August 1980 was that the Helsinki Final Act be reprinted and widely disseminated in Poland. We have kept in close touch with representatives of the Solidarity movement in Europe and the United States, and we have helped communicate their messages to the delegations in Madrid.

Trade Unions

The Helsinki Final Act of 1975 did not include any language on trade unions. The Madrid document reflects a Western initiative stemming directly from the suppression of Solidarity in Poland. It clearly states that participating states "will ensure the right of workers freely to establish and join trade unions, the right of trade unions freely to exercise their activities and their rights as laid down in relative international instruments." This, of course, clearly refers to the conventions of the International Labor Organization (ILO). A reference to "the law of the State" follows, thereby referring to the fact that all states have laws which in some measure define union rights and activities. But that reference is associated with another provision asserting the requirement that such measures be "in conformity with the state's obligation under international law," again a reference to the ILO.

This provision also calls upon states to encourage direct contacts among trade unions and their representatives. The West, which has always made the point that unions freely organized in the West are not to be confused with the totalitarian state-controlled organizations known as unions in the East, was able successfully to insist that this provision be applicable only to "such" unions which are indeed freely organized by workers and free to function under ILO standards.

Monitors

The Helsinki Final Act of 1975 provided a very clear basis of legitimacy to the courageous men and women who formed Helsinki monitoring groups within their own countries. Their purpose was to keep watch on how their states were complying with the provisions of the accords, a right they had under the 1975 agreement. In deliberate decisions to violate the provisions of the act, authorities in the U.S.S.R., Czechoslovakia, and elsewhere in Eastern Europe persecuted and imprisoned those who exercised that right "to know and act upon their rights."

In Madrid, 14 states mentioned the names of 123 victims of repression, many of them monitors. This was in contrast to the Belgrade meeting where the United States was one of only two countries to mention the names of victims, and we mentioned six. The Netherlands was the other.

The language on monitors in the Helsinki Final Act is quite clear and should not require elaboration. Indeed, within the rules of Madrid requiring consensus, it was very difficult to formulate appropriate additional language more clearly. We

Tensions

Negotiations for a concluding document continued amid rising rhetorical tensions at Madrid. The next phase of the conference would run from October 27 to December 18, 1981. Increasingly, Ambassador Kampelman voiced the U.S. position that if a concluding statement were to be regarded as acceptable to the American people, it had to be accompanied by perceptibly changed behavior of the Soviet Union.

As the session was ending, martial law was declared in Poland. Ambassador Kampelman addressed this major development in his speech of December 18.

October 30, 1981 ZAPAD-81 and SOYUZ-81

The American delegation wishes at the very outset to associate itself fully with the message of the delegate from the United Kingdom, who spoke on the opening day of these renewed sessions in behalf of ten of our participating states. The contribution of the delegate of France this morning was particularly wise and statesmanlike, and we commend it with respect.

Our delegation did not speak on that first day. We wanted to assess the atmosphere that we would find here. We hoped that we would discern a more constructive intent to comply with the spirit and words of the Helsinki Final Act, so that we could together proceed to negotiate a substantive and balanced agreement. It is with disappointment that we note the absence of that determination. Indeed, judging from events in some of the drafting groups this week, there has been a deterioration of that spirit, and a retreat from the purposeful dedication that is required of all of us.

I note sadly that the efforts made by many of us to advance the objectives of human rights under the Helsinki Final Act were again characterized in plenary as "cheap propaganda" and "sterile polemics," as if that is the way to deal with a serious problem of interest to millions of people. The Soviet Union, furthermore, continues to maintain its extraordinary and incomprehensible position that their willingness to consider CBM coverage extended to the Urals somehow requires a compensatory move outside of Europe.

The American delegation again comes here committed to the pursuit of an agreement designed to achieve peace. We believe that the terms and spirit of the Helsinki Final Act provide the formula for that goal. The remarks this morning of the delegates from Sweden and Switzerland are very important in this regard. Extensive violations of that Act create serious obstacles to agreement and to peace; and those violations continue.

We doubt the commitment to peace of any state which uses its troops, its tanks, its weapons of destruction to invade and subjugate a neighboring people. It is, furthermore, difficult to accept as genuine, new proposals to strengthen cooperation among the states by those who continue to ignore agreements undertaken by them in 1975. We question the commitment to the Helsinki process and to "détente" of any state which continues to act in many areas as if the Helsinki Final Act did not exist.

It was our hope that the convening of this review meeting a year ago would produce evidence of a greater commitment to the Helsinki Final Act. We looked for some sign of good faith in complying with its provisions, some glimmer of respect for the Madrid meeting. Instead, we have found defiance—85,000 Soviet troops remain in Afghanistan where they do not belong and where they have caused untold suffering to people who desire nothing more than to live in peace in their own land. We find growing intimidation of Helsinki monitors and other human rights advocates, with new arrests and imprisonments taking place during the very period that we are in session. And this summer, Mr. Chairman, there was failure to comply with the Final Act in yet another area, that of military security. We can find no reasonable explanation for this failure, during a crucial phase of our Madrid negotiations while we're discussing a conference to deal with confidence-building measures (CBMs). We fear it may be an intent to demonstrate, in this area too, further disdain for the Act. What we see is disdain for the individual, disdain for other states, and disdain for the Helsinki process.

And now about the military events of this summer. On August 14, the Soviet Union notified the participating states that it would hold a military maneuver between September 4 and 12 in the Byelorussian and Baltic military districts and in the Baltic Sea. The Final Act specifies that notification of major military maneuvers "will contain information of the designation" of such exercises. The Soviet notification gave none. We had to learn from press reports that its name was ZAPAD-81. The Final Act specifies that notifications will provide information on the "numerical strength of the forces engaged." The Soviet notification provided none. We had to learn from their press that "approximately 100,000" were engaged, after an initial press report that the numbers were "extremely limited." And this in spite of the provisions of the Act that notification should take place "through usual diplomatic channels." It is significant that in response to representations requesting the missing information, we were told that the provisions of the Act on notification of major maneuvers were, after all, only " "guidelines," not requirements!

The maneuver notification, such as it was, was also unduly vague and unrevealing, not at all consistent with the very purpose of the CBM concept, which is to build mutual confidence among states. Rather than build confidence, the apparent Soviet disdain for the notification requirement generated suspicion and mistrust. What we have seen in the ZAPAD-81 maneuver notification is a sham. It leads us to strengthen our resolve that if we are, as we wish, to go forward with a conference on CBMs, the French proposal, which insists on firm and unambiguous criteria, must be its framework. We see no room, in the light of this year's experience, for voluntarism and vagueness in implementation.

Let me go on. Earlier this year, the Warsaw Pact engaged in another massive military exercise, SOYUZ-81. We previously referred to this military event as one which, in our view, had as one of its purposes the intimidation of a neighboring state in violation of the Helsinki Final Act. It is appropriate now for us to look at it within the standards of the CBM requirements.

During our most recent recess I took the occasion to review texts of radio broadcasts describing the exercise, heard over the state-owned facilities of Warsaw Pact countries. What stands out in bold relief is that SOYUZ-81 was a major Warsaw Pact military exercise which lasted from March 17 to April 7, 1981.

Why were those maneuvers not announced under the CBM requirements? Two reasons were given: The first was that it was a routine "command/staff exercise"; and the other, that the maneuvers did not involve more than 25,000 troops. Let us see what we have learned from official radio reports emanating from the very countries which participated in the exercise:

1. On March 21 the Polish press agency, PAP, explained that joint exercises of Polish, Soviet, Czechoslovakian, and GDR troops would continue on Polish territory "to test the attained level of training of each of the four armies as well as cooperation between them." That same day, the Warsaw Domestic Radio Service broadcast the voice of a commander in the field referring to reservists in action, an entire regiment in military operation, and helicopter activities.

2. That same radio service on March 22 and March 23 reported an amphibious exercise involving the Soviet Baltic Fleet, and the live firing of rocket artillery followed by paratroopers jumping from "successive waves of planes." A correspondent reports: "I witnessed a head-on clash between selected sub-units from various tactical groups. . . . The seizure of a line suitable for the launching of an attack was assisted by a helicopter landing and air support. A similar helicopter landing was, of course, employed by the enemy. Today has been a busy day. At the moment I am at the rocket artillery firing post. I am waiting for the firing of the rocket. . . . We can now hear the siren; the firing command is given. . . ." There was a reference to "many complex operations," on land, sea, and in the air, with Polish soldiers cooperating with units of the Soviet army in evacuating casualties from the battlefield.

3. On March 23, a correspondent from the Silesian military district is heard to say: "At this moment we are being approached from above the forest over there by transport helicopters, screened by assault helicopters. . . . A moment ago we

saw the gunship helicopter. . . . We have here a regular battlefield with shots being fired. . . ', an enemy and our troops." The same service reported that pontoon bridge-building units were operative.

4. On March 24, the voice of the GDR domestic service referred to "mass air, land and naval attacks by the assumed enemy."

5. On March 27 the East German international service reported the presence of motorized tank troops, artillery, signal units, engineers. That same news service, the next day, referred to motorized riflemen and gunners. Interesting also was a reference on the following day to the fact that many of the troops participating "returned to their garrisons and were replaced by new units."

6. On March 29 the GDR international service referred to "maneuvers... annihilating an assumed enemy," amphibious landings, the throwing of grenades, the firing of machine guns and antitank rifles, motorized infantry, tank and artillery soldiers, reservists, antisubmarine warfare, MIG aircraft, rockets, minesweepers, motor torpedo boats, reconnaissance troops—all were involved in what was described as "the concluding high point of the first half" of the 1980-81 training year.

7. On April 2, from the GDR international service: "On Thursday, the 'enemy' again tried to land troops on the coast. Fighter planes were ordered to foil the plan together with units of the ground forces and the People's Navy. . . . One after the other the MIG's dashed over the waves of the Baltic. A brief flash under the wings and . . . the unguided rockets explode with a muffled roar in the target area. Swoop follows swoop. . . ." A colonel then declares: "the operations during SOYUZ-81 confirm that the pilots, technicians, mechanics and other experts of the supporting staff are able under all circumstances to carry out their tasks. . . ." This theme was expanded on April 5 with a reference to "the high level of combat readiness of the allied armies," while on April 3, a GDR army general asserts that SOYUZ-81 "had a high political value" as well.

Mr. Chairman, I could go on with pages and pages of these broadcasts. We have the texts of more than fifty of them. But I have said enough to describe the extent, seriousness, and wide-ranging activity of the SOYUZ-81. Furthermore, many of us here saw on our television screens the pictures of large-scale troop movements and amphibious landings. Are we to believe that this was "a routine command/staff exercise"? On March 24 there was a report that napalm was used. Against whom? The staff against their commanders?

The facts also seem quite clear as to the large numbers of troops used in these exercises. There can be no other conclusion from the Eastern broadcasts:

● four armies were involved

● concurrent activities took place in three different military districts in Poland

● at least two amphibious landings were carried out, each involving waves of troops from three countries

● there was at least a partial mobilization of reservists in both Poland and the GDR

● airborne landings were practiced, as was antisubmarine warfare

● virtually every branch of the ground forces of the GDR and Poland were exercised at the unit or sub-unit level

● infantry combat vehicles and tanks and personnel were used "in battle combat," frequently with the use of live ammunition and rockets

- Soviet naval aviation, Polish tactical aviation, and East German air force units participated

- casualties were evacuated and other rear service functions were exercised

Mr. Chairman, it is clear that there is something wrong with a system under which military activities such as the kind I have described are either not reported or not required to be reported by technical definitions.

Furthermore, we find questionable articles in the Soviet press about CBM practice. A September 10 *Tass* article praises CBMs and asserts that the CSCE participating states in Madrid not only provide advance notification but also "invite... observers from other countries." The clear and erroneous message is that the Soviet Union engages in this confidence-building practice. But were observers from Western or neutral or non-aligned states invited by the Soviets to ZAPAD-81? They were not. In fact, the Soviet Union has invited observers to less than half of the major maneuvers it has announced since the Final Act was signed.

The threat or possible use of military force in a surprise military attack in Europe is of direct concern to all of us. Our role at Madrid is to help relieve that concern. Our goal is to diminish the danger that armed conflict might result from misunderstanding or misinterpretation of military activities. The record of ZAPAD-81 and SOYUZ-81 is not encouraging in that regard. We cannot accept a result which has most of us believing that notification provisions are requirements, while the Soviet Union dismisses them as mere guidelines. We cannot and should not accept a result under which a state can define the presence of 100,000 troops in the field as an "extremely limited" number not worthy of proper disclosure in a notification. We cannot support a result where widespread and intense combined-arms military activity involving all military branches and specialists, during a period of political tension, falls through the cracks of a CBM system because it can be billed as a "command and staff exercise." It is a charade to accept a result where the states participating in a CBM regime have no negotiated means to help verify the nature of military activities by other states about which they are concerned. We cannot accept a result where one power, the largest military power on the continent, engaged in the largest military buildup in the history of the world, benefits from an exemption that excludes most of its European territory.

Mr. Chairman, the United States and its friends earnestly desire here in Madrid to provide for a serious security conference, based on firm criteria, designed to achieve a more secure and militarily stable Europe. We wish to begin the process of devising new and effective confidence and security building measures. We are determined to do what we can to achieve that objective. We intend to use our energies between now and mid-December to help achieve that goal as part of a necessary balanced result.

In July, our delegation presented to this conference an initiative designed to achieve that end. We hope that those who could not then accept the proposal can perhaps now do so. The proposal does not in any way threaten or weaken the integrity or the security or the national interest of any participating state here. It serves the interests of all of us.

Our goal in Madrid has been to strengthen the CSCE process and thereby meet the aspirations of all of us for security and cooperation and peace in Europe. That is why we continue to assert our unconditional willingness to agree now to meet again in a third review meeting to take place in two or three years after the conclusion of the Madrid meeting. We do not want the Helsinki process to be held hostage by us or any state. We again invite a positive response to that offer from the Soviet Union.

We want an agreement. And we can get an agreement. Agreement, however, requires mutuality, consent. It requires a commitment to the Helsinki Final Act and a good faith effort toward its observance. We have yet to see that. We hope that it will be forthcoming.

November 6, 1981 Raoul Wallenberg

* * *

It was with keen interest that the American delegation, during the plenary of a week ago, heard the distinguished delegate of Sweden refer to Raoul Wallenberg, a Swedish citizen whose heroic deeds in the last two years of World War II saved thousands of Hungarian Jews from annihilation, and who has not been heard from directly since his detention by Soviet authorities and subsequent disappearance in January 1945. We have a special interest in associating ourselves with the concern expressed by the Swedish government because during the period of our most recent recess, Raoul Wallenberg, by an act of Congress signed by our president, became an honorary citizen of the United States. Our interest in Raoul Wallenberg is thus a humanitarian one; but it is now also one on behalf of one of our newest citizens. Only once before in our nation's history has a non-American been accorded honorary citizenship.

My continued expression of deep concern about the fate of this missing hero of the Holocaust reflects an overwhelming sense of indignation at the highest levels of my government. I read now from a statement personally delivered by President Ronald Reagan on October 5, while signing the official document:

Raoul Wallenberg is the Swedish savior of almost 100,000 men, women and children. What he did, what he accomplished, was of Biblical proportions. Sir Winston Churchill, another man of force and fortitude, is the only other person who has received honorary United States citizenship, and as John F. Kennedy said at that signing ceremony, "Indifferent himself to danger, he wept over the sorrows of others."

That compassion also exemplifies the man we are gathered here for today. In 1944, the United States requested Sweden's cooperation in protecting the lives of Hungarian Jews facing extermination at the hands of the Nazis. In the months that followed, the United States supplied the funds and the directives and Raoul Wallenberg supplied the courage and the passion. How can we comprehend the moral worth of a man who saved tens of thousands of lives?

In 1945, in violation of diplomatic immunity and international law, he was seized by the Soviet Union. The Nazis were gone and the Soviets had come in as an ally, and yet today there is evidence that he is still imprisoned by the Soviets. Wherever he is, his humanity burns like a torch.

Mr. Chairman, there have been persistent and reliable reports that Raoul Wallenberg was alive and imprisoned in the Soviet Union long after the Soviet authorities, after first denying knowledge of his existence, reported him dead. There are recent reports that he may still be alive. His family and his fellow citizens have every right to expect a full and honest account as to his status. It has been more than thirty-six years since his imprisonment, but he would today be only sixty-eight years of age.

Referring to the tragic fate of Raoul Wallenberg reminds us of the many others who are in Soviet prisons and labor camps for political or religious reasons. Last Friday, a week ago, "Political Prisoner Day" was observed in the Soviet Union. This unofficial event has been commemorated every October 30 since 1974. The American delegation notes this event with sadness here at Madrid because, as our distinguished British colleague so eloquently pointed out last week, in the last year—despite the Helsinki pledge to respect human rights—the ranks of political prisoners in the USSR have swelled.

During these past few days, too, Mr. Chairman, we received further word

Eastern Noncompliance With Helsinki Accords

We must, however, not be blind to the difficulties of the task ahead. These difficulties were dramatized by a first-page editorial in the July 14 issue of *Pravda*, which I read shortly after leaving this hall on Friday when 34 of us signified our provisional approval of a final document. The editorial sharpens for us not only the real meaning of the Madrid agreement but its decided limitations as well. The editorial's theme is the speech made to the June plenum of the Communist Party Central Committee by the leader of the Soviet Union, during which he said: "There is a struggle for the hearts and minds of billions of people on this planet." Concerned that the U.S.S.R. may not be doing too well in that struggle, *Pravda* urges that Soviet citizens be "immunized" against hostile ideas. Specifically, it aims at religion in the U.S.S.R. as a danger.

The United States understands the profound seriousness of the inherent contradictions between the Soviet totalitarian system and the system of liberty and individual dignity which is a hallmark of democratic governments. Reaching agreements such as we did in Helsinki and now in Madrid, do not, by themselves, automatically minimize those differences or end the competition. We intend to be in the competition for "hearts and minds" to which *Pravda* refers. We welcome a competition of ideas and values. In many ways the Madrid forum has been and remains a vehicle for that competition. What concerns us deeply, however, is that the U.S.S.R. may believe it cannot win a competition of ideas and values without the threat and use of armed force and repression, within and outside its borders.

The Helsinki Final Act and the Madrid agreement are efforts to channel the competition of values within civilized constraints and at the same time to strive for understanding so that we can learn to live with one another in peace. The fact that these agreements continue to be violated, even during this very period of negotiation and agreement, is discouraging.

We cannot in good conscience permit a limited negotiating success, important as we believe it to be, to make us forget, much to our regret, that signatures on a document do not necessarily produce compliance with its provisions. The continued fighting in Afghanistan, where more than 100,000 invading troups remain, violating the sovereignty of that unhappy country and abusing the humanity of its people, stands as an affront to the peace we in Helsinki professed to pursue. The people of Poland remain today subjugated by a martial law which attacked the legitimacy of their free trade union, Solidarity, and continues to keep in internment and imprisonment thousands of persons who declare and champion their human rights.

Our delegation believes in the importance of words. But we cannot permit an agreement on words to obfuscate unpleasant realities. We have sought and welcome the agreement represented by our decision in Madrid. We do not wish to minimize the importance of that agreement. But we also do not wish to minimize the consequence of undermining such agreements when they are not complied with in letter and in spirit.

What are we to think when at the very time we were coming to agreement on provisions dealing with religious rights, *Pravda Vostoka* of Uzbekistan informed us that leading members of the Seventh Day Adventist Church have been imprisoned by government authorities precisely because of their wish to practice their religion?

On December 1, 1981, I reluctantly brought to the attention of this body a detailed report of what clearly appeared to be a government-sponsored anti-Jewish campaign in the Soviet Union. It was my hope, obviously misplaced, that I would never have reason to raise that issue again. The facts, however, force me to do so. The decline in Soviet Jewish immigration is to the lowest levels since the

1960s, a tragic violation of the Helsinki accords. An important escape valve has thus been cut off for one of the most persecuted religious groups in that society. We note too, with sadness, that many Jewish scientists and professionals have been stripped of their educational degrees, that the teaching of the Hebrew language brings on police harassment and arrest, and, perhaps most disturbing of all, that extreme anti-Semitic articles are appearing in the Soviet press with increasing frequency.

Soviet officials sometimes respond to these facts with assertions of "indignation" and "libel." I fully understand such indignation in the light of the horrendous memories of anti-Semitism during and prior to World War II. As to libel, in many of our societies truth is a defense to a charge of libel. We pray that this issue may soon disappear as an issue between us. Until the facts justify that change, however, I quote from a statement made last week by President Reagan: "We have repeatedly stated that our concern for human rights in general, and Soviet Jewry in particular, is integral to our national interest and remains a major focus of our national policy."

The picture is no more encouraging when we turn to the very marrow of our objectives, the search for peace. A Soviet pacifist, Alexander Shatravka, was recently sentenced to three years in prison for circulating a petition calling for the universal abolition of nuclear weapons. The document had urged both the United States and the Soviet Union to scrap their nuclear arsenals. Mr. Shatravka had earlier been associated with a group of young people, who, a year ago, had been arrested for unfurling a banner in Red Square bearing only the Russian words for "bread, life, disarmament."

The arrest of these young Soviet citizens seeking peace stands in sharp contrast to the enthusiastic editorial which appeared in *Pravda* last January hailing antiwar movements in Western Europe as "vital causes of the people." Is it any wonder that we are reminded of a perceptive statement by Clausewitz: "The aggressor," he said, "is always peace loving. He would like to make his entry into our country undisturbed."

We know that the people of the Soviet Union, like all of our peoples, are peace loving. But we also know from the *Pravda* editorial of last week that Soviet authorities, who are not elected by their people, fear independent ideas and want their people "immunized" against them. General Aleksei Yepishev, the political head of the Soviet Army, recently complained that Soviet youth was being infected by pacifism. To stop independent ideas is a lost cause. Ideas, like the wind currents and the climate, reach all lands and cannot be stopped by artificial barriers.

It is the view of our delegation that in arresting and harassing those of its citizens who work for peace and universal nuclear disarmament, Soviet authorities not only maintain an indefensible double standard, they clearly demonstrate that the mantle of peace, in which they would like to cloak themselves, simply does not fit their shape, their ideology, or their practices; and it is not simply one country to which we wish to address these comments.

Similarly, a few weeks ago, more than 300 Czechoslovak young people were clubbed by the police, with many arrested, for holding a peace demonstration in Prague and chanting "we want peace and freedom." And in that country, Ladislav Lis, a spokesman for the Charter 77 human rights and peace organization Helsinki monitoring group, is expected to go on trial this week for his activities. Religious believers are also facing renewed repression for their expressions of faith.

In East Germany—where there is a growing unofficial peace movement that opposes all nuclear arms, including those of the Soviet Union and the United States—young people, many of them associated with churches, also find them any era. To be sure, the process is far from complete. But Americans, black and white, are proud of what has been accomplished.

We have not as a society eliminated prejudice from the hearts of all of our citizens, but that prejudice, when it exists, is contrary to the whole thrust of our national direction. Our laws and regulations, conscientiously enforced, are designed to eliminate the discriminatory acts that stem from prejudice. This is to be clearly distinguished from government support and encouragement of hate, bigotry, and discrimination. A government cannot fully eliminate prejudice within its people; but it certainly can choose not to dignify that prejudice to the level of official encouragement.

The Soviet delegate referred to the existence of anti-Semitism in the United States. While sporadic and isolated anti-Semitic incidents do regrettably occur, never in the history of our country have our Jewish citizens enjoyed greater equality, more rights, and as much dignity and appreciation as today.

But the Soviet delegation is fully familiar with our deep concern about anti-Semitism in the Soviet Union. This is not the occasion to develop that theme further, but it is illustrative of the distinction that must be made between individual acts, on the one hand, and actions that have government acquiescence or stimulation. Where the government participates, serious questions of Final Act implementation are raised.

During last Friday's Soviet intervention, it was suggested to us that one must judge a country's commitment to human rights, not by judging the rights of the individual, particularly those who are in disfavor within the society—the dissidents—but by judging the lives of the masses of people. This concept should be examined more carefully.

The chief criticism against the West, produced to demonstrate the superiority of the Soviet ideology, is the large number of people unemployed in the West. Let me speak about my own country. The most recent figures announced a few days ago for the month of October showed that our unemployment rate was 8 percent, our highest in six years. This represents a total of 8.5 million men and women who do not now have regular employment, a figure which is much too high. Our unemployment rate has been a fluctuating one. In recent years it has been down to 5 percent and as high as 9 percent. When it climbs, our government, no matter which administration is in office, makes strenuous efforts to put people back to work. In the meantime, those who are unemployed receive public benefits designed to minimize the economic impact of joblessness. We care for those who are temporarily afflicted; and every Western society has a series of welfare programs designed to express that care with compassion.

The Soviet Union has traditionally asserted that there is no unemployment in its society. Indeed, since all employment in that country is controlled by the state, it is not unusual in that society to penalize those who are in disfavor with the state by denying them employment. The irony of all this is that once they are without work, they are guilty of the crime of "parasitism." We do not know what parasitism means. What we do know is that when an individual does not have the right to refrain from working, then his labor is forced labor. What we do know is that in May 1980, the International Labor Organization found that the parasitism law in the Soviet Union constituted forced labor and condemned it as a violation of the vital international convention on the subject.

It is disturbing, furthermore, to hear the boast that there is no unemployment, when we know that forced labor is an essential part of that society's economic structure. In that connection, I refer to Document No. 85 issued by the Moscow Helsinki group on April 21, 1979, dealing with "the right to work." A portion of its conclusion reads: "If the Western concept of unemployment—formulated through many years of practical experience in the labor movement—were to be applied to the USSR, the myth of the country of no unemployment would be dispelled.''

There is reason to believe that there are now more than 1,700,000 people incarcerated in the vast Soviet system of forced labor camps; another 1,000,000 people in government-imposed correctional tasks while living at home; and more than 1,400,000 Soviet citizens, on probation from labor camp sentences, are engaged in compulsory labor, at low wage rates, frequently in distant and often dangerous construction, mining, and industrial projects. The Soviet delegate also referred on Friday to a recent strike in the United States by a union of air traffic controllers. I do not understand why this issue was raised by him. In my country a law was passed a number of years ago, after energetic discussion and debate, which made strikes by Federal employees illegal. When the air controller strike took place, the law was enforced; those employees who had signed an oath not to strike were discharged. It seems ironic to have this incident raised by the representatives of a society which declares all strikes to be illegal, strikes by any workers in any industry.

This leads me to the question of trade unions for working men and women. Western society is characterized by a free labor movement. Working men and women in my country can choose freely to be represented or not by a trade union. In Western societies the free trade unions are influential, strong and effective representatives of their members. I remind this group, however, that in May 1979, the International Labor Organization conlcuded that there were no free trade unions in the Soviet Union and that the provisions of the labor code of the Soviet Union violated Article No. 87 of the ILO convention concerning the rights of workers to establish organizations of their own free choosing.

Efforts by Soviet citizens to form independent trade unions have resulted in their imprisonment or commitment to psychiatric hospitals. When the Association of Free Trade Unions was formed in 1977, eight of its founders were sent to psychiatric wards by the Soviet authorities. When the Free Interprofessional Association of Workers (SMOT) was organized in 1978, a number of their leaders, too, were imprisoned or forcibly detained in psychiatric hospitals. It is not persuasive for these courageous men and women to be called "outcasts." It is more telling to note the condemnation of Soviet labor practices by the International Labor Organization.

Mr. Chairman, I conclude with the following observations. None of us, East or West, is free from internal social and economic problems. We are all victims, as well as beneficiaries, of modern-day life with its stresses. All governments represented at this conference share the burden of coping with these strains. While our efforts may not always be met with immediate success, we must, nonetheless, constantly strive to improve the quality of life for our citizens. A government may not always be able to manage its economy to prevent unemployment; but a government does have the power to end the bondage of forced labor. A government cannot, with the passage of laws alone, entirely eradicate its social problems; but a government can refrain from so misusing the healing sciences, for example, as to make them an instrument of political repression. A government cannot eliminate racism and prejudice in a generation; but it certainly can choose not to elevate that prejudice so as to become an instrument of government policy.

We in the United States and our colleagues in the West live in democratic societies. We have periodically scheduled competitive free elections which allow for frequent changes in leadership. The right of all citizens to participate freely in the political process is a cherished ingredient of democracy. Other societies may reject that system. We will not interfere with that reality, but we will express ourselves when those societies act in a manner contrary to the commitments of the Helsinki Final Act.

To act as if these differences do not exist, or are unimportant, is to build on sand and not be true to ourselves. But we do have the obligation to try to understand one another; for, above all, we must learn to live in peace with each other. Our battles should be limited to the realm of ideas. This forum gives us that opportunity. Our exchanges may be sharp, but they reflect the depth of our respective convictions. The American delegation has confidence that the Helsinki Final Act and this process of debate and discussion in which we are engaged are indispensable parts of our search for peace and understanding.

December 1, 1981 Anti-Semitism

Today is the ninth day since Dr. Andrei Sakharov and his wife, Elena Bonner, began a hunger strike in the city of Gorky, where he has been exiled by the authorities of the Soviet Union. A week ago today, the United States Senate unanimously—Republicans and Democrats, liberals and conservatives, representing all of our fifty states—adopted a resolution associating itself "fully and completely" with that protest. They joined in his condemnation of the Soviet Union for its "flagrant violation of the Helsinki Accords." I have no doubt that the Senate, in doing so, spoke for an outraged American people indignant at the harassment inflicted on Dr. Sakharov and his family.

We have noted on several occasions during the past year that harassment and mistreatment and repression have intensified in the Soviet Union. There is persecution of individuals and persecution of groups. Many ethnic and religious minorities have been particular victims. The pattern of ethnic and religious oppression, officially sanctioned, takes many forms: the repressive legal restrictions on Crimean Tatars which prohibit them from returning to their historic homeland; forced Russification of the Baltic States; biased employment practices against Evangelical Christians; prohibition against manifestations of Ukrainian culture. We have talked of these and of others.

Last fall the delegate of Belgium eloquently addressed a particularly pernicious aspect of Soviet repression: anti-Semitism. The delegate of the United Kingdom has forcefully, on a number of occasions, brought this problem to our attention as well. Last Friday he did so again. This distasteful phenomenon has grown in intensity and in ugliness.

Speaking personally for a moment, I am Jewish by ancestry and commitment. My personal stake in this subject is, therefore, clear. Wherever anti-Semitism exists, Jews elsewhere react with concern and with the thought, "There but for the grace of God go I." My intervention today, affected as all our statements may be by our personal values and beliefs, is nevertheless an expression of my government's deep concern.

The roots of anti-Semitism run deep in the human experience. It has commanded the attention and the profound intellectual energies of experts in psychology, sociology, religion, and politics. The phenomenon is not yet fully understood, but we do know that the human being requires an avenue of release for his personal frustrations; and that, through a confluence of accidental and historical forces, the Jew often has become the focus of the anger associated with that frustration and disappointment.

The task of civilized society has been to harness and redirect the energy of that anger into more constructive channels, so that the basis of frustration may be understood and thus overcome. Regrettably, all too often totalitarian societies—unable to resolve the internal problems which beset them—have diverted the attention of their citizens away from the actual source of their frustration by finding targets on which to place the blame. Time and again, that scapegoat has been the Jew.

History has taught us that anti-Semitism is a contagious disease, a virus that
dangers not only Jews but also the societies in which they live. It becomes our
ncern here in Madrid when and where anti-Semitism has government sanction.
that form, it is destructive to the Helsinki Final Act.

It is with regret that our delegation has concluded that the Soviet Union is
early identified with a pattern of anti-Semitic behavior that could not function
ithout government support and acquiescence. Despite Soviet protestations to
e contrary; despite the Soviet Constitution's prohibition of any "advocacy of
cial or national . . . hostility"; despite Chairman Brezhnev's call at the 26th Party
ongress in February to "fight resolutely against . . . anti-Semitism"; despite
ese words, government-condoned and government-propagated anti-Semitism
urishes in the Soviet Union today.

The anti-Semitic campaign has intensified since the first CSCE review meeting.
has become more fearsome during our meeting here in Madrid. This latest
rge, I assert without hesitation, is an officially sanctioned campaign, stimulated
state-controlled publication and exhibition of overtly anti-Semitic books, arti-
es, cartoons and exhibitions. The issue, Mr. Chairman, is too serious to exagger-
e, and I will do my utmost not to do so. The label of anti-Semitism is too terrible
apply loosely, and I will guard against doing so. I proceed, therefore, with care
address this problem as a problem that dare not be ignored. The evidence is
verwhelming. I will refer to only a few out of the hundreds of examples:

Fact: A book published in 150,000 copies in Moscow in 1977 and republished in
79, written by Vladimir Begun and entitled *Invasion Without Arms*, characterizes
e Torah, the Old Testament of the Bible, as, among other things, "an unsur-
assed textbook [of] . . . hypocrisy, treachery, perfidy and moral degeneracy—all
e basest human qualities." He writes: "Jewish and Christian hypocrites alike
eep silent over this."

Fact: There are frequent cartoons—we have them here—representations in the
fficial Soviet press portraying Jews with large hooked noses and evil-looking
nshaven jowls. Indeed, in September 1975, after the Helsinki Final Act was
gned, the *Kazakhstanskaya Pravda* reproduced a cover cartoon of the 1934 edition
f the notoriously poisonous "Protocols of the Elders of Zion," depicting an
vil-appearing Jewish figure under the caption "The Jewish Peril" digging his
ngers into a globe of the world and making it bleed.

Fact: A 1979 exhibition of paintings in Minsk by the official Soviet artist Mikhail
. Savitsky included a canvas depicting the brutalities of the Nazi occupation of
yelorussia. The painting, entitled "Summer Theater," showed a pile of naked
rpses in a concentration camp. Standing over them and grinning sadistically at
ach other are a helmeted Nazi officer and a Jew with the stereotype hooked nose
nd wearing a Star of David, presumably a camp trusty. Despite protestations
gainst the work's blatant anti-Semitic character, a reprint of the painting also
ppeared in the Byelorussian Ministry of Culture's official journal.

Fact: Jews are repeatedly characterized in Soviet articles as criminals and
angsters. One illustration, an article by A. Filipenko, "Zionism and Crime,"
ates that although "the myth has become established that gangster bands
onsist exclusively of Italians, the facts prove that an active role is also played in
e United States criminal syndicates by persons of Jewish origin." There are
eferences in other Soviet publications to "the Jewish-Sicilian Mafia." (L. Kor-
eyev, "The Most Zionist Business," in *Ogonyok*, November 28, 1978; and, same
uthor, "Leaders—Gangsters," in *Nedelya*, November 1977, pp. 21-27.)

Fact: A television program entitled "Traders of the Souls" was broadcast on
rime time throughout the Soviet Union. The constant theme of this documentary
as the Jew as moneychanger, "a trader of souls."

Fact: There is constant derogatory reference in the official Soviet press to persons with obvious Jewish names and background. Thus I quote a reference to American capitalism as being "led by the Lehmans, Lazards, Blausteins, Stillmans, Warburgs, Kuhns, Guggenheims, Loebs, Kahns, Rosenwalds and Schiffs." (B. Bannov, "A Provocative Confluence," *Vechernaya Moskva*, September 3, 1977.)

Fact: Reference to Jewish ownership of "death concerns," to "growing financial might," to the "Zionist Mafia of death," to Jewish control of media and banks and crime and multilateral corporations, government, and the theater—all these abound. (L. Korneyev, "The Secret Wars of Zionism," *Neva*, No. 4, 1978; L. Korneyev, "The Most Zionist Business" [part one], *Ogonyok*, No. 28, 1978; V. Meshcheryakov, "With Someone Else's Voice," *Zhurnalist*, No. 4, 1976; and B. Antanov, "America in the Web of the Zionists," *Moskovskaya Pravda*, March 1, 1978.)

Fact: Soviet authorities in 1979 issued the *White Book*, which purported to reveal, as the subtitle states, "Espionage and Deception in the Name of Defense for Human Rights." Instead, the publication is replete with preposterous accusations and anti-Semitic attacks on Soviet Jewish activists and Western correspondents of Jewish origin. The *White Book* was first published by the Juridical Literature Printing House and edited by the director of the prestigious Association of Soviet Jurists. Even after this despicable work received worldwide condemnation, a second edition was released in December 1979.

Fact: Last year, it was announced that the book *Judaism and Zionism* by Trofim K. Kichko was to be published. Designed for a "mass audience," the book pretends to "unmask the criminal activities of various Zionist organizations and Zionist-oriented Judaism." The author's previous work of seventeen years ago, *Judaism Without Embellishment*, was so virulent in its anti-Semitism that after international protests were made—including some from the major Western Communist parties—Soviet authorities were forced to withdraw the book for "erroneous statements."

Fact: Articles accusing Jews of collaborating with Hitler to destroy the European Jewish community, to destroy the Soviet Union, and to strengthen a Jewish state are disseminated widely. Jews have furthermore been accused in the Soviet press of stimulating anti-Semitism and setting fire to synagogues in order to settle Israel. (L. Komcyev, "The Sinister Secrets of Zionism" [part two], *Ogonyok*, No. 35, 1975; [Colonel] I. Tsvetkov, "The Tool of Imperialist Aggression," *Krasnaya Zvezda*, October 27, 1976; *Kono*, August 1975, a review of the anti-Semitic film "The Secret and the Overt"; L. Korneyev, "Zionism's Octopus of Espionage," *Ogonyok*, No. 5, 1977; V. Chernyavski, "Conversations with a Reader," *New Times*, No. 37, 1977; T. Kichko and D. Koretsky, "Trap for the Youth," *Dnipro*, No 7, 1975.)

Fact: Anti-Jewish material has been distributed to Red Army recruits and is published in official journals of the Soviet armed forces. (Captain Y. Makulin, "Rabbis amd Soldiers" in *Sovietskyvoin*, November 10, 1976.)

Fact: Jewish history is deleted from Soviet elementary and secondary school textbooks. Indeed, the Russian pogroms of the late nineteenth century against the Jews are justified in a Soviet publication as part of the class struggle. (V. Ya Begun, [Ibid. pp. 55-56.)

Fact: The Soviet Union—with the third largest Jewish community in the world—is the only country with a Jewish population in which there is not a single approved Jewish school and no means for teaching Jewish history and tradition. The private teaching of Hebrew is outlawed, while the official study of the language is restricted to a very few non-Jews. In recent weeks, over eighty Jewish teachers of Hebrew, in Moscow alone, received threats of prosecution and banishment should they continue their instructions.

Mr. Chairman, all of the evidence for the above facts reflects events taking place after the signing of the Helsinki Final Act. During the past fifteen years, a total of at least 112 Soviet books and brochures with anti-Semitic overtones of various degrees have been identified, some of them printed and reprinted in editions of 150,000-200,000 copies. Anti-Semitic propaganda is also carried out through lectures, stimulated by the Communist Party and the state.

Soviet anti-Semitism is not limited to domestic consumption. It is also widely exported to Arab, African, and other Third World countries. The writings of outspoken Soviet anti-Semites—Kichko, Begun, Korneyev, and others—have been featured prominently in publications of the PLO, for instance. In addition, their writings are often published in English and distributed throughout the English-speaking world.

A publication of the Novosti Press Agency, the seventy-seven-page *Sword of David* by Leo Korn, has been widely distributed at Soviet Embassies and international fairs. Clearly aimed at Western readers, the pamphlet purports to reveal the "monstrous lie of Zionism" which is called "the most reactionary force of Jewish bourgeois nationalism." The booklet alleges that anti-Semitism is, after all, the fault of the Jews themselves, an understandable "result of the non-Jewish workers' hatred of their exploiters who belonged to the rich Jewish bourgeois caste." Canadian authorities demanded the publication's removal from the Ontario Science Center in 1978, where it was being given away by Soviet representatives.

In March of 1979, this same author raised the spectre of an international Jewish conspiracy, a familiar anti-Semitic theme, in the journal *Communist of the Armed Forces*. In an article entitled "Zionism— The Tool of Imperialistic Expansion and New-Colonialism," he wrote: "The Jewish financiers and industrialists strive to direct the domestic and foreign policies of the USA, England, France, the FRG, Belgium and of other capitalist states. . . ."

Now, it may be said that these books, articles and films are mere reflections of their authors, who have the right to their own opinions, no matter how repulsive. But we all know that nothing can be published openly or distributed in the Soviet Union without the official imprimatur of the government censoring agency, Glavlit. Indeed, the chairman of the Soviet State Committee for Printing, in justifying the Soviet banning of Western publications at the September 1979 International Book Fair in Moscow, cited legislation prohibiting books on racism and those that "stir up hatred and hostility between people." It is significant that anti-Semitic books, pamphlets, films and articles published in the Soviet Union are not required to meet that noble standard.

This is not a pretty picture that we have painted, Mr. Chairman. We have done so with profound regret and sadness. We have cited but a few deplorable examples. At our last session, the delegate from the United Kingdom cited others. There are many more instances of blatant government-condoned anti-Semitism in the Soviet Union. These are accompanied by harassment and imprisonment of Jewish leaders, discrimination against Jews in education and employment, active and frequently violent interference with the study of Hebrew and the possession of articles of prayer, and by a drastic reduction in the number of Jews being allowed to escape this pervasive anti-Semitism through emigration.

I respectfully suggest that there should be no room for anti-Semitism in a society that professes its commitment to the teachings of Marx, a Jew. The early roots of socialism were idealistic. They had their philosophic justification in a commitment to human brotherhood and to the dignity of the individual. Where there is anti-Semitism, Mr. Chairman, there is a corruption of those ideals.

I make this plea once again. The Soviet Union is a society that is large and powerful and has existed for more than sixty years. There is no need for that society to crush human beings, small and insignificant as they may appear in the broader perspective of history. There should be no need to stimulate hatred

first requires an agreement as to its meaning and a joint commitment to its realization.

Within this forum of the Helsinki process, our delegation feels obliged to recall how moved we and the American people have been by the developments in Poland during the past year and a half. We have seen in that country a growing respect for human rights and fundamental freedoms. Poland has been a living demonstration for the world of the vitality of the process launched at Helsinki which is embodied at this meeting today.

Our regret at recent developments is, therefore, a profound one. Arbitrary detentions and beatings and killings; interference with the free flow of information, ideas and people; the wholesale repression of civil liberties, the imposition of military control at the workplace; the use of violence against Polish workers; and the attempt to stifle and possibly destroy Solidarity, the legitimate expression of the yearning of Polish working men and women for dignity—all these represent gross violations of the Final Act.

We note these developments with sadness. We would deplore any reversal of the movement of the Polish people towards a more open and just society. That would inevitably damage the vital process launched by the Final Act and would be tragedy for the people of Poland.

Yesterday, President Reagan said that it is difficult to believe that these acts of aggression against the Polish people could have happened without the full knowledge and support of the Soviet Union. Noting the "sharp reversal of the movement toward a better society," he said: "Coercion and violation of human rights on a massive scale have taken the place of negotiation and compromise. All of this is in gross violation of the Helsinki pact. . . ." "We view," he said, "the current situation in Poland in the gravest of terms. . . . We call upon all the free people to join in urging the government of Poland to reestablish conditions that will make constructive negotiations and compromise possible."

I remind this body of the obligation assumed by all of us to refrain from the threat of use of force; and of the pledge of nonintervention in the internal affairs of other states. The Polish people have the right, under the Act, "in full freedom, to determine, when and as they will, their political status." They have the right "to pursue their political, economic, social and cultural development." This is their right, "without external interference."

The government of Poland has been well represented here in Madrid by able professionals. I trust that they will communicate to the thirty-six million men, women, and children who live in Poland the warm feelings of compassion, friendship, and support for them that is universally held by the American people. We are proud of the spirit and courage of the Polish people in their aspiration for freedom.

* * *

Stalemate

The next phase of the conference began February 9, 1982 with an analysis by Secretary of State Haig of the crackdown in Poland. He said the first principles of the Final Act were under attack in Poland. He described how seven of these basic principles had been violated recently in Poland.

Ambassador Kampelman in succeeding days described the growing repression in Poland and its impact on the Helsinki process. The Western states unifiedly refused to negotiate the final document for Madrid until Poland significantly improved the condition of its citizens.

This phase ended on an ominous note, March 12, 1982, and pointed toward a return in November. If agreement could not be reached then, said Ambassador Kampelman, "it will be due to the continued use of Soviet military power to subjugate its neighbors.'

February 10, 1982 Bronislaw Geremek

Yesterday was a sad day for the Helsinki process. The moment at hand is grave one, and it requires honest and direct language.

For more than seventeen months we have been meeting here in Madrid i serious, earnest, intensive discourse. During that time, our differences of percep tion about our obligations to one another and to the Helsinki Final Act have bee fully aired. The West has set forth in detail a whole series of actions engaged in b the Soviet Union which, in our view, represented contempt for, if not defiance o the substantive provisions of the Helsinki Final Act. We took notice of thes actions out of a conviction that if all thirty-five of us were going to build the fabr of peace and cooperation demanded by our publics and by reason, we neede understanding among us.

It was of great importance that we used the Helsinki process fully to exchang views and to negotiate with one another. We respected the rules of courtes which have characterized the Helsinki process since its beginning. We differed but we did not seek to destroy the fabric of our intercourse here. Our procedure mutually arrived at, were present, except for the Soviet Union and those whom directs through the threat of military and police power. The chairman yesterda received no support from any delegation other than those few whose destinies ar controlled by the Soviet Union. Every other delegate who spoke protested th arbitrary, stubborn and improper behavior of the chairman.

The chair kept reiterating that it was not making rules, that it was a prisoner the rules and of this body, that it did not have power. And yet, it was the initiativ of the chair and the gross misinterpretation of the rules by the chair that led t yesterday's destructive confrontation. Never before in the history of this proces has a delegation, inscribed on the speaking rolls, been denied the right to talk tha day. We witnessed a blatant usurpation of power by the chairman, perhaps quit representative of the practices engaged in by his government but highly ir appropriate for the CSCE.

It is important, however, that we not let this violent affront to the Helsink process divert our energies from the substance of what was said by six foreig ministers yesterday in behalf of the free world, and what will continue to b expressed by others at this meeting.

Our broad concerns about the destruction of human liberty in Poland, ou objections to the threat of the use of force by the Soviet Union against the people Poland—all this has been and will continue to be clearly enunciated. Basic to it a however, and to the very purpose of diplomacy must be the consciousness tha the human being and his welfare are primary. The strength of the Helsinki Fin Act is that the human dimension is recognized for its primary role in achievin security, cooperation, and peace among us.

In this context, I wish to comment for a few brief moments about one ind vidual, one distinguished citizen of Poland, one human being with a wife an child, a man deeply respected in my country, who is today a victim of martial la in his own.

It has been my privilege, while these meetings have been in session, to serv also as Chairman of the Board of Trustees of the Woodrow Wilson Internation Center for Scholars in Washington. In 1978, Professor Bronislaw Geremek Poland served as a distinguished Fellow at our Center. He came to us as one of th world's most distinguished and productive medieval scholars. He had graduate from the University of Warsaw in 1955 with a special thesis dealing with th fourteenth century, which earned for him great distinction. His thesis on medie val Paris led him to receive his doctorate in 1960 from the Polish Academy Sciences; and that thesis in turn has been published in a number of languages. H was Director of the Center of Polish Culture and taught Polish history at th

University of Paris in the early 1960s. He did further work on Paris of the fourteenth and fifteenth centuries, on the basis of which he received an even higher degree from the Polish Academy of Sciences in 1970. This work gained for him as well the *Prix d'Histoire de l'Académie Française* in 1977.

During Professor Geremek's stay in the United States as a Wilson Fellow, he produced an absolutely remarkable piece of work on the role of the gypsies in the late medieval culture. This paper was published in Poland in the spring of 1980 and was called "The World of the Beggars' Opera." He subsequently completed another book on "Social Attitudes Toward Poverty in the Middle Ages and Modern Times."

Professor Geremek's great scholarship was accompanied by a characteristic of many scholars, the possession of a free mind and a free soul. In 1968 he turned in his Communist Party membership card in protest against the Soviet invasion of Czechoslovakia. In 1980 he joined the Solidarity movement of his country, assisting the Gdansk strikers in their negotiations and then later serving as an unpaid chairman of that movement's Board of Academic Advisers. During the period of his people's struggle for human dignity and freedom, this outstanding citizen of Poland represented his people last November at a conference summoned by Pope John Paul II at the Vatican on "The Common Spiritual Roots of Europe."

With the retreat of Poland into the darkness of martial law and repression, this outstanding Pole, this internationally respected scholar, was jailed by the military rulers of his country, one of more than a score of leading historians of his country so incarcerated.

This man, considered by his colleagues to be the center of "Europe's common spiritual roots," has now been maligned as a "political gangster." His outstanding and creative medieval studies, particularly his work about the gypsies, were shamelessly characterized by Moscow Radio as "writing about degenerates," another blatant example of the racism which governs that society. On December 18 Radio Moscow further attacked him as a Zionist writing about "psychotic social movements." This courageous young man and remarkable scholar, who until the age of nine was held by the Nazis at Auschwitz, has once more suffered direct anti-Semitic attacks.

Is this the image that the military leaders of Poland intend to convey about the nature of their society to a world which looks upon the evolving tragedy of that country in anguish and outrage? Is this the respect for learning which has characterized Polish history over the ages, or is it, rather, clear evidence of this military regime's repudiation of that lofty civilization?

Professor Geremek is a scholar who has linked Eastern and Western history, social and traditional history, the distant past and the troubled present. Today the military rulers of his country show their disdain for the tradition of learning represented by him by imprisoning and punishing him through a whole series of indignities. It is our information that he has been moved to the Drawsko Prison far from Warsaw, far from his family. In his role as the elected chairman of the prisoners at Bialoleka Juvenile Prison, which was turned into a detention camp, he has recently completed a two-week hunger strike in protest against the inhuman treatment he and his fellow prisoners were receiving.

Those in my country who know Professor Geremek have joined with countless others who respect him as a scholar and as a human being in a plea for his release from prison. On December 23, a letter was addressed to General Jaruzelski, signed by past presidents and the present president of the American Historical Association, expressing particular concern about their colleague's fate. I am informed that Professor Geremek has been proposed for honorary membership in that distinguished professional association.

There is great skepticism in my country about the genuineness of statements made by representatives of the Polish military regime that their intent is to continue the process of renewal and dialogue which began in their country and was abruptly interrupted. The fate of Bronislaw Geremek and his colleagues will be an important yardstick by which we will measure that genuineness. Their release would go far in dealing with that skepticism.

We say to our friend Bronislaw Geremek, a historian, that the teachings of history demonstrate that at no period can we say that "it is over." The Polish people have seen this inhumanity before in their lifetime. Today is not the last day. It is just today. And there will be tomorrow.

Editors note: *The debate turned bitter. The Soviet delegate responded to the preceding statement by referring in abusive terms to human rights activists. They are, he said, threats to the existing Soviet order. Ambassador Kampelman used his right of reply to note the fate suffered by one such activist. The Polish delegate did not challenge the facts in the case of Professor Geremek but declared that such criticism would be counterproductive. Ambassador Kampelman replied.*

February 10, 1982 Right of Reply Statements

A few moments ago, as we listened to the remarks of the head of the Soviet delegation, I was struck by the fact that today is the fifth anniversary of the arrest of Professor Yuri Orlov, founder of the Moscow Helsinki group. Dr. Orlov, a leading physicist, was elected to associate membership in the Armenian Academy of Sciences. In prison camp, where Dr. Orlov was sentenced by a Soviet court for a seven-year term, he has been threatened with death by his camp wardens. He has been told by the wardens that he will never leave camp alive. When we think of Professor Orlov and the arrests of forty-three other Soviet citizens who have taken the Helsinki Final Act seriously by calling on their government to live up to its commitments, we have a sufficient response to the assertion by the Soviet delegate that his governnient is observing its commitments to the Helsinki Final Act.

* * *

I must again ask for the floor to respond to the informal comments made by Mr. Konarski, who served as our chairman yesterday. I appreciate his candor, but his remarks are most troublesome.

Mr. Konarski quite openly acknowledged that it was the content of the speeches made yesterday morning, the substance of what was said by the ministers, which governed his judgments as chairman. This reaffirms our view that the judgments were not based on proper procedures.

But even more seriously, we heard him a few minutes ago tell us that if other Western speakers continue to express themselves openly and directly, critically of Polish military authorities, the meeting will face continued procedural harassments and interruptions. This threat is improper and unacceptable to the American delegation. It is a violation of the Helsinki spirit, and we again thoroughly condemn it.

February 16, 1982 Chemical Warfare

* * *

The Soviet delegate criticized my government for engaging in chemical warfare preparation. The reason I describe this reference as "surprising" and "strange" is that I would have thought this to be a subject that the Soviet Union would want to keep away from, since they have made every effort to hide from the world their own priority attention to this form of brutality.

All of mankind lives with the horrible reality that the unravelling mysteries of science and technology have so intensified man's capacity to be brutal to man that he runs the risk of destroying himself and his planet. This conference in Madrid is another in a long series of searching steps to seek means of minimizing the threat of war and violence for us and our children. This is why so many of us here have expressed our deep concerns about the tragic developments in Poland.

Reason and conscience demand that we continue to work for agreements and treaties among ourselves to increase the degree of sanity governing relations among states. Principle X of the Helsinki Final Act is based on the premise that if there is to be any confidence in our capacity to begin weaving the fabric of understanding among us so essential to our survival, those international treaties must be looked upon as sacred ones, to be scrupulously observed. When they are not observed, we must, as we did all of last week on Poland, and as we will continue to do, express our outrage and disappointment.

As early as 1925, with the expansion of new frontiers of knowledge, statesmen with vision understood the need to deal with the awful realization that man then had the capacity to unleash poisons in the air. In that year, the Geneva Protocol was signed banning the use of chemical and bacteriological gases.

Science continued to evolve and prove the maxim that the devil too evolves. The more powerful nations, including our own, found themselves in a race to adapt new learning to wartime use. The growing sophistication of bacteriology and chemistry now provided additional instruments of horrible destruction.

The United States, in an effort to inject sanity into the process, unilaterally renounced its use of those weapons in 1969. A sensible solution then emerged: let us agree mutually to renounce the use of biological or toxic weapons. An international convention toward that end was signed in 1972 by 111 countries. The pledge taken was not to "develop, produce, stockpile or otherwise acquire and retain" these biological weapons.

Most of the world greeted that step with enthusiasm. This was not an arms limitation; it was a disarmament agreement. We knew that the treaty did not provide for ways to insure verifiability, but we were convinced that the treaty would be observed because the alternative was too awful to be contemplated by the rational mind. This proved to be a naive error.

It is with regret, Mr. Chairman, that I bring to the attention of this meeting that the Geneva Convention of 1925 and the 1972 Biological Weapons Convention have both been seriously and deliberately violated by the Soviet Union. The consequences are most serious. The realization that even in this area the Soviet Union operates without restraint affects our confidence in any agreement signed by the Soviet Union. The need for absolute and unmistakable verification of any agreement to be entered into is now for us unconditional.

But the violation of Principle X of the Helsinki Final Act represented by these transgressions, serious as it is, is not our only deep concern arising from this disregard for international law and human decency. There is an intense moral and practical concern as well.

It is unmistakable that innocent people in Laos, Kampuchea, and Afghanistan have been victims of a deadly poison rained down upon them by airplanes carrying, among other lethal agents, potent mycotoxins of the trichothecene group. Death, often with victims choking on their own blood, occurs within an hour after exposure. This biological warfare agent has either been used by Soviet planes and Soviet pilots, or supplied by the Soviet Union to the pilots and planes of others.

Soviet scientists have been working on biological weapons since the 1930s.

in the Soviet Union. Their use, in defiance and violation of international agreements, merits the condemnation of civilization.

Now let me move to the related question of chemical warfare, raised by the Soviet delegate. The record will show that in 1969 the United States ceased the production of all weapons and has today only one chemical weapon production facility, which is no longer usable or used. The record will also show that today the Soviet Union operates at least fourteen chemical weapon production facilities. Its armies are better equipped, better organized and better trained in chemical warfare than any others in the world. Each Soviet combat unit, down to the regimental level, has a sizeable chemical warfare contingent. Chemical warfare specialists are assigned at the company level. It is estimated that there are close to 100,000 personnel with chemical warfare training, a training which uses actual chemical agents. Soviet artillery units are regularly equipped with various kinds of chemical warfare shells and other weapons. The Soviet Union has without doubt invested heavily in all aspects of chemical warfare.

My government, therefore, found itself in a position of having unilaterally renounced production of all chemical weapons in 1969 while the Soviet Union recklessly proceeded in an effort to gain world supremacy in this area of warfare. To meet this dilemma constructively, we initiated in the 1970s an attempt to reach an agreement with the Soviet Union on a comprehensive and verifiable joint ban on all chemical weapons.

I have been informed by experts that the question of verification is a complex and difficult one. We concluded that on-site inspection was a prerequisite for agreement. We found that the Soviet Union rejected all suggestions for on-site inspection. It appeared to us that the Soviets had no incentive to enter into an agreement with us. They possessed a decisive advantage in this field because of our inactivity and saw no reason to give it up. Nevertheless, they continued to talk, without decision; and we saw that their purpose in going through the form of the negotiation was to impede the ability of the United States to protect its own interests by building an adequate deterrent capability. We concluded that it was essential to demonstrate to the Soviet Union that we would now deny them any significant military advantage from using chemical weapons. We would improve our defenses against their use and thereby prayerfully reduce casualties; but it was also necessary for us to maintain a capability to retaliate so as to reduce any incentive that the Soviets might have for the first use of these awful weapons.

It is thus the reluctant policy of the United States to build and maintain a chemical munitions stockpile to deny a significant military advantage to any who would seek to initiate their use. We are making only those improvements necessary to provide us with a credible and effective deterrent. It is our fervent hope that this program will provide an incentive to the Soviet Union to join us in seeking a complete and verifiable ban on the production, development, and stockpiling of all such weapons.

Our objective is not to produce chemical weapons. We have demonstrated the genuineness of that objective by our unilateral action of 1969. Our objective is to achieve a complete and verifiable prohibition of chemical warfare. Our unilateral restraint has not worked and has instead only resulted in a significant imbalance between our capability and that of the Soviets. It is necessary for us to try another approach. We are doing so.

The official position of our government was stated in the following announcement from the White House:

The administration's ultimate goal in the area of chemical warfare (CW) is a complete and verifiable ban on the production and stockpiling of chemical weapons. Until such a ban can be obtained, our objective, consistent with existing treaties and international law, is to deter the use of chemical weapons. The U.S. will not use chemical weapons unless chemical weapons are first used against us or our allies. The U.S. does not and will not possess biological or toxic weapons.

We have had enough self-serving and misleading allegations and assertions by the Soviet Union here and elsewhere. The search for peace will not be achieved by propaganda. The search for peace will be achieved by actions consistent with peace. That is what our delegation has been asking for at this meeting. When we see action which merits a constructive response from us, I want to assure this body that our response will be immediately and generously and enthusiastically forthcoming. Until then we will expose the propaganda for what it is, just as we will continue to use this forum to expose the violations of the Helsinki Final Act, including the violence against the people of Poland, for what they are.

February 19, 1982 Martial Law in Poland

* * *

Genuine effort toward compliance with the Helsinki Final Act is required if we are to build upon that Act by new agreements designed to advance our aspirations. We doubt the sincerity and the good faith of those who speak peace but engage in war; of those who speak peace and threaten their neighbors with the use of force; of those who speak peace and engage in a form of warfare against their own citizens.

Daily events in Poland constantly remind us with dramatic intensity that the Helsinki Final Act, which guides our deliberations, is being openly defied in many respects by a number of states here. This is most discouraging to our prospects.

The martial law which was declared in Poland on December 13 had as a primary purpose the imposition of a regime designed to prevent the people of Poland from exercising their rights as human beings, basic rights assured them at Helsinki. Today, martial law remains; arrests continue; threats against the people intensify; tensions increase—all for one reason: the military regime is unwelcome, and its repressive measures are deeply resented by millions of Polish men and women who wish to renew their striving for liberty.

It is difficult to understand what those who imposed martial law might have expected. Did they believe the Polish people would submit to armed control without protest? Here was a people gripped by the prospect of freedom. They became excited, perhaps unrealistically, by the dream of national reconciliation under the banner of democracy. They saw developing in Solidarity a free trade union movement incorporating the hope of solving their own grievances through participatory dialogue within the broader context of solving their nation's economic crises. Suddenly the troops appeared, with every reason to believe that behind the orders for them to appear was the massive power of the Soviet Union, with its more than 50,000 troops, and their tanks and their planes, on their Polish soil.

What did those troops and their generals bring with them? With them came martial law with provisions for the preventive detention of anyone over the age of seventeen who is suspected of possible violations of that martial law; with them came the seizure of factories, mines amd universities; the rescinding of university reforms; the arrests of thousands of workers and intellectuals; miners killed by militia bullets; beatings of strikers; the loss of jobs for activists and those suspected of independent thought and action; summary prison sentences by military judges; the imposition of loyalty oaths; the total centralized control over all broadcast and print media; the renewal of anti-Semitism; the destruction of social organizations; the appointment of commissars to control other organizations; the loss of freedom of speech and assembly; and the crushing of their own popular Solidarity.

What else but passive resistance, subdued defiance and sullen protest on the part of the Polish people could be expected? Yes, there are leaflets and couriers; there are pastoral letters; there are sermons; there are work slowdowns; there are broadcasts; there are protests of all kinds—of course there are. These are the Polish people who are being victimized, a people with a noble history, strong religious and family ties, deep convictions. Is it any wonder that the scrawled slogans read: "Winter is yours, but spring will be ours"?

Newsmen report that in Warsaw a few days ago a Solidarity member was sentenced to a three-year prison term for distributing leaflets calling for a strike at the Ursus factory. About 200 spectators protested the trial and the sentence by singing the Polish national anthem.

But the regime continues with its repression. The Gdansk prosecutor recently announced that Miroslaw Krupinski, deputy chairman of Solidarity, now ill in a local hospital with a heart condition, will be tried by a military court. A correspondent is reported as saying that this is tantamount to trying the whole of Solidarity. Is this the way to proceed toward the goal of reconciliation?

On February 9, Ewa Kubasiewicz was sentenced to ten years in prison for organizing a strike, the longest sentence reported for a violation of martial law regulations. Is this the lessening of coercion that we have been promised? Last night's news reports quote official Polish radio sharply attacking Polish priests and, indirectly, primate Archbishop Josef Glemp for "perfidious activity" sympathetic to Solidarity leaders and for urging the faithful to resist the removal of crucifixes. Is this the way to unify a society?

Mr. Chairman, the Helsinki Final Act teaches us that respect for the human dimension is vital to international understanding. Our delegation, on occasion, concerns itself in detail with the individual human being, because we believe it is a vivid and accurate measure of a society's commitment to that human dimension.

Thus we note again that a few days ago, in the city of Gdynia, Mr. Wladislaw Jerzy Trycinski, a man with a wife and a daughter, a worker and not a leader, was sentenced to a term of nine years in a trial which lasted just a few hours. The sentence was by a presiding military judge; the charge was that Mr. Trycinski attended a meeting at a student hostel. There was no evidence presented that day to the effect that he did anything else at that hostel other than play cards with friends. Only his wife, in addition to his attorney, was permitted to be present during the trial, and she was surrounded by military policemen. His daughter was turned away from the courthouse steps after being strip-searched and her shoes cut open by military police looking, they said, for illegal publications. It had been expected that there would be prosecution witnesses against Mr. Trycinski, but several prosecution witnesses recanted. They said their earlier statements had been extracted by force, with police officials holding guns to their heads to force them to testify.

In one prison in Gdynia, on Kurkowa Street, 180 members of Solidarity await trial in a dingy jail built by the Nazis during the occupation. They have no medical care, no exercise facilities. In the Bialoleka Prison in northern Warsaw, where according to recent reports more than 260 detainees are being held, at least eighty of these men and women went on a hunger strike to protest the cruelty of their conditions. Riot police entered the grounds on January 1 wearing gas masks and carrying clubs, threatening the internees with beatings unless they stopped singing Christmas carols. There are fifty such internment camps.

Mr. Chairman, what we have been recently witnessing in Poland is working peoples, peoples of all walks of life, searching for dignity and an opportunity to breathe the fresh air of freedom. The significance of this move is not yet clear to us. The process is still evolving. What is clear is that there has been a melting away of the Communist Party of Poland like snow in the spring. There has been a revolt of the Polish working class against the Polish United Workers' Party which governed that society, a revolt against a "dictatorship of the proletariat." What is also clear to us is that the Communist Party was helpless to resist that workers' revolution; and it had to call on the army to help save its place and position. The rule of a repudiated Communist Party has been replaced by the rule of the Army. Those who concern themselves with Communist ideology may well wonder whether Lenin's fear of "Bonapartism" may not now be of topical concern to all who embrace that ideology.

We also note with interest that the Soviet Union, whose ideological obligation it is to express "fraternal duty in support of Socialism," is interpreting that requirement by proclaiming its comradeship with a cadre of police, a military elite, a massive bureaucracy, at the expense of a legitimate workers' movement in Poland, which it is attempting to destroy. Here we have yet additional reason to conclude that the Soviet society has repudiated any claim it may have to call itself a "workers' state."

Mr. Chairman, our delegation has used this forum on many occasions over the past seventeen months. During much of that time we have expressed our disappointment and even our anguish at the repeated and continued attacks against the Helsinki Final Act by some of the states here. We do not at all relish that role. To be silent, however, in the face of those violations would have been to condone them and thus make a sham of the Helsinki standards.

We stay here, we work here, we will return here out of a conviction that the Helsinki Process is vital to peace and thus vital to our national interests and to the interests of our people. The spirit and the letter of the Act show us the path to cooperation and to our mutual security. Within that framework we say to all of the participating states here: "Listen to your people; listen to your workers; listen to your artists, poets and writers who plead for dignity and emancipation from the depth of their souls. Do not put them away in prisons, in mental hospitals, in exile. Their voices will not thereby be stilled. Their voices will rather be heightened and sharpened with the contrast you create. The people have much to teach you and to teach us all. They know that the true worth of a nation is not in its massive military forces. It is in the welfare and liberties of its people."

I conclude, Mr. Chairman, by quoting from the words of the famous German playwright, Bertolt Brecht, a particularly apt source in this forum. On another occasion similar to today's, when force was used to crush the aspirations of his country's people, referred to by some as the "proletariat," Herr Brecht made this wry observation: "The people have lost confidence in their government. The government has, therefore, decided to elect a new people."

February 24, 1982 Psychiatric Hospitals

Since we reconvened these meetings on February 9 many important words have been spoken here about the most recent of a continued pattern of Helsinki Accord violations, the violence against the people of Poland. It is important to recall, however, that the excesses that disturb us in Poland are not only the result of Soviet military and political pressure, they reflect a pattern of even greater repression in Soviet society.

On Human Rights Day, in this hall, the Soviet delegate called our human rights concerns a "fuss being made over a bunch of dropouts"; he charged us with using "barefaced inventions" for the purpose of "damaging polemics." He obviously considers our expectation that the Soviet Union will observe its Helsinki commitments of 1975 to be an "undermining" of his country's "sociopolitical rights."

The Polish people understand, as the Final Act clearly directs, that human rights have directly to do with the individual's right to live in liberty and with dignity. Those who would redefine this concept by referring to economic and social rights of "masses" are attempting to obscure the absence of human rights in their own societies. Large groupings of people consist of individuals. Where the integrity of the human being is not respected, there are no human rights for the many. It is also noteworthy that those states who deny the human rights of the individual are unable to provide for his economic and social needs as well.

Recent news reports illustrate again with dramatic impact the consequences for a society and its people where there is a lack of concern and sensitivity for individual human rights. Allow me, Mr. Chairman, to give one vivid illustration of the extremes to which a failing society will go to suppress criticism of its own deficiencies.

In the Soviet Union, psychiatry, a healing science, has been perverted into an instrument of cruel political repression. Men and women, sane and exercising their rights as human beings under the Helsinki Final Act, have been, usually without trial, brutally condemned to the grotesque world of politically controlled psychiatric institutions, where they have been silenced through drugs and violated in a manner reminiscent of the Middle Ages. The logic of this travesty is cruel and simple: the authorities can commit a dissenter to a mental institution by administrative action. In the criminal commitment procedure, the defendant can be ruled "not accountable" and ordered by the court to receive compulsory psychiatric treatment, without the right to participate in his own defense or be present at his own trial. The trial itself is closed to the public.

Psychiatric incarceration spares the authorities the embarrassment of staging full-scale trials of political dissidents; a person's views are discredited by calling them crazy. Indefinite sentences without the *de facto* right of appeal are then thrust upon those whose continued activity is a nuisance to the state. Once in an institution, the victim is administered powerful drugs with painful and debilitating side effects in order to induce recantation. Others on the outside are then dissuaded from exercising their rights by the threat of psychiatric institutionalization.

No wonder this practice led the Sixth World Congress of the World Psychiatric Association in 1977 unprecedentedly to single out the Soviet Union for condemnation! In recent weeks, as a result of yet new disclosures, the Royal College of Psychiatrists in England has voted to ask the World Psychiatric Association to expel the Soviet Union when it next meets in 1983.

We are all here aware that the repression of human rights in the Soviet Union has increased in intensity—clearly an act of defiance and disdain for this meeting and the Helsinki process. As part of that repression, all of the founding members of the Working Commission for the Investigation of the Use of Psychiatry for Political Purposes have also been imprisoned or exiled.

Let us examine this abnormal phenomenon in human terms, using a few current examples:

• Dr. Anatoly Koryagin, a consulting psychiatrist with the working commission had examined numerous people confined for alleged psychiatric illness and found them to be normal, sane individuals. For such activity he was sentenced last June to seven years in strict regimen camp plus five years internal exile. In taking his moral stand, Dr. Koryagin knew that Dr. Semyon Gluzman, a young psychiatrist, had been sentenced ten years earlier for refusing to cooperate with this abuse of medical science. We hope that when Dr. Gluzman's long incarceration and exile is over, he will be permitted to emigrate.

A recent letter of Dr. Koryagin's, written in Soviet labor camp Perm #37, appeared in a British medical journal, *Lancet*. He writes: "Let there be no doubt that Soviet authorities have turned our most humane branch of medicine into an instrument for achieving the main aim of their internal policy—the suppression of dissent.... I appeal to you not for a moment to forget...." To show that we have not forgotten, let us go on.

• Aleksandr Podrabinek wrote a monograph, *Punitive Medicine*, in which he described Soviet medical malpractices against dissidents. He was sentenced this last year to three years in a labor camp.

• Felix Serebrov was sentenced last July to a total of nine years in severe regime labor camp and internal exile for, among other things, appealing to this very CSCE meeting to help stop the practice of psychiatric abuse in the Soviet Union.

• During the same month, Irina Grivnina, mother of a small child, was sentenced to five years in internal exile for having passed along information which helped to expose the misuse of psychiatry.

• Last February, Yuri Valov, a member of a group formed to defend the rights of invalids in the Soviet Union, was sentenced to a psychiatric hospital for his samizdat paper, "An Invalid's Message." This, Mr. Chairman, in the year proclaimed by the United Nations as "The Year of the Invalid."

• Dr. Leonard Ternovsky was sentenced a year ago to three years in labor camp for having been unafraid to speak up against the political abuse of psychiatry. Dr. Ternovsky's words at his trial are illuminating: "I have felt a particular responsibilty as a doctor for things done in the name of medicine. I became convinced that psychiatry is in fact being misused, and that it is necessary to oppose such misuses.... I would have been happier if my activities and statements were not needed.... I foresaw my arrest and this trial. That does not mean I wanted to go to prison. I am almost fifty, not fifteen. I no longer need romantic notions. I would much prefer to escape years of imprisonment. But I only did what I considered necessary. If I had failed to do so, I would have lost my self-respect."

Dr. Ternovsky and Dr. Koryagin are by no means alone. Other Soviet physicians are now in prison for their defense of human rights and their protest of the Soviet abuse of medical science. We here recognize the heroism of Dr. Mykola Plakhotnyuk, Dr. Zinovy Krisivsky, Dr. Algirdas Statkevicius.

Copious documentation of the torture we have described exists for more than five hundred persons, out of the thousands so punished. Nor can the existence of the inhumane abuse be denied. The evidence is too great, and it has been confirmed by Soviet Ministry of Health officials. In a paper prepared under the direction of the chief psychiatrist at the Ministry of Health for presentation to a congress of Soviet psychiatrists this past summer, we learned officially that persons are indeed confined in mental institutions because they made "groundless" and "slanderous" statements against the government.

Keeping pace with the growth of the human rights movement, the government has increased the number of Special Psychiatric Hospitals from three in the early

1960s to twelve in 1981. These hospitals are managed by the Ministry of the Interior, the same ministry that runs the Soviet prison system. Dissenters confined there live in constant danger from the truly criminally insane patients.

Nor is the confinement of dissenters limited to political dissidents, Religious activists are frequently similarly victimized. Valeriya Makeeva, an Orthodox nun, was confined in Kazan Special Psychiatric Hospital from 1979 until her transfer to an Ordinary Psychiatric Hospital near Moscow in early 1981. Intensive treatment with drugs left her right arm paralyzed. Members of unregistered Christian groups in several regions of the Soviet Union have also been forced into psychiatric hospitals. A case in point is Vladimir Pavolovich Khailo, a worker with fifteen children, member of the Reform Baptist Church, a faith not recognized as legal by the Soviet government, and long the target of persecution. On September 22, 1980, with our Madrid preparatory meeting in session, Khailo was forcibly interned in a mental hospital. On December 1, 1980, he was ruled "not responsible" for his actions on the grounds of insanity and sentenced by a closed court. Khailo remains in psychiatric confinement to this day in spite of his desire to emigrate.

Soviet authorities also have used psychiatry to suppress incipient free labor organizations. Mr. Chairman, we have joined here with many in condemning the military government in Warsaw for its efforts to crush Solidarity. It is useful to remind ourselves that Soviet workers, who have fought for reforms similar to Solidarity's, are themselves too often persecuted and too often condemned to mental hospital cells.

A number of workers formed a group in Moscow in 1976 collectively to protest violations of their labor rights. By early 1978, no fewer than five of the group's leading members had been confined to psychiatric institutions. Later that year, another group announced that they were forming a similar unofficial trade union group. Within three weeks, one founding member was in a psychiatric hospital, while other members were sentenced to imprisonment or exile.

When Mikhail Zotov publicized a lockout at an auto plant in Togliatti, doctors declared him "mentally incompetent" and committed him to the Togliatti General Psychiatric Hospital. Vladimir Klebanov, a foreman in a Ukrainian coal mine, once complained to superiors that his men were dying in accidents because they were exhausted from too much overtime work. When Klebanov went on to announce the formation of an independent union, he was sent to the Dnepropetrovsk Special Hospital, where he is still being held.

In 1980, Soviet officials moved against an outspoken coalminer and former member of the Communist Party named Aleksei Nikitin, who first had protested lax safety precautions in the Donetsk mines eleven years ago. This led to his confinement in the Dnepropetrovsk Special Hospital, and he has been in mental hospitals nearly all of the last decade. Although he was examined in September 1980 by the psychiatrist, Dr. Anatoly Koryagin, and pronounced absolutely sane (which pronouncement led to the doctor's arrest), Soviet authorities ended Nikitin's efforts to form a free trade union in Donetsk and locked him up again just a few months ago in a special psychiatric hospital in Kazakhstan in distant Central Asia, far from family and friends. He is being injected with sulfazin, not an accepted therapeutic drug; and he writes that it "is like a drill boring into your body that gets worse and worse until it's more than you can stand."

We realize, Mr. Chairman, that the people of Poland are not free to determine their own destiny. We have no doubt, however, that the full knowledge of the nature of the Soviet Union and its inhuman repressions are well known to them. They know the fate of the Aleksei Nikitins and they want no part of this barbarism in their own country.

It is tragic that the Soviet government regards independent opinions as threats to its security and labels them mental diseases. We remind them that the winds of change cross the world as inevitably as the winds of winter. It is obligatory that Helsinki signatory states not manipulate the minds of their citizens; that they not step between a man and his conscience or his God; and that they not prevent his thoughts from finding expression through peaceful action. We are all painfully aware, furthermore, that governments which systematically disregard the rights of their own people are not likely to respect the rights of other nations and other people.

Scientific developments do not occur with an even frequency among states. Soviet medicine has in the past made great advances in many areas. The widespread misuse of psychiatry to serve the ends of political punishment places this sector of Soviet medicine back into the realm of the dark ages of medical science. This tragic situation has been brought to the attention of the Soviet Society for Neurologists and Psychiatrists. We plead with the Soviet authorities to end the barbarism. It is not worthy of a great people.

Editors note: The Soviet delegate responded angrily, charging the American sought "confrontation." Only one minor U.S. point was challenged. Ambassador Kampelman replied.

February 24, 1982 Right of Reply Statement

We have just heard the Soviet delegate exercise his right of reply to our delegation's deep concerns about the inhuman exploitation of psychiatry in his country for political purposes. I have on many occasions privately and in this forum, in writing and orally, informed the Soviet delegate that if there are factual errors of substance in any of our statements to this body, I would like him to bring those to our attention so that we might correct the record. This morning he tells us that no person is sent to a mental institution unless a doctor certifies as to his mental illness. Of course we know that the testimony of one doctor is required in the administrative proceeding prior to the condemnation of an individual to a psychiatric institution—only one doctor. That in no way goes to the essence of the statement we made, a statement that we reaffirm with conviction.

A few days ago the head of the Soviet delegation noted a tension in my voice. He will recognize it again as I respond to the remarks made by his delegation. It is, however, not tension that he hears. It was, and is, anger at the system of repression which his society represents, an outrage at the brazen attempts to have us diverted from the main thrust of our concerns.

We have been hearing the refrains, "Our delegation is ready to carry on constructive work here," and, "It is high time to do something concrete." Mr. Chairman, it is with reluctance but candor that I must say those statements are sheer hypocrisy. The Helsinki Final Act has been pummeled to near death by the Soviet Union. We hear the misleading, repetitious chirping of "Let's get to work" by those who have demonstrated by their actions their utter contempt for our process. What kind of "work" are they talking about? The only work I know they are doing on the Act is flagrantly to undermine it. The work I see them performing is the continued military invasion of Afghanistan by 100,000 of their troops who are subjugating an innocent people. On Friday, the Soviet delegate called the events in Afghanistan "irrelevant." Imagine the utter disdain for our process reflected in the use of that word "irrelevant." It is in effect to call the provisions of our Act "irrelavant."

The work I see them performing is to threaten the use of force against a neighbor, Poland, which led to the use of martial law in that tragic land with its violence against the Polish people.

The work I see them performing is to continue to imprison and send to mental institutions a continuous stream of men and women who seek to exercise their rights as human beings under the Helsinki Final Act.

That is the only work dealing with the Helsinki Final Act that they engage in—wrecking work! Everything else they do here has been talk!

Meaningless talk! Empty talk!—all in a transparent effort to turn the attention of the world away from their transgressions as they use their organs of propaganda to evade the real issues here. Nobody but the readers of a controlled press can be taken in by this obvious sham, and we know the healthy skepticism that those deprived people have about the information provided them by the controlled organs of the media in their societies.

Are they offering us more talk? More words? More words on paper that they can disregard? More promises that they will not keep? The words are useless in the face of their deeds of violence against our Act. Let them demonstrate their intent to do something to restore confidence—acts—and then we'll look at their words. Until then, we do not accept or believe their words.

February 26, 1982 Soviet View of Détente

It is always difficult to decide whether to respond to the Soviet delegation when, as they did this morning, they make outlandish, unsubstantiated, and excessive statements at these meetings. It was not my intent to speak today. I reply as part of our continuing effort to try to have the Soviet Union understand the extent of the damage they are inflicting on the Helsinki Final Act which they profess to support.

Soviet statements here are made without regard to what they hear from the rest of us at these meetings. This is discouraging for the purposes of dialogue and understanding. In many ways Soviet interventions here remind me of the one who said: "I know it is true beacusce I have said it before." We can only hope that higher authorities of the Soviet Union are listening, taking heed, and registering the overwhelming message coming out of these meetings—that the Helsinki Final Act should be complied with if we are to achieve the security and stability sought by our peoples.

We are told that the United States is engaged in "destructive action" designed to "poison the atmosphere." We are told that our interventions here, our refusing to do business as usual, are nothing but a "stilted pretext." They would have us believe that the Soviet invasion of Afghanistan and the continued presence of 100,000 Soviet troops there to inflict violence on the people of that put-upon country is a "stilted pretext." This is as irresponsible as the Soviet delegate's statements a few days ago that Afghanistan is "irrelevant." Here we have a flagrant violation of the Helsinki Final Act, and the Soviet delegate has the temerity to call it a "stilted pretext."

We have been told by the head of the Soviet delegation that his country has never here spoken out for the cause of war. But his country engages in war. And we here have heard him defend that war and other aggressions waged by his government.

For the Soviet threat of force against the people of Poland and for the violence against those people by their military authorities to be labeled "stilted pretext" only reflects the insensitivity of the Soviet Union to their obligations under the Helsinki Final Act.

Many of us here have documented our assertions that the imprisonment and persecution of Soviet citizens who seek to serve as Helsinki monitors within their own country, the jamming of radio broadcasts, the interference in the free exercise of one's religious convictions, the refusal to grant permission to emigrate to thousands of citizens who seek to reunite with their families—that all of these actions of Soviet authorities are in defiance of their 1975 commitments. The only response we get is that the persecuted are "scum," and "criminals." And so long as their written constitution contains noble words, we have no right to point out that their deeds deny and defy our commitments.

"Stilted pretext" indeed!

The issue is clear to all of us. Do we or do we not take the Helsinki Final act seriously? The American delegation does. The Soviet Union obviously does not. Until we see that they do, their speeches and promises are meaningless to us.

We find ourselves in a Kafkaesque situation. The Soviet Union and its followers break our agreed upon Helsinki standards; and then they attack us for taking note of those violations and speaking to those transgressions. Once again today, we heard the accusation of "confrontation." This word "confrontation" is another of the many superficial and meaningless slogans designed to obscure reality. From the very beginning of the Helsinki period, shortly after the Helsinki Final Act was signed, Soviet propagandists continued with their "ideological struggle" and with their massive military buildup against the West. They feel historically justified in attacking democratic societies at any time and do not wish to be criticized for those aggressions.

To those of us governed by rational analysis, these Soviet attacks would appear to be contrary to the so-called "spirit of détente" and to "peaceful coexistence." But to those in the grips of dialectical analysis rather than rational analysis, there is no inconsistency. They are justified in attacking, because the laws of history justify whatever they choose to do. But Western attacks against Soviet aggression are "confrontational" or a "return to the Cold War." This Orwellian distortion of language makes rational international dialogue extremely difficult, if not impossible. It fools nobody. We reject it.

The Soviet Union is fond of using the word *détente*. They know that most of us who hear the word identify it with the equivalent of peace and the relaxation of tensions. They would like us to believe that they share our interpretation of that word. That, however, is not the case. The evidence is overwhelming that the Soviet Union sees "détente" as a device to cause a relaxation of Western efforts to protect themselves rather than a relaxation of tensions. This then permits the Soviet Union to pursue its aggressive intentions.

We question the good faith of the Soviet Union when we see an authoritative article issued as late as October 1980, on the eve of the formal opening of our main session, which reads: "Peaceful coexistence creates the optimum conditions for the class struggle.... Thus détente creates favorable conditions for the class struggle." (A. S. Milovidov and Mr. Ya. A. Zhdanov, in *Voprosy Filosofii*, No. 10) This followed upon an earlier statement in the May 1979 issue of *International Affairs*, by Vadim Kortunov: "Détente creates a much more favorable international setting for each of the three revolutionary streams of our day—world socialism, the international working-class movement, and the national liberation revolution—to achieve their goals.... Détente is not only a *political* but also a *social* factor characterizing a new and important stage in the anti-imperialist struggle the world over."

It is not my intent to belabor this point. It is rather to set forth the reasons for the perception by many of us here that the motives and objectives of the Soviet Union are threatening to our security and to our desire to build a society characterized by confidence and cooperation among us. We look to deeds rather than words to allay our concerns. Until then, we will act to protect our interests. The Soviet Union does not interpret "peaceful coexistence" or "détente" in any manner which can give the West any comfort. The Soviet battle against the West has never stopped, ideologically, politically, or militarily, and it continues today.

The Soviet delegate this morning would have this body believe that my country, which was the first in the world to have the atom bomb and the first and only state in the world to offer to share nuclear power with the world when it proposed the Baruch Plan, is responsible for the nuclear arms race. Most of us look upon war in this nuclear age as unthinkable. We want to end the threat of nuclear war. This profound hope unites all of our peoples—those who choose to pray to achieve that goal, those who choose to demonstrate in the streets, those who choose the political process, those who choose to work for peace through diplomacy and negotiation—all of us are united in seeking the end of the threat of nuclear war.

To most of us, nuclear war is indeed "unthinkable." It is a matter of concern, however, that this is not universally shared. I read from a statement by Soviet General Major A. S. Milovidor: "There is profound error and harm in the disorienting claims of bourgeois ideologues that there will be no victor in thermal nuclear war. . . ." I read next from Marshal V. D. Sokolovskiy in his book (1968) *Soviet Military Strategy:* "The armed forces of the Soviet Union and the other socialist countries must be prepared, above all, to wage war under the conditions of the mass use of nuclear weapons by both belligerent parties. . . . The preparation and waging of just such a war must be regarded as the main task of the theory of military strategy and strategic leadership." I read next from an official publication of the Soviet Army: "Today's weapons make it possible to achieve strategic objectives very quickly. The very first nuclear attack on the enemy may inflict such immense casualties and produce such vast destruction that his economic, moral-political and military capabilities will collapse, making it impossible for him to continue the struggle, and presenting him with the fact of defeat." (Colonel M. P. Skirdo, *The People, the Army, the Commander,* Voyenizdat, Moscow 1973, p. 78) And from *The Soviet Dictionary of Basic Military Terms:* "Surprise—One of the basic conditions for achieving success in battle. . . . Surprise is achieved by the use of various ways. . . by leading the enemy into error concerning one's own intentions, by preserving in secret the plan of battle, by speedy action, by hidden artificial maneuvers, *by the unexpected use of the nuclear weapon . . .*" [Emphasis supplied]

We have here the essence of much of our problem. Are we to ignore these authoritative military statements which we do not believe have been repudiated, or should we believe the political statements urging peace that are being propagated massively throughout Europe by the Soviet Union? It is difficult for us to know which of these messages to believe. We, therefore, look to the deeds, and we find a pattern of aggression and militarization, which adds to our concern. The Soviet Union talks about "détente" and talks about peace and disarmament at the same time as they continue to build up the massive nuclear forces that threaten the rest of us at an alarming rate.

When I last addressed myself to this question here a few months ago, I brought to the attention of this body that the Soviet Union possessed 250 SS-20 missiles with three massive warheads each. During the intervening days between that last comment and today, the Soviets have increased the number of their dangerous and destructive SS-20 missiles so that today they have 280 such missiles, each with three warheads. In addition, the Soviet Union possesses 300 SS-4 and SS-5 missiles still in place. Today, therefore, there are 1,100 such warheads, nearly all of which are aimed at the cities and at the people of Europe. The American supply of similar land-based missiles is none. The West will redress the balance.

The United States is strategically committed to Europe. We understand full well that there are no safe harbors in this age of nuclear warfare.

The United States abhors the possibility of nuclear war as much as any country because we believe, as President Reagan recently stated, "In nuclear war, all mankind would lose."

I conclude, Mr. Chairman, with the following observation. Students of totalitarian societies of both the right and the left tell us that the technique of the totalitarian is to respond to criticism and factual allegations by first denying them boldly; they then make counterstatements of an outlandish nature and of all kinds, not necessarily to the subject matter under discussion. The purpose is obvious. It is to set up an extreme position in the hope it will lead observers to conclude that the truth may be someplace in between the original factual criticism directed against them and their own extremism, thus obfuscating the thrust of the initial factual allegation. A further objective is the belief that repetition of a lie may make it believable by some. I suggest to the Soviet delegation that they are here demonstrating the validity of the analysis to which I have referred.

Free societies, Mr. Chairman, are not perfect societies. We have imperfections in my own country which we continue to try to correct. We believe that the Helsinki Final Act provides the standards to which we should aspire. We invite the Soviet Union to join us in that process of growth. It is our best assurance of peace.

March 3, 1982 Imperialism and the Baltic States

On Friday, the head of the Soviet delegation spoke of "imperialism." It is not my purpose today to engage in a fruitless discussion of Marxist ideology. Thinking of his comments, however, I was struck by the fact that he spoke on our last working day in February; and that during the month of February, Estonians and Lithuanians throughout the world were marking their countries' declarations of independence.

The Baltic states of Latvia, Lithuania, and Estonia understand the meaning of imperialism and the loss of liberties that follow it. Between 1918 and 1939, these three Baltic republics were proud members of the world's community of free nations. In 1940, consistent with the earlier Molotov-Ribbentrop Pact, these nations were forcibly annexed by the Soviet Union. The United States condemned that annexation then, and we reaffirm our opposition to it now. We do not recognize the forcible incorporation of the Baltic states into the Soviet Union. Our commitment to the principles of liberty and self-determination requires no less.

Lenin, in his first decree to the Second All-Russia Congress of Soviets, known in the Communist world as the "Decree of Peace," said on the first day that he took power: "If any people is held by force in defiance of its expressed wish . . . is not given the right of decision, free from every duress, by free elections, without the presence of those armed forces of the incorporating state or any more powerful state, of what form of national existence it wishes to have . . . then the incorporation of such a state should be called annexation, an act of seizure and force." We have here indeed an act of "annexation," an "act of seizure and force" against the Baltic states.

I am well aware that the Soviet Union calls itself a "socialist" state and that by definition, *its* definition, it can never be guilty of imperialism, regardless of what it may do. There is an American saying: "If it walks like a duck, talks like a duck, and looks like a duck—it's a duck." Some may wish to call the duck a goose, or a chicken, Mr. Chairman. But it is still a duck. The acts of aggression against the three Baltic states were acts of imperialism.

I respectfully suggest to the Soviet authorities that those nations of the world which, in the course of their own histories, have experimented with imperialism have learned that there are decided limits to imperial attainments. Those that have abandoned the imperial mode have found relief from its burdens, not regret at their loss. Universal opinion today rejects the right of any power to conquer and subjugate other peoples. Furthermore, formal imperial powers have learned that they gain little from their efforts. I suggest that the Soviet Union is now finding that its imperial objectives, its dangerous adventurism have proven to be and will continue to be extremely expensive, an unnecessary burden.

The Helsinki Final Act will have renewed meaning and strength for all of us when that lesson is finally learned and acted upon.

March 10, 1982 Soviet Responsibility in Poland*

Our delegation and others have expressed the view that the threat of the use of force played a major role in influencing developments in Poland. This has been denied. It is appropriate that we share with all delegations here the basis of our conclusion. The descriptive chronology which follows provides that information:

On September 1, 1980, less than one month after the dramatic emergence of Solidarity into Polish life, a lead editorial in *Pravda* criticized Polish authorities for working out a settlement with the union, described as an "antisocialist element." Polish authorities were reminded of their Warsaw Pact obligations. The editorial included an implicit threat of economic reprisals. A week later a Polish government economic mission went to Moscow.

On September 8, 400,000 Warsaw Pact troops began four days of maneuvers in East Germany.

Two months later, Warsaw television showed films of maneuvers on Polish soil in which units of the Polish army and the Soviet Northern Group of Forces participated.

In early December, there were further authoritative reports of Soviet troops active in Western military districts.

On January 13, 1981, Warsaw Pact commander-in-chief Viktor Kulikov made a surprise visit to Warsaw. More will be heard of Marshal Kulikov, who was present in Warsaw prior to and during the declaration of martial law.

On March 4, First Secretary Kania and General Jaruzelski met in Moscow with Chairman Brezhnev and other Soviet leaders, who told them that they expected the Poles "to turn the course of events" because developments in Poland were of concern to "the entire Socialist community."

The very next day the USSR announced plans for Warsaw Pact maneuvers along the Polish-Czech border north to the Baltic; and shortly thereafter, the Polish news agency PAP announced the SOYUZ-81 maneuvers, with the Polish army participating to "fulfill its duty" to "defend socialism."

Significantly, on March 9, Deputy Premier Rakowski informed Solidarity leaders that SOYUZ-81 maneuvers would be extended "because of the situation in Poland." He warned Solidarity that its continued activity could bring in Soviet tanks.

During that same month, Polish Ambassador to Japan Rurarz, who later sought freedom in the United States after martial law was declared, received word from Warsaw that plans for a state of emergency were imminent.

The month of March was characterized by higher levels of Warsaw Pact military activity, with increased Soviet troops near Poland. Added supply stockpiles and new Soviet transport helicopters, planes, pilots, and technicians were flown into Soviet headquarters in southwest Poland.

On March 23, Soviet Politburo member Mikhail Suslov unexpectedly arrived in Warsaw. The Polish press reported that the talks stressed the need to "remove the danger to the gains of socialism." It appears, understandably, that the talks about the "gains of socialism" met with little response in Poland. The poor outcome of

---

Addendum in the form of a letter to chiefs of delegation from Max M. Kampelman.

the visit was reflected in *TASS* of March 25, which attacked "revisionist elements" within the party itself, the first such Soviet accusation.

At the Czechoslovak Party Congress on April 6, with Chairman Brezhnev present, President Husak reiterated the right of the Warsaw Pact to intervene to preserve Poland's socialist system (a clear admission that intervention was and would continue to take place, and a so-called "right" which runs directly contrary to the Helsinki Final Act).

On June 6, the Soviet Communist Party sent a harshly worded, seven-page "warning" letter to the Central Committee of the Polish Communist Party severely critical of their complacency and granting of concessions. Developments in Poland were called a "threat to our common security." The letter insisted that the party must "change the course of events" and clearly referred to the "threat. . . to the very existence of the independent Polish state."

Later in the month, on June 20, chief Kremlin spokesman Zamyatin continued Soviet pressure with a declaration that "the time has come for decisive action. . . to avert a national catastrophe."

Two days later, Marshal Kulikov, making his military presence again evident, denounced Polish "counterrevolutionary forces." This was immediately followed by a Polish news agency's report of joint Polish-Soviet military exercises in Silesia, later extended to the northwest province of Pomerania.

On July 2, Soviet troops in the western Ukraine on the Polish border underwent, according to Moscow sources, a two-day intensive training period for full mobilization.

By September 4, ZAPAD-81, which we earlier discussed at these meetings, began. With these military exercises, Soviet pressures intensified.

On September 17, Soviet Ambassador Aristov warned Mr. Kania and General Jaruzelski that the "growth of anti-Sovietism in Poland. . . has reached dangerous limits." On November 22, Soviet Deputy Premier Baybakov was in Warsaw warning about possible Soviet use of economic pressure on Poland. The next day *TASS* criticized Polish leadership for not acting decisively and urged that "all existing means" be used.

A statement of the Soviet Communist Party on September 18 is here noteworthy. The Soviet ambassador on the previous day had complained about the "growth of anti-Sovietism in Poland." The official statement talked about an "acute and unbridled campaign against the Soviet Union" and its policies, which were "not isolated." It reported threats against Soviet soldiers. Polish nationalism was characterized as "distinctly anti-Soviet." There are further threats in the Soviet statement and insistence that the Polish authorities "stop the malicious anti-Soviet propaganda and acts which are hostile to the Soviet Union" and that they do so "without delay." [What a devastating commentary on fraternal solidarity!]

On October 13, *Pravda* continued the pressure with further implied threats of intervention. The next day, Mr. Suslov promised Polish authorities that any positive action that they would take would find the support of the Soviet Union behind that action. Two days later, Premier Jaruzelski removed First Secretary Kania from office.

The pressure on General Jaruzelski was intensified. In early November, the Soviets warned the Polish authorities that Soviet economic assistance would be reduced and that Moscow would insist on a trade balance beginning in 1982.

There is no need to go on with this chronology as we move closer to December 13. By late October and early November, the Polish military had already sent task forces into some 2,000 villages and parishes. These were later transferred to towns and cities. On November 13, another Soviet-Polish military exercise took place in Silesia; and the Polish government's position toward Solidarity hardened. More significantly, Soviet Marshal Viktor Kulikov reappeared in Warsaw on November 23. He was accompanied by Soviet General Anatolii Gribkov, Chief of Staff of the Warsaw Pact Forces. They met with Generals Jaruzelski and Siwicki. We also know that Marshal Kulikov was in Warsaw precisely on the fateful day of December 13, as well as before and after that date.

My government also knows, as President Reagan stated on December 23, that the actual printing of the Polish martial law proclamation took place in Moscow in September.

Polish authorities were unable to continue with the process of dialogue and reconciliation because the Soviet Union gave every sign that it refused to tolerate such a peaceful solution to Poland's internal problems. Those signs were backed up by massive Soviet military forces on Poland's borders. The interference in Poland's internal affairs and the threat of force against the people of Poland were violations of the Helsinki Final Act.

March 12, 1982 Concluding Statement

Our meeting in Madrid has been a difficult one. The current session which we are now closing has been a particularly sad one. The disturbing vibrations emanating from East-West tensions have clearly affected our deliberations. We end this phase of our meetings today fully conscious that the Helsinki Process is in danger.

Our meeting opened in September 1980 under the shadow of the Soviet invasion of Afghanistan and the continued armed occupation of that nation. Each passing week of that meeting and of the main meeting which began in November of that year brought with it new tensions as we perceived Soviet behavior which could only be interpreted as disdain, if not defiance, of the Helsinki Final Act.

Soviet repression of human rights has taken place on a scale unsurpassed in recent years. During the period of our Madrid sessions there have been at least 248 new political arrests, most of them individuals attempting to exercise their religious rights. Fifty-two members of the Soviet Helsinki Watch Committees are in prison or in internal exile, fifteen of them having been imprisoned since we began our deliberations.

Even while Soviet delegates here were proclaiming their government's allegiance to the human contacts provisions of Basket III, emigration from the Soviet Union kept declining drastically. Last month, for example, fewer than 300 Jews were allowed to leave the Soviet Union, the lowest number in the last twelve years.

The jamming of broadcasts has been intensified—a defiance of the Act, but a useless and a costly gesture in the face of the knowledge that oppressors can no longer be hidden from the eyes of the outside world.

And then there was Poland. During the first week of this phase of our meetings, a month ago, nearly twenty foreign ministers spoke here, the largest such gathering since the Helsinki Agreement was signed in 1975. However differently and eloquently they chose their words, their message was the same: The Soviet Union and the Polish authorities must respect and adhere to their commitments under the Helsinki Final Act if this meeting is to attain its objectives.

* * *

We talk here, we have stayed here, we will return here, we try, we propose, we decry, and we try again. We do so because the stakes for us are the blessings of peace. These are stakes too precious for us to abandon. We therefore work to preserve the process. We work in spite of the frustration, the disappointment, the lengthy meetings, the argumentation, and even the occasional personal calumnies that regrettably appear to be an inevitable part of the exchange.

The objective of our effort is peace. Peace is a complicated idea. It is the supreme achievement of statesmanship. In one limited sense, it is the absence of war, and that in itself is a cherished goal. In an important sense, however, it must be more than that. It must be a network of relationships based on order, on cooperation, and on law if it is to be lasting.

History, I am confident, will proclaim the Helsinki Final Act as one of our century's most important milestones on the path to peace. Its distinction is that it has established a set of standards, attested to by the signatures of all our heads of state, whose fulfillment is indispensable to the achievement of peace.

Our modern age of diplomacy has been characterized by the striving for arms control agreements. These are important. On our own agenda has been a conference on confidence-building measures to deal with our concerns over surprise military attack. Conscientious observance of the Helsinki Final Act, however, may well prove to be of greater importance in the search for peace. The disarmament agreements after the First World War did not prevent the Second World War. The SALT I agreement and the SALT II negotiations did not prevent the worst decade of the cold war or halt the extraordinary buildup of the world's nuclear arsenal. We must seize every opportunity to negotiate for arms control and arms reduction. But the achievement of peace requires more.

The unique ingredient of the Helsinki Final Act is that it reflects the integrated totality of our relationships. The commitment to human rights, which all of us· assumed in 1975, is as necessary to peace as is our commitment to respect one another's borders and to refrain from the use of force against any state. The emphasis of the Act on cultural and scientific exchange, human contacts, trade, emigration and the reunification of families represents essential components in the weaving of the fabric of peace.

The standards of the Helsinki Final Act are based on the principle that the human being is the center of it all. Our quest for peace is to preserve the human being and the civilization he is continuing to build. Alexander Solzhenitsyn said it this way: "It is high time to remember that we belong first and foremost to humanity, and that man has separated himself from the animal world by *thought* and by *speech*. These, naturally, should be *free*. If they are put in chains, we shall return to the state of animals."

* * *

A few days ago, the distinguished head of the Yugoslav delegation made an impressive talk here, a portion of which made an important contribution to this discussion. In referring to the Yalta Agreement, he said that the Helsinki Final Act establishes a principle which rejects the notion of "spheres of influence." On New Year's Day, President Mitterrand of France in a similar message stated that it was time to consider "getting out of Yalta."

Historians frequently refer to the "myth" of Yalta. They say that to equate Yalta with spheres of influence is to misread history. The Yalta Agreement was based on the assumption that the peoples of Eastern Europe were to be guaranteed free elections so that they might choose their own governments and those governments would then be free to select their own alliances. That did not take place.

The partition of Europe along predetermined lines cannot and should not become a permanent part of our geopolitics. The myth of Yalta, together with its concomitant so-called "Brezhnev Doctrine," is a danger to peace. It stands in the way of necessary peaceful change and can only, if it remains, produce later upheavals which will threaten our stability, in the East as well as in the West. Change will come. Its winds will reach us as inevitably as do the winds of the seasons. It will come to the East as it comes to all of us, because life requires change. The great challenge is whether that change can come peacefully.

* * *

Rulers who fear the people they govern end up fearing one another, fearing their nightmares, fearing the unknown, fearing the future, fearing for themselves and their states. They then try to instill fear in others. But fear does not produce loyalty. Affection and pride in one's government and in one's society must be earned by respect, not by fear. Peace cannot evolve in an atmosphere of fear. That, too, is a lesson implicit in the Helsinki Final Act.

The striving for economic and social liberty is on the agenda of the twentieth and twenty-first centuries; it joins the striving for political liberty which began in the eighteenth and nineteenth centuries and continues today on its steady path. To believe that the economic and social needs of people can be achieved without political liberty, or that bread and circuses will satisfy peoples and make them forget about their need for liberty, is to make a serious miscalculation. To believe that political liberty can survive alongside economic and social deprivation is to be guilty of a similar grievous error. My own government is fully aware that these political, social, and economic goals are complementary. To regard them as antithetical undermines and endangers our search for peace.

I dwell upon this because of a real concern that must be aired and considered. Those heavily influenced by the teachings of Lenin look upon the interests of the East and the West as irreconcilable. This belief in historic "irreconcilability" is incompatible with the stark reality of the nuclear age. I suggest that it requires earnest reconsideration. We reject the notion that world peace can be assured only after "just wars." To believe that only the ultimate defeat of capitalism, which will require violence, can bring about a "just peace" is in effect to challenge the Helsinki Final Act and to threaten world peace.

We for ourselves cannot accept declarations of peace as genuine if they are accompanied by a belief in the doctrine that war is a law of history and that there is a duty to prepare for, encourage, and fight that war to inevitable victory over the existing order. That philosophy is inconsistent with the objectives and principles of the Helsinki Final Act. It has no place in a world envisaged by the Act. It certainly has no place in a nuclear age. It is a threat to our security and to peace.

I conclude, Mr. Chairman, with some frank observations about the future of our meeting and the prospects for agreement when we reconvene in November.

The concerns of many of us have been fully expressed. The transgressions against the Helsinki Final Act which have led to our current impasse have been fully documented. The only response has been an attempt to drown this conference with empty exhortations to work. But the sole objective of these urgings has been to make us forget the oppressive reality that has been imposed upon us by the Soviet Union. We do not forget that our commitment to genuine security and cooperation in Europe does not permit us to be lured by offers of easy but empty agreement, an agreement that would be dishonored at the moment of its signing.

The objective of the American delegation is to achieve agreement if we can thereby strengthen and advance our mutual security and our objective of peace and cooperation in Europe. We patiently await developments; we await concrete actions; only these will justify our renewed energies toward agreement when we meet again. To be offered only the narcotic of words while continued violence is perpetrated against the provisions of the Helsinki Final Act cannot produce the agreement we seek.

* * *

We seek the substantive concluding document that we and so many here have worked so long to achieve. We believe that RM.39, proposed to us by the eight neutral and non-aligned states after laborious and conscientious effort, can well provide the basis for such an agreement, amended, as it must be, by proposals that have already been noted, and supplemented, as it should be, by a reflection of what has transpired here since the paper was prepared.

Our delegation in November will be ready to continue the effort to achieve genuine security, cooperation, and peace among all our peoples. We genuinely urge those who have jeopardized the work of this conference to take the necessary steps outside of this meeting that would permit the active and serious negotiation toward the constructive completion of our work in Madrid.

What we ask here is nothing more and nothing less than a genuine effort to comply with the Helsinki Final Act. We do not seek argument. What we seek is a joint and a genuine effort for peace.

Amendments

Eight months after recessing, the review resumed on November 9, 1982. Before the delegates was the revised draft of a concluding document prepared by the neutral/nonaligned states, and amendments submitted by a group of Western states. The amendments include an affirmation of free trade unionism; a strengthening of the principle that citizens may express themselves freely on Final Act implementation; extending religious freedom; providing for an experts meeting to help solve the humanitarian problems that the Act was intended to meet; providing that there should be public access to missions; a commitment not to jam or otherwise interfere with one another's radio broadcasts; and the assurance of expanded rights of journalists.

Mr. Kampelman stated on November 16 that "the integrity and credibility of the Helsinki process are now at stake." This phase of the conference concluded at the Christmas recess. Before leaving, Ambassador Kampelman noted that the Western amendments were now "an agreed upon basis for our continuing work here"—a "positive sign," he said, despite "some unduly sharp exchanges" the previous six weeks. He hoped that the conferees would return in February to produce a "balanced and substantial document."

The eighth phase of the Madrid conference began February 8, 1983 on a note of hope. The Yugoslav added that his delegation "could hardly accept another adjournment of the Madrid meeting and its prolonged negotiations into uncertainty."

Ambassador Kampelman responded, "We await the evidence of a mutuality of political will to face realistically the need to add substance to the words of good will."

Ambassador Kampelman repeatedly used appropriate occasions—anniversaries of violations of human rights, international women's day, Karl Marx's birthday, Afghanistan Day, and a new assassination—as themes to focus attention on the amending process.

On July 15, 1983 Ambassador Kampelman could announce an approaching agreement on a final document.

November 16, 1982 **Poland and the CSCE**

* * *

The Polish delegate's harsh reference to my country requires a response. It is, of course, not surprising that a totalitarian military regime, unable to earn the confidence of the people over whom it has imposed itself and unable to meet the needs of its people, will attempt to hide its failures by attacking others. There was a reference to the "arrogance of power," a worthy reminder. I suggest there are none more arrogant than those who foolishly believe that the temporary power that ensues from the bayonets and clubs of riot police and militia can last. The historic aspirations of the Polish people for freedom will, in time, prevail. They will enjoy the "freedom to choose" now deprived them. A few days ago, Mr. Chairman, Poland's military authorities announced the release from jail of Lech Walesa, leader of Solidarity. We are immensely pleased for him, his wife and children. That release has been long overdue for humanitarian as well as Helsinki reasons. We hope this move will be followed by the release of the other leaders, members and advisors of Solidarity now in confinement; and that this will lead to a renewed dialogue between the Government, Solidarity and the Church. Mr. Walesa was imprisoned for eleven months, the last seven reportedly in virtual solitary confinement. His crime was that he sought to achieve rights for workers by organizing a free trade union. A state, which calls itself a workers' state, renounced its right to the dignity of that name by punishing him and then recently declaring Solidarity to be illegal:

The Solidarity trade union movement has become the symbol of the aspirations of the Polish people. Among the first items of Solidarity's program was the request that the text of the Helsinki Final Act be printed in the Polish press. The decision by the Polish military authorities to destroy Solidarity is a blow to the very essence of the Act, is in violation of ILO Conventions 87, 98 and 105; and in human terms represents a declaration of war by the military against the working men and women of Poland.

Pope John Paul II assailed this massive act of repression by declaring that it "violates the basic rights of man and society"(October 10, 1982). Archbishop Jozef Glemp sadly stated that the Polish military authorities were "embittering the nation" by their "trampling of man," their "disrespect for man's dignity." He prayed for the day that his country could be "free...from such evil."

The spirit of the Polish people cannot be kept behind bars. There is no permanence in a system imposed by the tips of bayonets.

The Polish delegate referred to what he termed my country's "nostalgic yearning." It is not nostalgic. It is a practical yearning for peace and freedom and individual human dignity for all peoples. That is the guiding principle of the American people and their freely elected government. That is the guiding principle of the Helsinki Final Act.

Mr. Chairman, there is no more urgent requirement on our human agenda than the achievement of real peace among us. The task of harmonizing the differing interests and the differing philosophies represented at this meeting is not an easy one. There are no quick short-cuts; it takes hard work and patience on all sides. It also requires determination. This Madrid meeting provides us the forum in which to exercise that patience, in which to express our concerns, in which to exchange views; in which to discuss our differences and our agreements. The United States is committed to the CSCE objective of peace, security and human dignity. We are prepared to dedicate ourselves to that task by giving it the hard work and the patience that will be required for our objectives to be realized. We are prepared to welcome tangible indications that others will join us in that noble task.

November 24, 1982 Words Require Deeds

I believe that the previous interventions this morning have been helpful in serving to clarify some of the issues that we face at our meeting. But, I must emphasize to our Hungarian colleague that if we are to make progress here, there must be full understanding that the amendments submitted by the Western countries are not a "pretext." It is essential that the seriousness and bonafide nature of the Western proposals be appreciated if we are to find constructive solutions to the serious problems we face here.

In essence, it must be recognized that there are many delegations here, including our own, who believe that there must be an organic connection between words and deeds. Words are suspect if deeds run contrary to them. This is a logical view and if some delegations are skeptical of it, I am at a loss to understand their skepticism. Indeed, we have here the essence of the difficult problem that faces us at this meeting and has been with us for two years.

I listened attentively to the statement made by the Soviet delegate yesterday, in response to a statement made by our delegation. I was struck by the fact that he emphasized the compromise nature of the Helsinki Final Act. This is important. We agree. But it must be understood that in our view the essence of the compromise arrived at in 1975 will be destroyed if states here choose only selectively to abide by the commitments made and feel free to disregard other commitments made by them which are of particular importance to that compromise.

When we complain, as we have for two years, about Afghanistan, we are told that there was no invasion because Soviet troops were invited by the Afghan authorities. When we talk, as we have since last December, about the Soviet military pressure on Poland, we are told that the Soviets had no role. When we discuss blatant human rights violations, we are told that we are interfering in their internal affairs. In effect, we are told to disregard the very essense of the compromise arrived at in 1975. States must understand that this is not and will not be acceptable to us; and is no basis for reaching an agreement.

The issue of the non-use of force and our Helsinki humanitarian commitments are all issues that are basic to our interests. They are integral parts of the Helsinki compromise of 1975. We insist that these concerns of ours be dealt with around this table. We cannot accept the notion that a pattern of defiant behavior contrary to the provisions of the Accords is consistent with the notion of "détente" or with the letter and spirit of the Helsinki Final Act. It would be a disservice to the objective that we seek if we were to condone or disregard those actions of defiance or in any way make them accepted or acceptable parts of international life.

The amendments introduced by the Western countries to RM-39 are designed to make absolutely certain that we do not in any way unwittingly condone the irresponsibility implicit in these actions. Nor do we want our position to be interpreted as condoning irresponsible behavior that is contrary to the standards of the Helsinki Final Act. It is important that this body understand that we view such behavior as a serious matter.

We and many delegations here have been making this statement continually for two years or more. It obviously must be repeated. The proposed Western amendments must be viewed in this context.

We opened this meeting on November 9. On that day many people in my country, many in other countries around the world, and many people in the Soviet Union, marked the sixth anniversary of the founding of the Ukrainian Helsinki Monitoring Group. Out of 30 members of that group, 27 commemorated that occasion behind prison bars. RM-39 was introduced in December of last year. Since then, three of these 27 members of that Helsinki monitor group, Yuri Lytvyn and Petro and Vasyl Sychko—a father and son—were sentenced to labor camp and internal exile. This treatment demonstrates vividly the necessity for the language found in Paragraph 2 of RM-39.

In the Final Act, we agreed to deal "in a positive and humanitarian spirit" with the requests of our citizens to be reunited or to visit with relatives in other countries. We all pledged to make extra efforts in cases involving elderly or ill persons. Yet, Francesca Yanson, the 74-year-old cancer-ridden mother of a United States citizen, continues to be denied permission by Soviet authorities to join her son.

Seven years ago, the participating states agreed that applicants for family reunification would not be subject to recriminations. Yet, Feliks Kochubievsky, a Jewish refusenik and activist from Novosibirsk, who, together with his wife, has been trying since 1978 to secure emigration approval to join their two sons and his sister in Israel, were arrested on September 10 and charged with defaming the Soviet state.

In Basket III, we agreed to promote tourism and agreed to facilitate freer movement and contacts. Yet, just four weeks ago, a train traveling from Kiev to Bucharest was stopped at the Soviet border. There were eleven American tourists on that train. All eleven were hauled off the train, stripped, searched, and all their possessions — including bandaids and dental floss — were closely scrutinized. They asked why they were being singled out, out of all the passengers on that train, for such mistreatment. A Soviet border guard answered that it was because tensions between the U.S. and the USSR were increasing.

It must be understood that such incidents, multiplied by the hundreds and thousands, including one involving the wife of an American Congressman visiting the Soviet Union with her husband, continue to exacerbate relations between our states at this meeting. They lead to our conclusion that the words of the Helsinki Final Act are not consistent with the deeds of the Soviet Union and other delegations here. It is the strong view of many delegations around the table that the words to which we agree must be consonant with our actions. I urge all the delegates around the table to understand that we have serious, bonafide criticisms that will not be swept under the table by more rhetoric and empty words. Where old words are disregarded we question whether we should believe any new promises.

I was pleased to hear Ambassador Van Dongen (Netherlands) on the need to see new positive actions consistent with promises in order to give delegations that confidence. It makes sense to spend time elucidating our position. Otherwise, we have done serious damage to the Act that brings us here.

November 24, 1982 "Internal Affairs"—Right of Reply

I have asked for the floor again to assure [Soviet] Vice-Minister [Anatoli] Kovalev that I have respect for him personally. That is not the issue. I don't want any of my comments to be interpreted as other than a serious attempt to solve the problems of this meeting. We respect opposing views. He is an eloquent spokesman for his cause. He has a poor case, but he does well with it.

But that is not the issue before us. I don't think it is helpful to define "businesslike" in the manner suggested by the Soviet delegate. What we do must correspond to what we say. It is indeed "businesslike" when we pay serious attention to violations of "détente" by the Soviet Union, and when we try to explain why our amendments are necessary to preserve the integrity of the Act. That is "businesslike."

The real issue has been defined today. It is the Soviet view that discussion of our humanitarian interests is an interference in their internal affairs. That is unacceptable to us. Here is the essence of the problem. We do not believe that we interfere when we comment on compliance and judge behavior against the standards of the Act. We will continue to verbalize and discuss our position and we will continue to negotiate for acceptance of our position.

The Soviet delegate used the word "incorrect" as it was translated to me. If anything I have said at this meeting is factually incorrect, I will be pleased to be informed factually and will then be pleased in this body to acknowledge that error, if it exists. I have made that offer before and no such errors have been disclosed to me.

Ambassador Kovalev said he does not discuss Lebanon here. I do not think the subject of Lebanon is relevant, but I would be delighted to talk about Lebanon if the issue is of concern to the Soviet delegation in this format.

In regard to the subject of missiles raised by Mr. Kovalev, we have talked about the missiles on many occasions during these past two years. I would be pleased to send Mr. Kovalev the text of comments I have made here on missiles, on the SS-20's, on disarmament and arms control. We believe that such discussions are relevant and we are prepared to discuss them now as we have in the past.

Delegations at these meetings, including the Soviet delegation, have raised questions at these meetings about our compliance with the Helsinki Accords. We have attempted to respond to the specific questions raised. We have never refused to discuss these and similar issues on the ground that they constitute an interference in our internal affairs.

November 30, 1982 Soviet Behavior

At the outset I would like to welcome the participation today of a new member [Igor Andropov, son of Chairman Andropov] of the Soviet Delegation who presented his government's case in a clear and precise manner. The process of direct exchange is helpful to each of us in our efforts to achieve understanding between us. The subsequent contribution of the head of the French delegation very appropriately put the issue before us in its proper context. He said that it is vital at these meetings that we know what it is that each of us considers important if we are to achieve understanding between us. The Soviet contribution makes it clear what is important to that delegation, but we see in the interventions of these recent weeks by the Soviet delegation that they fail to take into account that which is important to other states. We see this Eastern failure over and over again.

The Soviet representative today referred to our different social systems. Those differences are crucial and create problems for us here in Madrid, but their existence is what makes dialogue here indispensible as well. For an understanding of our system, it must be appreciated that public opinion plays a vital role in a democracy.

The intervention of the French delegate brings to mind in that connection an article which I read last night on my flight to Madrid which explains the basis of our concerns at this meeting. I shall read from an English translation of an editorial in the French newspaper *Le Monde* which was published on the eve (November 10) of the opening of our meeting:

> The unreality of the exercise which the representatives of the 35 East and West European and North American governments are resuming in Madrid ...will spark off a great deal of sarcasm. It requires a large dose of unawareness or cynicism to aspire seriously to discuss respect for human rights, "confidence-building measures" and disarmament...when the Red Army's battle against the Afghan resistance is dragging on, when the military dictatorship in Poland is becoming more oppressive, when nuclear modernization programs are in full swing and when Anatoly Shcharansky—one well known name among many unknown people—guilty only of demanding that his government honor its Helsinki Act pledges, is rotting in Soviet prison.

It is essential that other delegations here understand the deep feeling about Soviet behavior which exists among many governments and peoples represented here. We hope to reach the stage where we can see the Soviets address themselves to these concerns of ours in a constructive manner. When we reach that point, we will be on the road to progress towards a substantive and positive agreement on a concluding document.

December 3, 1982 Escalating Repression

A few days ago, I read the English translation of a commentary on our CSCE meeting which appeared on October 27 in the Moscow *Komsomolskaya Pravda*. The theme of the article was reflected in the question: "How to stop the world's slide toward a nuclear catastrophe...and to secure changes for the better in the general climate of international relations?"

Putting aside the expected automatic condemnation of the United States as the devil and the equally unbelievable description of the Soviet Union as the paragon of virtue and excellence, it is clear that the question raised concerns all of us. It is of paramount importance to my government.

We agree that in "the present complex and dangerous situation, any kind of talks, contacts or dialogue between states relating to the most important issues...assumes special importance." That is why the United States has been here in Madrid, is here in Madrid, and has every intention to remain at these meetings so long as they last. The continued assertion of the Soviet press that my government does not want a successful completion of this meeting and would prefer to "wreck" it is not true.

The article complains of our "grating, bogus arguments about 'human rights.'" The words "human rights" are in quotation marks as if to question the legitimacy of the concept. The article also rather harshly protests our objections to the invasion of Afghanistan by Soviet troops, an invasion which earlier this week was overwhelmingly condemned by a vote of 114-21 at the U.N. General Assembly.

I respectfully suggest that castigating our position will not alter it or prevent it being repeated here. Only a constructive response will make the issues disappear at this meeting. The emphasis in the article is on the proposed Conference on Confidence and Security-Building Measures and Disarmament In Europe. In spite of what is written, I hasten to assure the Soviet delegation that they should not believe everything they read in their press. The United States has favored and continues to favor such a conference and very much hopes that a decision to hold such a conference, under an agreed upon specific mandate, will be made in Madrid as part of a balanced result from this meeting.

There are many reasons why we favor such a conference, the most important of which is our dedication to peace and freedom. The United States is now actively engaged in many disarmament forums, but a special virtue of the conference proposed by the French delegation at this delegation meeting is that all 35 states will participate as sovereign equals in the search for security. Large or small, every state represented here has a right to deal effectively with decisions of life and death that affect its citizens.

The United States also supports the idea of such a conference because we feel there is an urgent need to deal with the threat of surprise military attack. The confidence building measures to be formulated at this conference are specifically designed to minimize that threat.

It is no secret that my Government believes there is a serious threat to peace and security in Europe from what we perceive to be Soviet imperialism. We would like to be persuaded that our perception is wrong. Imperialist policies by any state are totally outmoded in this age. That is why we so frequently emphasize the need for compliance with the standards of civilized international behavior, including its humanitarian component, established by the Helsinki Final Act.

The policy of the United States is to work for peace, real peace, based on the relaxation of tensions. We seek mutually accepted and verifiable reduction of arms, both nuclear and conventional, that will lead to disarmament. We seek a peace that does not represent an advantage of one country or system over another. We do not seek military superiority; it is unattainable. We know that a nuclear war cannot be "won." Our purpose is to prevent and deter all wars.

What we look for and still do not find is a reciprocal and equally bonafide search for these goals. The traditional Soviet advocacy of "class war" and "wars of national liberation" is incompatible with this search for peace; and we fervently look to the time when we can have confidence that this outmoded ideology has been abandoned once and for all. There is one further thought in the Moscow article that calls for comment at this point. I quote: "There is practically no country taking part in the Madrid Meeting in which tens and hundreds of thousands of members of the anti-war movement have not made their views known — and in a very resolute form — in recent months."

My government believes that a dedication to peace is the mark of a civilized human being and a civilized society. The movement for peace in the West is an accurate reflection of the values that motivate our governments. Our peace movements function non-violently and are free of government restraint. This is regrettably in stark contrast to the manner in which their counterparts are treated in the Soviet Union. There, activists for peace, just as activists for human rights, are treated as anti-Soviet agitators and imprisoned.

In recent weeks Oleg Radzinsky, a 24-year-old member of a peace group calling itself "Group of Trust," a former literature student at Moscow University, was arrested by the Soviet police. One of his predecessors had been sent to a mental institution for his peace activities. Within the last week, the official Soviet news agency TASS described the independent peace activists as renegades and criminals. It is not surprising that many of us are skeptical of Soviet intentions.

The United States is committed to peace with liberty; we believe that military confidence-building measures can help establish conditions favorable for that peace. The essence of the Helsinki accords is the premise that real security and peace in Europe require the building of confidence, political as well as military confidence. When that confidence is undermined and we candidly express our reasons for it, measures to restore that confidence are called for.

We are profoundly disappointed that a number of states who urge us to be "businesslike" at these meetings are at the same time actively engaging in actions that undermine the Helsinki Final Act. The essence of our problem in Madrid is that many of us doubt the political will of some states here to comply with commitments they made at Helsinki. That lack of confidence cannot be ignored or distorted if we are to achieve the understanding that it is our duty to seek.

We are urged by some states to put aside this kind of candid talk at this time. After all, we are reminded, we did that in November and December of 1980. But, in the two years since that time, there has been no constructive response to our expressions; and the activities that undermine our confidence continue with intensity. It remains a sad puzzle to many of us, Mr. Chairman, why an impressive country like the Soviet Union, strong, powerful, ambitious to prevail, and eager to leave its mark on contemporary history, which rules great peoples with noble traditions, why that society should condemn itself in the eyes of the world by deliberately identifying itself with the brutal side of human history.

Is it really necessary to the security interests of that important state to threaten with arrest and imprisonment a 75-year-old grandmother (Sofia Kalistratova) suffering from a serious heart ailment because she is a member of the Moscow Helsinki Group? What does it prove when it compels the three members of that group remaining at liberty to cease their activities? Nobody doubts the power of a police state, willing to punish with ruthless determination, to assert itself over a handful of individuals. But is this the way it desires to be recorded in history?

There has apparently been a determined effort by Soviet authorities to escalate its campaign of repression against dissidents and potential dissidents within its borders. Police have been sent throughout the country warning Soviet citizens to cease all unofficial contacts with the West. Dr. Andrei Sakharov remains isolated from his family and friends, his personal memoirs taken from him, including a manuscript that he worked on for four and one-half years. Does the Soviet Union feel so insecure and uncertain of its position with its own people that it is required to engage in this kind of cruel and petty harassment?

For eleven years, a distinguished Soviet scientist has been trying to emigrate to join his daughter in Israel. He has been coerced into cutting off all contacts with Western tourists, journalists and diplomats. Why? How does that country demonstrate its greatness by this obvious repression?

Soviet spouses of American citizens — like Yuri Balovlenkov, married to a nurse in Baltimore and the father of a two-year-old girl — are unable to emigrate and join their families and a number of them were forced to undertake life-risking hunger strikes in an effort to attain recognition of their plight. Another of these men, Sergei Petrov, a 29-year-old photographer, explained his stand after 51 days of starvation: "...I have no job, and they will not give me one. They deny me the right to express myself through my work, and they deny me the right to seek a future elsewhere. Above all, they deny me the right to live with the woman I love, and to have a family." What threat does fulfillment of these simple human hopes pose to Soviet society? He says: "I am not a dissident." How can the world-wide publication of this story and the distribution of photographs of these emaciated young people be in the interest of the Soviet Union? What benefit is there to the USSR in advertising this kind of meanness?

I have already referred to the arrests of the organizers of an independent peace group. How can a society engaged in a campaign to persuade the rest of us that it believes in peace not recognize that its words appear to be hypocritical in the light of these arrests of pacifists in their society?

There are many millions of devout Christians, all over the world. Can they be anything else but angry and resentful at the Government responsible for the persecution of their fellow Christians, Catholics, Eastern Rite Catholics, Russian Orthodox, Seventh-Day Adventists, Evangelical Baptists, Pentecostals, Jehovah's Witnesses and others? Can they be anything but appalled when they learn that a Reform Baptist Pastor, Ivan Antonov, was arrested for the fifth time six months ago by Soviet authorities, after having already served a total of 18 years in prison for following the dictates of his religious conscience? His son, Pavel, and son-in-law have also been arrested. There are at least 154 known Reform Baptists now in jail, suffering for their religious beliefs. What must their fellow Christians in freedom think of a society which sentenced Pyotr Rumachik, Vice-President of the Soviet Council of Evangelical Baptist Churches, to a four year prison term and then for more than a year has prevented family visits to this seriously ill man?

And, Mr. Chairman, I must again raise the case of Anatoly Shcharansky, now possibly in his 67th day of a hunger strike. He was tried, convicted and remains in jail on the charge of being an American spy, but his real crime is that he was a Helsinki monitor and an activist in support of Jewish emigration. Prison authorities may keep Mr. Shcharansky's body alive by forcibly feeding him, but the decision to imprison him and frustrate his deep desire to emigrate to Israel also keeps his name alive as a symbol of man's striving for human dignity in the face of an oppressive state. How can that be helpful to the Soviet Union?

This man, savagely persecuted by the Soviet authorities, has not been permitted to see his mother or receive any mail for almost a year. Cannot the authorities see that they thereby pollute the atmosphere for rational and constructive international discourse and agreement? What is achieved by this brutality?

It is easy to respond to these questions I have raised by virtually ignoring them and asserting that they are an unwarranted interference in the internal affairs of another state. Such a response, which we have heard, is unfortunate. Our expressions are not acts of interference. We do not interfere when we point to events and accurately describe them as barriers to mutual confidence and the strenghtening of the Helsinki process.

The United States is convinced that significant steps taken to respect the concerns felt by many delegations here will help this meeting's move to a successful conclusion. We remain prepared to sit down with our co-signatories in an effort to find some constructive way in which our mutual goals might be brought closer to realization. We have been impelled to criticize, but we would much rather find a basis for further understanding, agreement and joint effort in the search for peace and security.

My country is a young one by European standards. Our Government, however, is an old and well-established one by modern standards. I trust this will permit me to refer, with due respect to all states here, to our founding document, our Declaration of Independence of 1776. Our fathers in that document began by affirming that we owe "a decent respect to the opinions of mankind."

This has proved to be wise counsel. It is all the more necessary in our modern world. No country can expect that its actions will be free of scrutiny by others, whether the actions be toward its own citizens or toward others. My own country, throughout our history, has been aware of this reality. It has contributed to our strength.

Let me assure every delegation here that we do not seek to remake others in our own image. We have problems and inadequacies of our own which have our attention. We do not seek to undermine the security of any other state. What we do seek, emphatically seek, are ways to remove the basic suspicions, tensions and hostilities that often arise between us. It is not easy for differing social systems to attempt to relate to one another. But the task must be undertaken. The pursuit of peace, cooperation and security demands it.

Our delegation will patiently pursue that difficult task of understanding and reconcilation. We know we will be joined in the effort by others. The goal of peace requires and deserves the patient and relentless energy that we are giving it. We trust that Madrid will open the door for us and point the way toward that goal of peace with freedom.

December 10, 1982 Human Rights Day

* * *

I urge that we never lose sight of the fact that overwhelming numbers of our citizens have taken our speeches and declarations to heart. They take us at our word; and have a right to do so. Many proceeded to act on what was perceived to be the promises we made in 1975 and in 1948 on behalf of our governments. But those who believed the declarations and acted upon them not only found disappointment and frustration, but too often they met tragedy. Many who attempted to exercise, in certain countries, rights they believed had been assured them by international agreement learned to their misfortune that they did so to their extreme peril. Our delegation believes that all of us who participated in the drafting of those agreements have a responsibility to those men and women who have been forced to suffer by reason of their faith in the words we wrote.

Many of these persons have had their names mentioned at our meetings. Many more names could be added; and there is always the temptation to do so to assure them that they are not forgotten. This morning, I wish only to mention the name of one other, a Byelorussian, Mikhail Kukobaka, who, during our recess last July, received a three-year sentence to a labor camp. He had already spent a majority of his adult years in forced psychiatric confinement and labor camp. Among the reasons for the charge of "anti-Soviet slander" brought against him was an article he wrote entitled "Détente and Human Rights are Inseparable."

Mr. Chairman, the men and women who have been punished because they believed they were assured the exercise of their rights by the Universal Declaration of Ruman Rights and the Helsinki Final Act are inextricably linked to the Helsinki process. They will be as much a part of its history as the concluding document of our Madrid meeting.

The Helsinki Final Act gave us a sound body of principles and provisions from which to build a healthy relationship. The language of our concluding document from Madrid will, we hope, give it added strength and sinew. At the same time, the people of participating States who have paid a price for sharing our aspirations also contribute, and in a most important way, to its heart and soul.

Today, on Human Rights Day, therefore, our delegation salutes the many extraordinary individuals who, at great personal sacrifice, continue to make lasting contributions to the realization of the ideals of the Helsinki Final Act.

December 10, 1982 Right of Reply

I was disappointed in the response of the Soviet delegate to our comments a few minutes ago about the declaration on human rights that his authorities signed in 1948. Although, as I consider it, we have here another agreement signed by the Soviet Union which they have blatantly disregarded. That may explain the delegate's unhappiness with my comments.

It would normally not be my purpose to respond to this attack on my Government, were it not for the fact that one of the delegate's comments was an outright lie. It is important, Mr. Chairman, that I correct that lie.

The delegate said that the United States, in the early days of this meeting, spoke out against the Conference on Security and Confidence-Building Measures. That is not so. The United States was a co-sponsor of the French proposal and has supported it throughout this meeting. At no time have we expressed opposition to the idea of having a meaningful conference to deal with surprise military attack, which would be the subject matter of the French proposal.

I will not dignify by reasonable comment the rest of what I consider to be the outrageous comments of the Soviet delegate, other than to note his criticism of the military policy of the United States, a strange criticism indeed from the Soviet Union which now has 333 SS-20's within its borders carrying 999 warheads with every city in Europe within its aim.

February 10, 1983 Remembering Yuri Orlov

Six years ago today, Dr. Yuri Orlov, a distinguished physicist and dedicated humanitarian, was arrested by Soviet authorities. He remains in strict regimen labor camp where he is forced to engage in harsh labor under cruel conditions.

His health has been endangered as a result of being frequently placed in solitary confinement and in a special punishment jail where he is deprived of adequate food, sleep and protection against the cold.

He is isolated from his wife and family, denied formal prisoner visitation rights and cut off from correspondence. His wife has been denied the opportunity to see him or talk to him since August, 1979—three and one-half long years.

Why is this giant of a human being punished so vindictively, harassed and physically beaten by hoodlums in jail?

It is because he believed in 1975 that his country, the Soviet Union, intended to live up to the Helsinki Final Act which its leader signed. He, therefore, founded the Moscow Helsinki Monitoring Group.

The agreement which his country signed said that citizens in each country could do what Dr. Orlov decided to do. His government in signing the Helsinki Final Act undertook to respect the human rights of its citizens. It turned out to be all a lie. And this courageous man of science, this humanitarian, who has so much to give to the world has been treated worse than a common criminal by a cynical and brutal system.

Yuri Orlov is not forgotten by men and women all over the world who believe in human dignity. He is not forgotten in Madrid where delegates from Western Europe, the United States and Canada are insisting that the human rights provisions of the Helsinki agreement must be lived up to by the Soviet Union if we are to believe other promises they make to us.

We will not forget and we will not stop our efforts until Yuri Orlov and Anatoly Shcharansky and the other members of the Moscow, Ukrainian, Lithuanian, Georgian and the Armenian Monitors now imprisoned are free — not until the members of the Charter '77 Group of Czechoslovakia now in jail are free — not until the members of the Polish Committee for Social Self-Defense (KOR) are free.

Only when these men and women of conscience are free can we all be assured that the peace and security promised us by the Helsinki Final Act can be achieved.

That is a task which the American delegation today rededicates itself to fulfill.

March 8, 1983 Issues to be Faced

Yesterday as we entered the fifth week of our current session, we heard a series of lucid assessments of where we stand in our negotiations. We respect those comments by our indispensable coordinators and believe it is now appropriate for our delegation to make some observations of our own.

There is growing sentiment at this meeting to produce a substantive concluding document, as part of a balanced result, prior to the onset of the Easter holidays. The American Delegation believes that it is possible for us to achieve that goal and we are prepared to assist in that direction, although we reiterate that an inability to reach that goal in timely fashion will not discourage us. We agree with the delegate from Finland who asserted yesterday that "time cannot be the decisive factor."

Differences in philosophy and values among us remain deep and are deeply held. Immense patience is required to overcome them. Our own delegation would like to see the Madrid meeting identified in history as an important beginning on the road back to peace, security, cooperation and understanding among us. But we all appreciate that delegations here will not set aside their basic values and their national interests in order to meet deadlines; and we have learned the hard, regrettable fact that written agreements by themselves do not produce "détente." What is required, as the delegate from Cyprus said, is "not only words but deeds as well." There has been discernible forward movement in our negotiations. A few of our difficulties have been narrowed and, in some cases, textually resolved. We agree with the statement of the Romanian Delegate that results here are "still modest." Other vital issues still remain unresolved. We will continue to discuss them. They are important to us.

• Our delegation feels that our concluding document should reflect provisions on freedom of religion to ensure the freedom to profess and practice that go beyond our tentative understandings.

- We believe that the jamming of Western radio broadcasts interferes with the spirit of "mutual understanding" which is a premise of the Helsinki Final Act.
- The right of working men and women freely to join and work through free trade unions of their own choosing should be asserted in our document.
- Our delegation, furthermore, cannot ignore the fact that men and women who believed in the Helsinki Final Act and its promise and acted upon that belief have been put in prison just for that reason. There are today 51 men and women, known as Helsinki monitors, in Soviet jails, labor camps, psychiatric hospitals and in internal exile. On this issue, the integrity of this meeting and of the Helsinki process is at stake.
- We believe that journalists should have access to their sources and protection against arbitrary expulsions. These questions are still open ones in our deliberations.
- And we do not understand why there is opposition to an experts' meeting on human contacts. It is essential that East and West explore ways of harmonizing and coming together on important issues that create tensions between us. The issue of human contacts and family reunification is one such irritant. We should find the means, through a meeting of experts, to help reduce the misunderstandings that surround this issue, so that when we return to the next follow-up meeting, we can do so already agreed on an approach to which we can all reassert our commitment. We believe such a constructive and professional dialogue would strengthen our process.
- In the security area, we still differ on the vital definition of the zone in which the security- and confidence-building measures should be applied.
- It should also not be surprising if our delegation and others believe that an absence of reference to the presence of our Ministers at this Meeting is in effect an act of disrespect to them. We do not believe that an insistence on such disrespect is helpful to our negotiation.

Mr. Chairman, in a bona fide negotiation there is room for flexibility. The American Delegation realizes that reality and we respect it. Such a negotiation, however, requires an appropriate atmosphere to inculcate a feeling of mutual confidence. It requires an awareness that there is a joint commitment to the integrity of the process. That atmosphere, I regret to say, is not yet evident to the American Delegation.

In an effort to expedite that spirit of negotiation, our delegation has not taken the floor at a Plenary Session since our opening day a month ago. It is, however, time for serious talk if we are to achieve the understanding so essential for agreement. Our chief concern is with developments outside of this meeting which continue to cast a shadow on our deliberations.

We have been disappointed at the continued defiance of the Helsinki principles by a number of states here. It saddens us, for example, to note that President Reagan, in response to a recent example of such defiance, was forced to make the following announcement last Friday:

> The Government of Romania has implemented a decree requiring any Romanian citizen wishing to emigrate to repay in convertible currency the costs of education received beyond the compulsory level. This decree conflicts with the letter and spirit of Section 402 of the Trade Act of 1974, which is intended to remove barriers to freedom of emigration. I therefore, declare my intention to terminate Romania's most-favored nation tariff status and other benefits effective June 30, 1983, if the education repayment decree remains in force on that date.

We are now, Mr. Chairman, in the third year of our Madrid meeting. During that time our delegation has seen no significant tangible movement to begin meeting the often-expressed view of many delegations here that developments outside of the meeting cast a dark shadow on our deliberations. We rather have seen and noted here a pattern of government action by some States which has appeared to us to reflect disdain for the Act and our Helsinki spirit.

● Political arrests in the Soviet Union continue to increase. A total of about 500 Soviet citizens have been arrested and convicted as political and religious prisoners since our meeting began.

● Last week, two human rights activists were given 12-year maximum terms: one, Valery Senderov, a 37-year-old mathematician, was imprisoned for wanting to organize a trade union and for writing a report on discrimination against Jews at Moscow State University; and another, a 29-year-old Ukrainian poet and physicist, Irina Ratushinskaya, for writing poetry that displeased the Soviet authorities.

● Jewish and other emigration has come to a virtual halt. In January, only 81 Jews were allowed by Soviet authorities to emigrate, a shamefully pitiful figure. Soviet citizens remain unable to unite with their spouses and children and families living in other lands, a direct disregard of the Act.

● There are still 110,000 Soviet troops in Afghanistan, where they have invaded a sovereign State and subjugate a proud and independent people.

● Too many of the effects of martial law continue to remain in Poland, even with its suspension, although we welcome even the small steps already taken. Solidarity, the free trade union of the Polish people, remains outlawed, and the harassment of its leaders and followers continues unabated.

● I have also noted continued personal attacks against me as my country's spokesman, designed to pollute rather than improve the negotiating atmosphere at this meeting. One of the most recent of these appeared on February 16 in the pages of the Soviet weekly, *Literary Gazette*. There, Vitaliy Kobysh, a prominent member of the staff of the International Information Department of the Central Committee of the Communist Party of the Soviet Union, characterized my concern for "human rights violations" as "buffoonery."

Mr. Chairman, the views we have expressed are legitimate concerns based on clear standards established by the Helsinki Final Act. The use of inept sarcasm and personal abuse does not alter their validity. I respectfully suggest that understanding among us would be better served by an effort to respect and understand one another's views. It is thus no wonder that large segments of our peoples question the wisdom and utility of new promises and new agreements when the old ones continue to be ignored.

We will here and elsewhere continue to express our views on the need for all the participating States to live up to the obligations assumed when we signed the Helsinki Final Act of 1975. When we believe that the Act is being violated or ignored or treated with disdain or neglect, we will continue to say so.

Mr. Chairman it is not too late. There is time. We speak as we do today because the issues we raise are dominant ones in this negotiation and act as barriers to the agreement most of us seek at Madrid. We do so in the hope that our views will be seriously noted. We could then proceed together to help restore the spirit of Helsinki and the spirit of "détente" and peace that our citizens deserve.

I realize that the response to this statement will probably be a charge of "confrontation" and Cold War. I suggest that it is not our reluctant comments which create confrontation. Our comments only describe it. It is the violence we note which creates the spirit of confrontation.

The distinguished and internationally respected Hungarian-born political man of letters and ideas, Arthur Koestler, died last week after a long illness. It is fitting that I close this plea with a sentence from one of his writings. "I plead guilty," he said, "to having placed the idea of man above the idea of mankind." It is the view of our delegation, Mr. Chairman, that only with this emphasis on the rights of man can the welfare of mankind be realized. That is the formula for peace.

March 11, 1983 Women as Victims

This week, International Women's Day was commemorated all over the world. It is fitting that we here in Madrid, well into the third year of our meetings seeking understanding under the Helsinki Final Act, take particular note of some of the extraordinary women of courage whose activities have clearly been felt in our deliberations.

The inhumane treatment by Soviet authorities of their country's citizens who have sought to instill the Helsinki spirit into that society knows no distinctions as to sex. Of the fifty-one Helsinki monitors arrested and sent by Soviet authorities to prisons, labor camps and internal exile, seven are women. The American Delegation wishes to honor them and others associated with them by publicly noting a number of their names so that they might be known and honored by others as well.

Oksana Meshko, a Ukrainian Helsinki Monitor, was sentenced in 1981, at age seventy-five and a diabetic suffering from hypertension, to six months labor camp and five years of internal exile.

Oksana Popovych, fifty-eight years old and an officially declared invalid, was consigned to a strict regimen labor camp, where she arrived on crutches in 1975 for anti-Soviet agitation and propaganda. She joined the Helsinki Monitoring Group while serving her seven-year term at hard labor and currently is in very frail health in internal exile.

Tatiana Velikanova, a long-time human rights activist, was sentenced in August 1980 to nine years of labor camp and exile.

Irina Grivnina, a member of the Working Commission on Psychiatric Abuse, affiliated with the Moscow Helsinki Monitoring Group, serving out a five-year term of internal exile under difficult conditions, is now six months pregnant, cruelly pressured to have an abortion and is required to perform heavy work at a construction site.

Raisa Rudenko, wife of Ukrainian Helsinki Monitor Mykola Rudenko, and Olha Heyko, married to Ukrainian Group Member Mykola Matusevych, watched as their husbands were dispatched to the camps. Subsequently, they were condemned to the same fate for speaking out in their behalf and for continuing their monitoring activity.

Three months ago Moscow Group Member Tatyana Osipova declared a hunger strike to protest the fact that she had not been permitted to communicate with her husband, prisoner of conscience Ivan Kovalev. There is serious concern for her health.

Galina Vilchinskaya, a twenty-four-year-old Baptist, was arrested for her religious beliefs and activities in November 1982 and is in pre-trial detention. She had been freed only three months earlier upon completion of a three-year labor camp term for having taught children's Bible classes.

Annasoltan Kekilova, a Turkmen, and Irina Ratushinskaya from Ukraine, follow a long and sad tradition of poets who have suffered at the hands of the Soviet Government because their verse pierces the conscience and touches the heart, revealing dark truths about Soviet society and human nature. Kekilova has been in psychiatric confinement for over a decade. Ratushinskaya was sentenced only a week ago to seven years labor camp to be followed by five years of internal exile. It is the harshest known sentence handed down to a woman prisoner of conscience in recent memory.

These women acted in defense of freedom and in doing so have lost their own. Now, they are enduring the rigors of punishment. The American Delegation salutes each of them for the immense contribution they have made to the process which will one day make the Helsinki Final Act a relevant and meaningful contributor to the achievement of peace for all of us.

March 14, 1983 Karl Marx—Anniversary

On March 14, 1883, a hundred years ago today, Karl Marx, 65 years of age, died at his home in a London suburb. Without analyzing the teachings of this historically important philosopher and social critic, it is significant to note that toward the end of his life, tired of the intense controversies carried out in his name, Marx told a French follower: "Mais moi, je ne suis pas Marxist'— "But, I am not a Marxist."

The passing of time has permitted history to highlight a number of ironies as we consider the aspirations of this social reformer:

1. The prediction of Marx that, as countries become more Communist, "the hostility of one nation to another will come to an end" is sharply contrasted by the fact that we are today witnessing intense rivalries and hostilities among Communist states.

2. Imperialism, far from being the last stage of capitalism, turns out to be the current dominant state of Communism.

3. Marx's assertion that the working classes would be the grave diggers of capitalism, producing a reign of Communism, has in itself been buried by the facts of history. We have seen uprisings by working men and women seeking dignity and free trade unions. These movements have been destroyed by forces in Communist societies.

4. Indeed, a totally unforeseen characteristic of contemporary Communism, as practiced by the Soviet Union, has been the use of military and secret police power by Communist countries to repress the rights of workers: 30 years ago in East Germany; Hungary in 1956; Czechoslovakia in 1968; and on three occasions in Poland.

A further irony is the ambiguously negative accomplishments of modern Communism, as we have seen it in Eastern Europe.

The Soviet Union has demonstrated an ability to produce large armies and armaments but it has done so at the price of meager rations for its people, shoddy consumer goods, and substandard housing. The standard of living for its people is below that of more than 30 other European nations. Its people have paid the price of deteriorating health conditions, with life expectancy lower than in any other European nation and with infant mortality rates now probably three times as high as in the United States and Western Europe; and all of this has been at the further price of subverting the human ingredient which was so essential in Marx's analysis and vision. It is reliably estimated that more than 4 million forced laborers live in approximately 1,100 forced labor camps. More than 10,000 of these are considered to be political and religious prisoners.

Finally, the Communist states of Eastern Europe have demonstrated an unusual ability to inspire their peoples to try to emigrate from Marxist-Leninist Communist societies to capitalist countries. The hideous Berlin Wall stands as a stark monument to this harsh reality.

Yes, Karl Marx, wherever he may be today, may well be recalling his comment of more than 100 years ago as he observes failure of the Communist societies who claim to be the inheritors of his teachings. He may still be saying, 65 years after the Russian Revolution, "But, I am not a Marxist."

March 25, 1983 Report from Solidarity

Before the Madrid meeting recesses today, I would like to acknowledge a remarkable and timely contribution to the aims of the Helsinki Final Act. The U.S. delegation recently has been presented with a detailed report, which was prepared by members of the Helsinki Watch Group in Poland at the request of the Temporary Coordinating Commission (TKK) of Solidarity.

This exhaustive and extensive work is remarkable for a number of reasons. First, it was compiled under very difficult conditions of official repression. Its authors assumed grave personal risks to collect information from across Poland. But the report is most remarkable for its scope and content. The report's 600 pages analyze legalized and extra-legal means of repression employed in Poland before and after December 1981; it documents wide-scale rights abuses which violate Poland's domestic law as well as international law obligations; it traces the enactment of legislation designed to institutionalize the massive repression undertaken; it cites the cases of thousands of Polish citizens who have suffered severe punitive measures for attempting to know and act upon their rights.

This chronicle serves to expose to the stark light of world public opinion countless oppressive actions of the Polish regime against its own people. But the determination of Solidarity to endure and continue in their peaceful pursuit of basic democratic freedoms also shines through the pages of the report.

In the cover letter introducing the report, the authors write: "We send this report with the conviction that it will serve the cause of peace and security in Europe, for there can be no peace without social justice." The American delegation shares that conviction and that aim.

April 29, 1983 Confidence-building Deeds

Some delegates asserted that what was urgently required to strengthen the Helsinki process were confidence-building deeds. It is indeed meaningless if a State makes promises and then acts in a manner contrary to those promises. We agree that this is the surest way to undermine détente and produce conflict. The future for the CSCE can best be assured by a common decision to fulfill our commitments to the best of our ability.

Thoughtful questions were raised by one delegation that deserve a response— Madrid is not a meeting in isolation. It is an integral part of the totality of East-West relations, or it will become irrelevant to the real world. The fact that some of us emphasize deeds in no way minimizes the importance of words. Words are important because they provide a standard toward which to aspire in the struggle for a more responsible and civilized international community. Words also provide a legitimate standard against which we can judge behavior. To expect the behavior of States to be consistent with their pledges does not, furthermore, make additional pledges superfluous. It rather, in the long run, strengthens the integrity of those pledges.

That is why it saddens us to report that on the very day, April 19, that our meeting reconvened, 72-year-old Dr. Naum Meiman was again threatened, harassed and intimidated as his apartment was invaded, ransacked and searched in the pained presence of his wife. How often must this couple be abused? Dr. Meiman, one of the three members of the recently disbanded Moscow Helsinki Monitoring Group remaining at liberty, has for more than seven years been denied permission to reunite in Israel with his only daughter, even though it is 28 years since he last engaged in any classified work.

In a recent letter to me, Dr. Meiman wrote: "In this day and age," he said, "agreements are the only alternative to an apocalyptical nuclear catastrophe." But no agreement is possible without a certain level of mutual trust. Outright violations of the Final Act can hardly help establish the trust necessary. That truth is reluctantly very much in the awareness of the American delegation as we contemplate our task at this reconvened meeting.

Mr. Chairman, on Wednesday, the distinguished head of the Soviet delegation called upon all of us to show "flexibility, reasonableness and responsibility." We were pleased to hear that call. We join in it and trust that we can together work to attain the balanced and substantive results in Madrid that are so essential for the peace we seek.

May 17, 1983 Dr. Sakharov Rejected Again

The Madrid meeting continues with its slow and ponderous attention to the question of how best to preserve and extend the principles of the Helsinki Final Act in the face of continued violations of its vital and life-giving provisions by the Soviet Union. It is clear to me, after a brief absence from these sessions, that the key attention of our populations has shifted away from these day-to-day negotiating frustrations. Rather, attention is riveted on specific events which continue to disturb the hopes of so many millions of us who look to the time when international stability and responsible behavior can become a norm of our lives.

The announcement by Soviet authorities that they will refuse an exit visa to one of its respected citizens, Dr. Andrei Sakharov, is an outrage. Dr. Sakharov and his wife, Elena Bonner, one of the founders of the Moscow Helsinki Monitoring Group, are being kept prisoners within their own country by authorities who do not appreciate the strength and nobility of their characters and of their role as citizens of the world.

To stifle Dr. Sakharov's talents, to steal his scientific and personal papers, to keep him in exile and under surveillance, to isolate him from the scientific atmosphere that has nourished his life, to harass and persecute him—these events in inhumanity are a blight on the government which perpetrates them.

The right freely to leave one's country and return to it is a fundamental human right which goes back to the ancient Greeks and to the Magna Charta. It is codified in formal agreements under the charter of the United Nations. It is an integral part of the Helsinki Final Act. Those who flaunt it stand condemned in the eyes of the civilized world and will suffer the opprobrium of history.

May 26, 1983 Information Revolution

* * *

There are a number of issues of varying degrees of importance that continue to divide us and that should be occupying our attention, perhaps at these drafting groups. One of them came to mind as I reviewed a series of press reports in the official press publications of a member State. Let me illustrate:

On May 17, *Izvestia* informed its readers that the United States has "not made a single move which might appear genuinely businesslike and constructive." Alleging that our delegation is against a Conference on Security and Confidence-building measures, which we have been actively negotiating to achieve, the report alleges we have a "desire to prolong" this meeting through "tactics of sabotage and obstruction."

It is understandable that the truth should be a prime casualty where the state has a monopoly of all sources of information. But more than truth is a casualty. A further casualty is the cement necessary to build understanding between peoples if the peace process is to prevail. Such understanding cannot be built on misinformation or disinformation.

The Helsinki Final Act reflects a clear understanding of this need in many of its provisions. At one point it states:

> The Participating States note the expansion in the dissemination of information broadcast by radio, and express the hope for the continuation of this process, so as to meet the interest of mutual understanding among peoples and the aims set forth by this Conference.

Article 19 of the Universal Declaration of Human Rights states that there is a human right to receive "information and ideas through any media and regardless of frontiers."

Article 35 of the Montreux International Telecommunications Convention provides that stations should not harmfully interfere with other radio services or communications.

The United Nations General Assembly Resolution against jamming, adopted in December 1950, calls it "a denial of the rights of all persons to be informed."

More recently, the Radio Regulations of the International Telecommunications Union of 1982 forbid all stations to transmit signals that interfere with the freedom of broadcasting by others.

We are told by one delegation here that it is indeed jamming Western broadcasts, but that it is justified in doing so because those broadcasts disseminate false information. In reality, they are objecting to broadcasts which run contrary to the established positions taken by their authorities. If we should choose to send programs glorifying the leadership and deeds of that State, they would, of course, be pleased to desist from the jamming.

There is no way, Mr. Chairman, that any State can prevent information and ideas from reaching its peoples. The extent to which totalitarian authorities attempt to do so, not only violates the human rights of those subject to their authority, and runs contrary to the spirit and letter of international agreements, but I respectfully suggest that those efforts are doomed to fail. They reflect a basic and profound lack of confidence in the stability of their system. Authorities who have confidence in the validity of their policies and in the loyalty of their citizens have no concern about unfriendly ideas reaching their peoples. My country does not jam broadcasts from the Soviet Union. We have confidence in the intelligence and maturity of our people to distinguish between fact and fiction.

Mr. Chairman, I hope that at this meeting we can begin to lift ourselves out of the narrow confines of our short-range national rigidities and leap forward to new and higher levels of being. There are periods in our human development when the mind stretches to new lengths and never shrinks back to its former dimensions; in our day, that increased growth has been in technology and science.

We still face a dismaying and overwhelming array of bitter religious and national conflicts. As old empires have collapsed in our day, we have witnessed the rise of more than 100 new States since 1945. We are threatened by accumulations of massive military power. We are caught up in the concerns and fears of nuclear war. Yet, our century has also produced the beginnings of the greatest political, economic and social change that the world has ever witnessed. More scientists are alive today than had lived in all of man's earlier history combined. More information is taught to university students today than was known even as late as ten years ago, let alone when I was a university student. The changes released by science encompass every aspect of our lives.

These changes have a profound impact on our political institutions and on the totality of international relations. This new world into which we are entering is still incomprehensible to many of us. There is a need to adapt to the new realities into which we have been thrust. Within this context, the new revolution in the age of information looms large. Those who govern rigid societies are finding it increasingly difficult to shield their peoples from new and outside influences. It is becoming increasingly difficult to control access to information. There is no way for any society, no matter how large and powerful it may be, to avoid the winds of change that are traveling with unmistakable speed throughout every corner of this earth.

To attempt to isolate a people from new ideas by jamming broadcasts is like seeking to hold back a torrential flow of wind currents by building a wall. The new world is one of satellites, coaxial cables, lasers, microwaves, computers, electronic miniaturization, fiber optics, semiconductor chips, and much more daily coming out of the experimental laboratories. The merger of the computer with telecommunications is producing a universal information network which will reach everyone everywhere at any time.

In my own country a tidal wave of electronics is going hand in hand with an explosion of knowledge. It makes possible the immediate and massive production, storage, and distribution of information which now involves close to half of our work force. These activities account for more than half of the American gross national product. The mentality of the printing press, which took decades to materialize and centuries to travel is no longer relevant. The current transformation travels at the speed of light and we are only at the birth of this new technology.

Frankly, it is strange to our delegation that the leadership of the Soviet Union, which from Lenin to Andropov has exalted the role of the "scientific and technical revolution" should still believe that it can withstand the impact of that revolution on its own people, on its own internal power relationships, and on its role with other nations.

The ability to control information is fast becoming an irrelevancy because it is becoming an impossibility. It is ludicrous to believe that one can hold back the inevitable consequences of the communication revolution by trying to end direct-dial telephoning between one country and another. This is like attempting to hold back a tidal wave with a row boat. It is as foolhardy to treat the telephone as a suspicious instrument as it is to lock up the mimeograph and Xerox machines. These temporary handcuffs of yesterday are being broken with ease in an age when new electronics and other devices are opening up the world to all of us as never before.

Within this context, some of us have suggested that here and now in Madrid, in 1983, a new document designed to strengthen the process of peace and understanding in Europe should reflect the reality that the dissemination of information contributes to the interest of mutual understanding among peoples and that we should all seek to promote the expansion of that information by radio broadcasting. Those, Mr. Chairman, who resist that suggested addition to the document before us do so at the risk of revealing their own limitations of vision and their own lack of confidence in the stability of the society they represent. They need have no such fears. The competition of ideas would be healthy for all of us, and would strengthen the fabric of peace.

June 16, 1983 Stumbling Blocks

The position of our government on the present rigid and inflexible "take it or leave it" attitude of a number of delegations here has already been clearly stated by us and need not be repeated. The words used this morning by the delegate from Poland to defend that current inflexibility does not alter the facts that we face at this meeting.

I do want to address, however, a specific comment made by that delegate, which has raised a vital issue for us. He suggested that the American Delegation and others supporting proposed changes in the document before us, are the "main stumbling block" to a satisfactory ending to the Madrid meeting. This comment requires me to remind this meeting again that there are indeed major stumbling blocks to our meeting that are continually being brought to our attention, not the least of which is the continued pattern of arrests and repression by the military authorities of Poland.

I might not raise this but for the fact that in the past few days I have received a number of communications on this subject. On previous occasions the American Delegation has introduced the name of Dr. Geremek, one of the world's outstanding medieval scholars, and reported that he had been arrested. It is with great regret we learn that Dr. Geremek has now been rearrested by the Polish military authorities. I have in my possession a letter signed by some of the most outstanding historians of my country expressing dismay at this most recent humiliation inflicted on Dr. Geremek. For large numbers of my countrymen, Dr. Geremek has become a symbol. His rearrest and imprisonment is a stark reminder that the people of Poland remain victims of Helsinki Final Act violations.

I also have a letter from the American Association for the Advancement of Science, the principal Association of the scientific societies of my country. Their letter was an expression of deep concern at the recent detention of the quantum theoretician, Janusz Onyszkiewicz, senior lecturer at the University of Warsaw. He was arrested after making a speech at the memorial for the Warsaw ghetto.

I suggest, Mr. Chairman, that the Polish delegate and his authorities, who say they are interested in removing stumbling blocks to progress at our meeting, should begin by taking positive and constructive steps to remove the stumbling blocks that they continue to place in the way of the healthy development of the Helsinki process.

Mr. Chairman, the delegate from the Soviet Union, who has just spoken, is aware that our delegation has restrained itself for many weeks with respect to our views on developments occurring in a number of states which, in our opinion, adversely affect the Helsinki process. We will continue to act, unless provoked, with that same restraint in the interests of pursuing our goal of arriving at a substantive concluding document. The American Delegation is prepared to negotiate as soon as any delegation indicates to us its willingness to pursue these negotiations in a constructive manner.

June 17, 1983 Concluding Initiative

We warmly welcome the initiative taken today by the Prime Minister, Mr. Felipe Gonzalez, on behalf of the Spanish Government.

* * *

Prime Minister Moran candidly told us on February 8 that this step was in his Government's contemplation. We welcomed that announcement then. Our delegation said at the time, in response to a press inquiry, that this special role as host was fully compatible with Spain's active and constructive participation in our Western NATO caucus at the Madrid meeting. We are an alliance of free and sovereign states and we respect one another's special responsibilities.

We, of course, cannot yet comment on the specifics of the proposal since we have not yet had the opportunity to study them. As President Gonzalez' proposals are directed to the heads of government, they will be forwarded to President Reagan for his consideration. When we have completed their examination, my Government will communicate with President Gonzalez and with our colleagues at the Madrid meeting.

We certainly hope that the Spanish initiative will lead to an expeditious and constructive final result from Madrid which will strengthen the Helsinki process and move all of us toward the lasting peace with liberty that we seek. Let us hope that historians will so interpret the "Spirit of Madrid."

Assessments

Ambassador Kampelman concluded as he had begun: warning that "We cannot. . .lull our publics into believing that words alone are adequate to erase the pressing threats to the integrity of the Helsinki and Madrid principles." The U.S. delegate quoted President Reagan on the new declaration: "We must ensure that good words are transformed into good deeds and that the ideals which they embody are given concrete expression." The ambassador assessed three years spent reviewing the implementation of the Final Act of 1975, and negotiating substantive amendments to those accords.

July 15, 1983 Assessment of the Meeting

The 35 states participating in the Madrid CSCE review conference, after almost three years of negotiation, are approaching agreement on a final document. This conclusion meets the Western criteria for an acceptable, balanced, and substantive result. It confirms and expands upon the original Helsinki Final Act of 1975. The United States is pleased at the result and believes that the two years and ten months spent negotiating in Madrid have been fruitful and well worth the extraordinary effort.

There follows a summary followed by an outline of the issues that have dominated the Madrid meeting, as well as a report on how the final document deals with those issues.

- The Madrid concluding document will add important new provisions to the Helsinki Final Act of 1975. These provisions deal with the rights of workers to organize, with human rights, with Helsinki monitors, religious rights, human contacts and family reunification, access to diplomatic and consular missions, information, rights of journalists, and measures against terrorism.
- It also provides for convening a conference on security- and confidence-building measures and disarmament in Stockholm next year to work out detailed measures to reduce the fear of surprise military attack. An important new element in this decision is that the measures to be adopted at Stockholm will apply to all of the European portion of the Soviet Union, right up to the Ural Mountains, rather than only to the 250-kilometer (150-mile) band provided for in the Final Act.
- In addition, the Madrid agreement schedules a series of additional meetings which are to take place over the next three years. There will be meetings on human rights, human contacts, and on the peaceful settlement of disputes; a cultural forum; and a seminar on economic, scientific, and cultural cooperation in the Mediterranean. A meeting is also scheduled in Helsinki during 1985 to mark the 10th anniversary of the Helsinki Final Act.
- Finally, the Madrid conference will agree to convene the next followup meeting in Vienna in November 1986 in order to carry forward the review process begun in Belgrade in 1977-78 and continued in Madrid over the past two years and ten months. One of the most important aspects of the CSCE process is the opportunity it provides for a thorough review of the implementation of the Helsinki Final Act. During this review in Madrid, there was general condemnation of the failure of the East European states to live up to their Helsinki commitments, with special criticism of the Soviet and Polish Governments for their policies of internal repression and, in the case of the U.S.S.R., its interference in the internal affairs of Poland and Afghanistan.

The establishment by the Madrid concluding document of a whole series of supplementary meetings will ensure that this critical attention to the behavior of the Soviet Union and other East European governments will continue during the next three and one half years. Those experts' meetings, and the Vienna followup conference, will ensure that any state's failure to live up to the undertakings made in Madrid and in Helsinki will again attract the full spotlight of public attention.

Implementation Review

The Madrid preparatory meeting — which began on September 9, 1980, and did not end until after the main meeting opened on November 11, 1980, a period of more than 9 weeks—focused on Western demands that discussions of new proposals on how best to strengthen the Helsinki process should be preceded by a review of how the provisions of the Helsinki Final Act of 1975 were being implemented. The agenda finally produced by the preparatory meeting provided that opportunity. The period of November 11 to December 19, 1980, was set aside for that review, and it was a thorough one. The Soviet invasion of Afghanistan and the record of human rights violations in the Soviet Union and Eastern Europe were explored and recorded in meticulous detail.

Continuing Soviet and other Eastern violations of the Helsinki Final Act made it necessary to extend this review of implementation throughout most of the Madrid deliberations.

The final document acknowledges that this review took place ("They . . . reaffirmed. . . the importance of the implementation of all the provisions. . . of the Final Act. . . as being. . . essential. . . . It was confirmed that the thorough exchange of views constitutes in itself a valuable contribution towards the achievement of the aims set by CSCE. In this context, it was agreed that those aims can only be attained by continuous implementation, unilaterally, bilaterally and multilaterally, of all the provisions and by respect for all the principles of the Final Act"), that the review is essential to the health of the process, and that there must be an improvement in compliance ("Serious violations of a number of these principles were deplored during the assessments. Therefore, the participating states. . . considered it necessary to state. . . that strict application of and respect for these principles, in all their aspects, are essential for the improvement of mutual relations between the participating states. . . ").

The United States is fully aware of the fact that the Helsinki Final Act cannot attain its objectives when certain states, particularly the U.S.S.R., continue to violate its provisions. There are no enforcement mechanisms under the act. The Madrid meeting has been, therefore, the appropriate forum at which to insert political and moral pressure into the process. The implementation review became the mechanism. The fact that it was efficiently undertaken by a united Western group of states, joined by most of the neutral and nonaligned states, made that possible.

Equally important, Madrid's implementation review afforded the opportunity for a large number of the participating states to communicate to the Soviet Union their deep concerns about violations of the accords. The message was clear: "Conform to the promises made in 1975 if you wish to be recognized as a responsible member of the international community."

Even as the pattern of Helsinki Final Act violations by the East continued, the United States took note of certain specific acts responding to Western concerns. The decision by Romania on its education immigration tax is an illustration. The suspension of some aspects of martial law in Poland and the release of Lech Walesa is another, although continued arrests and imprisonment of thousands and the continued outlawing of Solidarity put the *bona fides* of those steps into question. We have also noted and welcomed a few gestures from the Soviet Union and will continue to encourage further such steps. We hope there will be other developments in response to our concerns.

Poland

The imposition of martial law in Poland in December 1981 was a gross violation of the Helsinki Final Act even as the Madrid meeting was in session. This act of blatant defiance was met by a determined and unified presence of 20 foreign ministers, including U.S. Secretary of State Haig, during the week of February 9-12, 1982. From February 9 until March 12, 1982, negotiations at Madrid came to a complete halt as the West refused to engage in "business as usual" and instead detailed the Helsinki violations represented by Poland's martial law and continued repression in the Soviet Union. On March 12, 1982, in recognition of Western determination, the Madrid meeting recessed for eight months.

When the meeting reconvened on November 9, a group of Western states introduced a series of 14 amendments to a proposed compromise put forward by a group of neutral and nonaligned states (RM-39). The amendments were designed to reflect the view that "business as usual" remained impossible. The essence of many of these proposals was incorporated in a revised neutral and nonaligned document, submitted on March 15, 1983, after martial law was ostensibly and technically suspended (RM-39 revised). That revised document, with improvements to it produced by the Prime Minister of Spain on June 17, 1983, has become the official concluding document of Madrid.

A number of provisions of that document reflect our Polish concerns. They deal with trade unions, religious freedom, and renewed obligation to refrain from the threat or use of force. Summary language in the preamble further reflects Western attention to developments in Poland. The United States and its Western allies never forgot during the course of the Madrid meeting that among the first of Solidarity's demands in August 1980 was that the Helsinki Final Act be reprinted and widely disseminated in Poland. We have kept in close touch with representatives of the Solidarity movement in Europe and the United States, and we have helped communicate their messages to the delegations in Madrid.

Trade Unions

The Helsinki Final Act of 1975 did not include any language on trade unions. The Madrid document reflects a Western initiative stemming directly from the suppression of Solidarity in Poland. It clearly states that participating states "will ensure the right of workers freely to establish and join trade unions, the right of trade unions freely to exercise their activities and their rights as laid down in relative international instruments." This, of course, clearly refers to the conventions of the International Labor Organization (ILO). A reference to "the law of the State" follows, thereby referring to the fact that all states have laws which in some measure define union rights and activities. But that reference is associated with another provision asserting the requirement that such measures be "in conformity with the state's obligation under international law," again a reference to the ILO.

This provision also calls upon states to encourage direct contacts among trade unions and their representatives. The West, which has always made the point that unions freely organized in the West are not to be confused with the totalitarian state-controlled organizations known as unions in the East, was able successfully to insist that this provision be applicable only to "such" unions which are indeed freely organized by workers and free to function under ILO standards.

Monitors

The Helsinki Final Act of 1975 provided a very clear basis of legitimacy to the courageous men and women who formed Helsinki monitoring groups within their own countries. Their purpose was to keep watch on how their states were complying with the provisions of the accords, a right they had under the 1975 agreement. In deliberate decisions to violate the provisions of the act, authorities in the U.S.S.R., Czechoslovakia, and elsewhere in Eastern Europe persecuted and imprisoned those who exercised that right "to know and act upon their rights."

In Madrid, 14 states mentioned the names of 123 victims of repression, many of them monitors. This was in contrast to the Belgrade meeting where the United States was one of only two countries to mention the names of victims, and we mentioned six. The Netherlands was the other.

The language on monitors in the Helsinki Final Act is quite clear and should not require elaboration. Indeed, within the rules of Madrid requiring consensus, it was very difficult to formulate appropriate additional language more clearly. We were, however, able to incorporate language which, in some slight measure, further supports the legitimacy of monitor groups and other activities. In the introduction to the section on principles, for example, a sentence reads: "The participating states express their determination. . . to encourage genuine efforts to implement the Final Act." The Soviets may attempt to misinterpret this sentence in order to distort its meaning, but we take the justifiable position that the very act of urging compliance with the act is "genuine." This concluding document also states that "governments, institutions, organizations and *persons* have a role to play" in that endeavor.

An examination of the ninth paragraph of the principles section reveals significant strengthening of Principle VII of the Helsinki Final Act dealing with human rights. Recognizing that human rights "derive from the inherent dignity of the human person," it calls upon states to:

● "Assure constant and tangible progress. . . aiming at further and steady development. . . irrespective of their political, economic and social systems";

● "Ensure the effective exercise of these rights and freedoms"; and

● Recall "the right of the individual to know and act upon his rights and duties in the field of human rights and fundamental freedoms, as embodied in the Final Act." The provision goes on to assert that states "will take the necessary action in their respective countries to effectively ensure this right."

We have no illusions as to Soviet intentions in this important human rights area. Our own determination must, however, always remain clear. Our insistence—in this case with some success—on continuing to improve the original wording on the act is a clear indication of that intent. It is also important that we keep raising the standards for responsible international behavior.

Religion

The Madrid final document makes small but important gains over the Helsinki Final Act in four areas dealing with religious freedom:

● By extending and strengthening Principle VII to provide that states will *"take the action necessary to ensure the freedom* of the individual to profess and practice, alone or in community with others, religion or belief acting in accordance with the dictates of his own conscience";

● By specifying that states *"will consult,* whenever necessary, the religious faiths, institutions and organizations, which act within the constitutional framework of their respective countries";

● By a provision, urged by the Vatican, requiring states to "favorably consider" registering religious communities of believers practicing or prepared to practice within their constitutional frameworks; and

● By language in Basket III stating that participating states will:
    . . . Further implement the relevant provisions of the Final Act so that religious faiths, institutions, organizations and their representatives can, in the field of their activity, develop contacts and meetings among themselves and exchange information.

Human Contacts

The whole issue of human contacts has been highlighted in Madrid by the sadly unsatisfactory record of Soviet performance. Their record on reunification of families is abysmal. We responded to these violations of the act by continuing to highlight the issue throughout the meetings. In addition, some forward movement beyond the Final Act was achieved through six specific new provisions in the Madrid concluding document. The participating states have pledged:

- To "favorably deal with" and "decide upon" applications for family meetings, reunification, and marriage. The Final Act provided only that they would "consider" or "deal with applications in a positive and humanitarian spirit";
- That marriage and family reunification applications will be decided "within six months," the first reference to a definite time period. We believe this to be a useful improvement over the Final Act commitment to decide "as expeditiously as possible";
- That making or renewing applications for family reunification will not modify rights to "employment, housing, residence status, family support, access to social, economic or educational benefits";
- To provide the necessary forms and information on procedures and regulations followed in emigration cases. This has been a serious problem for many trying to emigrate from the East;
- To reduce fees charged in connection with emigration "to bring them to a moderate level in relation to the average monthly income." The reference to monthly income provides a new standard by which to judge fee levels which in some cases have been exorbitant; and
- To inform applicants as "expeditiously as possible of the decision" on their cases and inform them of "their right to renew applications after reasonably short intervals" in cases of refusal. Both the fact that applicants must be informed of decisions and the recognition of the right to reapply are important in that many refuseniks in the U.S.S.R. have been given "final refusals" and told they could not reapply. The Madrid concluding document also adds an important new element to the provisions of the Helsinki Final Act by specifying that visitors to diplomatic and other official missions and consular posts will be assured of access to them and reaffirming the importance of facilitating the normal functioning of those missions.

There was one additional step taken after months of debate and stalemate. The West believes that it is important to provide a forum after Madrid and before the next followup meeting for the issue of human contacts to be thoroughly explored at a meeting of experts attended by representatives of all 35 countries. We look upon an experts' meeting as a means of providing an opportunity for further clarity and, perhaps, understanding among us all, so that by the time of the next followup meeting this issue might be less of an irritant.

The Government of Switzerland shared our belief and invited the participating states to an experts' meeting to deal with human contacts during April 1986. This was finally accepted by the Soviet Union. A late date was selected so that we will have time to examine how the six new provisions in the Madrid agreement will have been complied with. We look upon this meeting as an important development.

Human Rights Experts' Meeting

The desirability of convening a human rights experts' meeting was first expressed by the West in Madrid in February 1981. We looked upon this highly controversial proposal as vital if we are ever to achieve understanding between East and West. We define human rights by what we consider to be the reasonable standard of individual freedom. Communists think of freedom in terms of "class" and the "state." We are pleased that the proposed experts' meeting received approval after more than two years of consideration. It is to take place in Ottawa, Canada, in May 1985. Its agenda focuses on the status of human rights "in their states," i.e., the participating states, so as not to broaden its scope to include other areas of the world.

Information

The Madrid document contains a number of new and helpful provisions designed to strengthen the Helsinki Final Act provisions in this important area. They are:

- A provision that participating states will encourage the public sale and distribution of printed matter from other states, including making them "accessible in reading rooms";
- A provision that prices of foreign publications should not be excessive in relation to prices in their country of origin. This language is somewhat qualified because Western governments find it difflcult to make commitments in this area;
- Language confirming that states will "further extend the possibilities" for the public to take out foreign subscriptions. In acknowledging that anyone can subscribe to foreign publications, this provision extends the Final Act which states only to "develop possibilities for taking out subscriptions according to modalities. . . . ";
- A reference endorsing "direct contacts among journalists" which is not in the Final Act;
- A pledge to decide visa applications from journalists without "undue delay" and to reexamine within a reasonable time applications which have been refused;
- A sentence stating that journalists traveling for personal reasons will receive the same treatment as other visitors. This is a new element, not found in the Final Act, and is in response to complaints by Western journalists;
- A commitment to grant permanent correspondents *and their families* multiple entry and exit visas *valid for a year*;
- A pledge to "examine the possibility" of coaccrediting journalists permanently accredited to other countries. This is a useful provision for most Western news organizations who have only one or two journalists covering all of Eastern Europe;
- A commitment to take "concrete measures" to provide more extensive travel opportunities for journalists and to "inform journalists in advance" of new areas closed for security reasons;
- A sentence pledging states to "increase the possibilities" and "improve the conditions" for foreign journalists to "establish and maintain personal contacts and communications with their sources." We look upon the word "personal" as implying individual contacts, thereby strengthening the Final Act;
- A provision that radio and television journalists may be accompanied by their own sound and film technicians and use their own equipment. This is another useful addition to the Final Act;
- A provision that journalists may carry with them reference material, including personal notes and files to be used for their professional purposes, an important addition to the Final Act. A qualifier acknowledging that import of printed matter may be subject to local regulation—and Western states also have such regulations—is itself qualified by a statement that these regulations "will be applied with due regard to the journalists' need for adequate working material";
- A provision on press centers open to national and foreign journalists may be helpful considering the paucity of such facilities in the U.S.S.R. and other Eastern countries;
- A sentence in the culture section committing states to "gradually lower custom duties" on books, films, and other forms of cultural expression, as well as "encourage wider dissemination of and access" to these items. This is a minor advance over the Final Act;
- A "cultural forum" to be held in Budapest in 1985. This will provide an opportunity for the West to raise, if necessary, a review of how artists and writers

in East European states are treated; and
- A provision in the education section calling upon states to encourage publication of "lists and catalogues of open archival material," an addition to the Final Act which may aid in negotiating future exchange programs and may be helpful to foreign scholars doing research in the Soviet Union.

Terrorism

The Helsinki Final Act does not deal with the subject of terrorism. The United States joined the Spanish delegation and others in urging that the Madrid final document include a provision on this vital threat to the security of all states. The final document does include such a provision. It includes:
- A statement that signatories will "take effective measures for the prevention and suppression of acts of terrorism, both at the national level and through international cooperation.... ";
- A provision that states will take measures to prevent their territories from being used for the preparation or organization of terrorist activities directed against other participating states and their citizens;
- A commitment to refrain from direct or indirect assistance, financing, encouraging, or tolerating terrorist or subversive activities directed at the violent overthrow of the government of other participating states; and
- A pledge that states will "do their utmost" to assure necessary security to all diplomatic, consular, and official representatives of other states.

Given the record of some of the states which approved this provision regarding international terrorism, there may be some understandable skepticism about such a provision. We strongly believe, however, that it is vital for an international modality to be established, and this provision helps to do so.

Security

The negotiations that led to the signing of the Helsinki Final Act in 1975 had their conceptual origins in an original plan calling for establishment of a European security conference. The agreement that finally came out of Geneva and Helsinki was one that included a very significant humanitarian dimension, which the United States and its Western friends consider to be one of their major accomplishments. Nevertherless, the security questions that are a part of the Helsinki process remain of great importance to all of the participating states.

The NATO group of states in February 1981 presented a French proposal calling for the establishment of a conference to take place after the Madrid meeting to deal with military confidence-building measures. The problem of surprise military attack is one uppermost in the minds of Europeans. The United States joined the Western resolve that a conference on surprise military attack had to be carefully structured in Madrid so that it did not become a vaguely worded mandate for a "disarmament" meeting in which propaganda speeches rather than constructive decisions would be the major element.

Fortunately, the neutral and nonaligned states agreed with this Western objective. The East abandoned its proposal, originally submitted by Warsaw, and after long and intensive debate a mandate for the conference fully acceptable to us was adopted. It meets our four essential criteria:
- The conference will be an integral part of the CSCE process;
- The conference will not interfere with ongoing arms negotiations, such as MBFR [mutual and balanced force reductions];
- The first stage of the conference will deal exclusively with confidence-building measures. This is stated in paragraphs two and six of the mandate for the

conference on confidence- and security-building measures and disarmament in Europe which provide that "... the first stage will be devoted to... confidence- and security-building measures designed to reduce the risk of military confrontation in Europe" and that "... a future follow-up meeting will consider ways and appropriate means for... supplementing the present mandate for the next stage of the Conference... "; and

• Confidence- and security-building measures agreed at the conference are to be militarily signiflcant, politically binding, verifiable, and applicable to the whole of Europe.

The extension of the area to the Urals is quite significant, because the limited confidence-building measures adopted in 1975 exempted the Soviet Union from their coverage, except for the first 250 kilometers within its borders. The Soviet Union, after first rejecting an extension to cover all of its European area, then urged that the geographic area be extended into the Atlantic Ocean as compensation for its extension to the Ural Mountains. The Soviet objective, of course, was to negate the international principle recognizing free use of the high seas and thus possibly to interfere with movement of U.S. forces in contingencies involving areas of the world outside Europe.

We presented a provision, which was in the original 1975 agreement, making certain that only "adjoining sea area and air space" would be included and only when activities in that area are a part of military activities taking place within Europe itself. This was eventually accepted by the East. We were pleased that this formulation was finally approved, because it clearly excluded independent air and naval activities from coverage. The mandate will now permit concentration at the meeting, which will be held in Stockholm, on the crucial confidence-building measures required to deal with the problem of surprise military attack on the European Continent.

Followup Meetings

During the preparatory meeting in 1980, the United States proposed to all of the delegations, most particularly to the Soviet Union, that all participants immediately commit themselves to hold a followup meeting within 3 years after Madrid. The Soviet Union refused to join us in that step and consistently refused to provide the West with such an unconditional commitment. This was apparently designed to intimidate other states into believing that the Helsinki process would end if the Madrid meeting did not conclude to Soviet satisfaction.

We are very pleased that the flnal Madrid document provides for another followup meeting which is to take place in Vienna in November 1986. This is a longer intervening period than we would have preferred, but the final document also provides that there will be a 10th anniversary commemoration meeting in Helsinki in 1985, the year we might ordinarily have held a followup meeting.

We also have decided to hold a series of supplementary meetings between those in Madrid and Vienna. We hope that these will help keep the Helsinki issues alive and at the same time strengthen the Helsinki process. Here is a list of the eight future meetings provided for in the Madrid document:

• The flrst stage of a conference on disarmament in Europe commencing January 17, 1984, in Stockholm, to be preceded by a 3-week preparatory meeting to take place beginning on October 25, 1983, in Helsinki;

• A 6-week experts' meeting on the peaceful settlement of disputes in Athens, beginning March 21, 1984;

• A seminar on Mediterranean cooperation in Venice, October 16 to 26, 1984.

• An experts' meeting on human rights in Ottawa, lasting 6 weeks and commencing on May 7, 1985;

- A commemorative meeting in Helsinki in 1985 marking the 10th anniversary of the signing of the Final Act;
- A cultural forum in Budapest sometime in 1985;
- An experts' meeting on human contacts in Bern, Switzerland, lasting 6 weeks and commencing April 16, 1986; and
- The third followup meeting of the CSCE in Vienna starting November 4, 1986.

July 18, 1983 **A Further Assessment**

After two years and more than ten months of negotiation we are close to the end of our Madrid meeting. We have just been informed by the delegate from Malta that he intends, as is his right, to continue to pursue the amendments about which he has fully informed us.* He is aware that our delegation, among others, will continue to oppose those amendments and will not provide the necessary consensus to them.

The American delegation is pleased with the draft concluding document that has emerged out of our deliberations. We consider it noteworthy that in a number of respects, such as in provisions dealing with the reunification of families, religious rights, trade unions, terrorism, rights of journalists, access to missions, and Helsinki monitors, the Madrid document goes beyond the Helsinki Final Act of 1975.

We also consider the decision to hold a conference on security- and confidence-building to be important. This can be a significant step toward strengthening security and cooperation in Europe. The need to minimize the risk of surprise military attack is of great significance to all of us. We welcome a decision to hold such a conference, a proposal we joined in supporting as early as February 1981.

We look for a conference which will produce more than vaguely worded declarations. We take very seriously the provisions in the mandate that the conference would concern itself with confidence- and security-building measures which are militarily significant, politically binding, verifiable, and applicable to the whole of Europe. The conference must complement, and not interfere, with other arms control negotiations. The United States will take a constructive approach to the work of the conference and hopes that others will do the same. Agreement to notify military activities which will take place on land in Europe is an example of the kind of measure we believe could be a valuable result of this conference.

It is also gratifying to all of us that Madrid is firmly establishing the continuity of the Helsinki process. We have done so explicitly; and we are doing so with our decision to hold another followup meeting in Vienna in 1986, preceded by a 10th anniversary meeting in Helsinki in 1985. This continuity is strengthened by a decision to hold meetings, between the sessions in Madrid and Vienna, on human rights, human contacts, cultural activities, the Mediterranean, and the peaceful resolution of international disputes.

The United States recognizes the special importance of arriving at an agreement in Madrid at a time when international tensions and differences continue to dominate our consciousness. We hope Madrid will be a significant signal of a new beginning in our earnest pursuit of peace.

---

*Malta, as the concluding ceremony neared, Sept. 7-9, withheld its consensus to the draft concluding document and insisted on discussion of amendments it proposed regarding security in the Mediterranean.

Eastern Noncompliance With Helsinki Accords

We must, however, not be blind to the difficulties of the task ahead. These difficulties were dramatized by a first-page editorial in the July 14 issue of *Pravda*, which I read shortly after leaving this hall on Friday when 34 of us signified our provisional approval of a final document. The editorial sharpens for us not only the real meaning of the Madrid agreement but its decided limitations as well. The editorial's theme is the speech made to the June plenum of the Communist Party Central Committee by the leader of the Soviet Union, during which he said: "There is a struggle for the hearts and minds of billions of people on this planet." Concerned that the U.S.S.R. may not be doing too well in that struggle, *Pravda* urges that Soviet citizens be "immunized" against hostile ideas. Specifically, it aims at religion in the U.S.S.R. as a danger.

The United States understands the profound seriousness of the inherent contradictions between the Soviet totalitarian system and the system of liberty and individual dignity which is a hallmark of democratic governments. Reaching agreements such as we did in Helsinki and now in Madrid, do not, by themselves, automatically minimize those differences or end the competition. We intend to be in the competition for "hearts and minds" to which *Pravda* refers. We welcome a competition of ideas and values. In many ways the Madrid forum has been and remains a vehicle for that competition. What concerns us deeply, however, is that the U.S.S.R. may believe it cannot win a competition of ideas and values without the threat and use of armed force and repression, within and outside its borders.

The Helsinki Final Act and the Madrid agreement are efforts to channel the competition of values within civilized constraints and at the same time to strive for understanding so that we can learn to live with one another in peace. The fact that these agreements continue to be violated, even during this very period of negotiation and agreement, is discouraging.

We cannot in good conscience permit a limited negotiating success, important as we believe it to be, to make us forget, much to our regret, that signatures on a document do not necessarily produce compliance with its provisions. The continued fighting in Afghanistan, where more than 100,000 invading troups remain, violating the sovereignty of that unhappy country and abusing the humanity of its people, stands as an affront to the peace we in Helsinki professed to pursue. The people of Poland remain today subjugated by a martial law which attacked the legitimacy of their free trade union, Solidarity, and continues to keep in internment and imprisonment thousands of persons who declare and champion their human rights.

Our delegation believes in the importance of words. But we cannot permit an agreement on words to obfuscate unpleasant realities. We have sought and welcome the agreement represented by our decision in Madrid. We do not wish to minimize the importance of that agreement. But we also do not wish to minimize the consequence of undermining such agreements when they are not complied with in letter and in spirit.

What are we to think when at the very time we were coming to agreement on provisions dealing with religious rights, *Pravda Vostoka* of Uzbekistan informed us that leading members of the Seventh Day Adventist Church have been imprisoned by government authorities precisely because of their wish to practice their religion?

On December 1, 1981, I reluctantly brought to the attention of this body a detailed report of what clearly appeared to be a government-sponsored anti-Jewish campaign in the Soviet Union. It was my hope, obviously misplaced, that I would never have reason to raise that issue again. The facts, however, force me to do so. The decline in Soviet Jewish immigration is to the lowest levels since the

1960s, a tragic violation of the Helsinki accords. An important escape valve has thus been cut off for one of the most persecuted religious groups in that society. We note too, with sadness, that many Jewish scientists and professionals have been stripped of their educational degrees; that the teaching of the Hebrew language brings on police harassment and arrest; and, perhaps most disturbing of all, that extreme anti-Semitic articles are appearing in the Soviet press with increasing frequency.

Soviet officials sometimes respond to these facts with assertions of "indignation" and "libel." I fully understand such indignation in the light of the horrendous memories of anti-Semitism during and prior to World War II. As to libel, in many of our societies truth is a defense to a charge of libel. We pray that this issue may soon disappear as an issue between us. Until the facts justify that change, however, I quote from a statement made last week by President Reagan: "We have repeatedly stated that our concern for human rights in general, and Soviet Jewry in particular, is integral to our national interest and remains a major focus of our national policy."

The picture is no more encouraging when we turn to the very marrow of our objectives, the search for peace. A Soviet pacifist, Alexander Shatravka, was recently sentenced to three years in prison for circulating a petition calling for the universal abolition of nuclear wespons. The document had urged both the United States and the Soviet Union to scrap their nuclear arsenals. Mr. Shatravka had earlier been associated with a group of young people, who, a year ago, had been arrested for unfurling a banner in Red Square bearing only the Russian words for "bread, life, disarmament."

The arrest of these young Soviet citizens seeking peace stands in sharp contrast to the enthusiastic editorial which appeared in *Pravda* last January hailing antiwar movements in Western Europe as "vital causes of the people." Is it any wonder that we are reminded of a perceptive statement by Clausewitz: "The aggressor," he said, "is always peace loving. He would like to make his entry into our country undisturbed."

We know that the people of the Soviet Union, like all of our peoples, are peace loving. But we also know from the *Pravda* editorial of last week that Soviet authorities, who are not elected by their people, fear independent ideas and want their people "immunized" against them. General Aleksei Yepishev, the political head of the Soviet Army, recently complained that Soviet youth was being infected by pacifism. To stop independent ideas is a lost cause. Ideas, like the wind currents and the climate, reach all lands and cannot be stopped by artificial barriers.

It is the view of our delegation that in arresting and harassing those of its citizens who work for peace and universal nuclear disarmament, Soviet authorities not only maintain an indefensible double standard, they clearly demonstrate that the mantle of peace, in which they would like to cloak themselves, simply does not fit their shape, their ideology, or their practices, and it is not simply one country to which we wish to address these comments.

Similarly, a few weeks ago, more than 300 Czechoslovak young people were clubbed by the police, with many arrested, for holding a peace demonstration in Prague and chanting "we want peace and freedom." And in that country, Ladislav Lis, a spokesman for the Charter 77 human rights and peace organization, a Helsinki monitoring group, is expected to go on trial this week for his activities. Religious believers are also facing renewed repression for their expressions of faith.

In East Germany—where there is a growing unofficial peace movement that opposes all nuclear arms, including those of the Soviet Union and the United States—young people, many of them associated with churches, also find themselves harassed. At least 22 members of this group have recently been expelled. Patches worn on clothing depicting "swords into plowshares," distributed by East German church leaders, have been outlawed as "the expression of a mentality hostile to the state and proof of membership in an illegal political association." Students wearing the patch were threatened with expulsion from their schools and workers from their jobs.

The irony is not lost on us as we remind ourselves that the statue of peace given by Moscow to the United Nations has the same motif of "swords into plowshares."

A double irony is that the harassment of those who try to demonstrate for peace stands in stark contradiction to a UN General Assembly resolution of last December, cosponsored by the United States, calling on all states "to encourage their citizens freely and publicly to express their own views on disarmament changes and to organize and to meet publicly for that purpose."

Once again, we have words; and we have deeds contrary to those words. We have the continuation of a pattern which has plagued the Helsinki process since 1975 and which continues to plague this meeting to this day.

The Helsinki Process Must Continue

The question might well be asked, therefore, and many in my country understandably ask, why do we negotiate about words? Why do we seek to forge a concluding document? Why do we enter into an agreement at a time when the repression of human beings in the Soviet Union is greater than at any time since the Helsinki Accords were signed in 1975?

The American delegation has pursued these activities here in Madrid because the pursuit of peace is too vital, the need for understanding too indispensable, the importance of the Helsinki Accords too great to permit us to be discouraged by the task or by the obstacles we face. We are convinced that the Helsinki Final Act has within it a formula for peace which is indispensable in this age of potential nuclear devastation. It is our conviction, furthermore, that unless these principles are taken seriously, the accords will become historically irrelevant. We, therefore, continue to express ourselves on this issue, even during these closing days of our meeting, in order to help mobilize a wider moral and political insistance upon universal respect for the Act by compliance with its provisions. Anything less threatens the integrity of our process and of our relationships under it.

The American Delegation makes this statement today not to irritate or offend any delegation here. We understand the need for patience in building the structure of peace and understanding among us. We cannot, however, lull our publics into believing that words alone are adequate to erase the pressing threats to the integrity of the Helsinki and Madrid principles.

We earnestly desire to enter into a constructive dialogue at all levels in order to achieve understanding and restore the "détente" contemplated in the Helsinki accords. We wish to negotiate reductions in arms of all kinds to ease the burdens of military spending on all of us. We wish peace with every state here. We wish to resolve all potential conflicts between us, bilateral, regional, and international. We seek to do so on the basis of reciprocity and mutuality.

We appreciate that in order to have a successful dialogue, we must be as attentive and responsive to the concerns of others as we ask them to be with respect to ours. We are prepared to do so.

I conclude with an extract from a statement issued by President Reagan in Washington last Friday evening:

In concluding the Madrid meeting, we reaffirm our commitment to the Helsinki process. We will not flag in our continued determination to work with all governments and peoples whose goal is the strengthening of peace in freedom. As Madrid has shown, dialogue, when based on realistic expectations and conducted with patience, can produce results. These results are often gradual and hard won, but they are the necessary building blocks for a more secure and stable world. The challenge remains: we must all consolidate and build on these gains; we must ensure that good words are transformed into good deeds and that the ideals which they embody are given concrete expression. Giving substance to the promises of Madrid and Helsinki will remain one of our prime objectives.

Acknowledgement

We are grateful to those who helped make possible the week-long ad hoc conference in Madrid in October 1980. This citizens' conference paralleled the official Helsinki review sessions which began that week and continued for almost three years. We acknowledge their support:

The American Federation of Labor-Congress of Industrial Organizations (AFL-CIO)

The Ford Foundation

International Ladies Garment Workers' Union (ILGWU)

Joyce Mertz-Gilmore Foundation

Konrad Adenauer Stiftung

United States Embassy, Madrid

Appendix

Mount the Helsinki Watch!

* * *

There should be no illusions. While the USSR agreed at Helsinki that all frontiers are "inviolable," her Brezhnev Doctrine, by which Soviet tanks subdued Czechoslovakia in 1968, has not been publicly annulled. The Soviet Union, furthermore, has systematically dodged or ignored agreements which tend to "open" its closed society. Yuri Kashiev, a Soviet foreign ministry official, just weeks after the signing at Helsinki, noted that western news media oppose communism. He asked, "Is there really anyone in the West who seriously hopes that the socialist countries will sometime allow the 'free circulation' of such 'information' in their society?"

Yet the promise of Helsinki is clear. It seeks to extend the process of détente—including the "free circulation" of diverse "information." If it is to be taken seriously, the Helsinki document should now be used as an international standard against which to test the actions of *all* the signatories. The West, particularly, should be pressed to implement even the stickiest exchanges described in the accords.

* * *

Human rights in a stable, peaceful world have been Freedom House's business for nearly 35 years. Our year-round Comparative Survey of Freedom, for example, tests the level of political and civil rights in every nation.

We are now launching the Helsinki Watch.

We begin, in this issue, with analyses by political scientists of the August accords. These specialists focus on ways to judge whether Helsinki is being honestly, earnestly implemented.

Freedom House will report to the American people hereafter on steps taken—or not taken—by America and others in fulfilling the pledges made at Helsinki.

Help us mount the Helsinki Watch. Make known your views as widely as possible, and please share them with us.—L.R.S.

from an editorial in Freedom at Issue
November–December 1975, number 33

Index

DATE DUE

DATE DUE			
FEB 2 0 1995			
FEB 1 9 1996			
APR 0 2 1996			
			Printed in USA